WHAT OTI

"A one-of-a-kind breakthrough strategy for problem solving is thoroughly and understandably presented in this book... The Holmes' strategy provides tools for analytically achieving the most effective problem solving skills... The author has provided a new, valuable and proven resource for businesses and education. The book's tools will provide users superior advantages in business and life choices."
—**Recommended and Reviewed in the Mindquest Review of Books, Lightword Publishing**

"A fine pick with plenty of useful wisdom... Reasoning and thinking come into play far more than one would expect in life. This book is a guide to empowering one's critical thinking skills to execute them well in everyday life. These deduction skills are made famous by Sherlock Holmes in criminal mysteries, but Gregg Young shows where they can be used in life. "Reasoning Backward" is a fine pick with plenty of useful wisdom."
—Midwest Book Reviews

"Never be stuck again! Now you have a Gameplan and a Toolbox to solve those sticky problems!"
—Don Linsenmann, Vice President Six Sigma, DuPont

"Gregg Young aka Sherlock has a way of taking the complex and making it seem logical, manageable and interesting. His ability to engage his audience in what to some is a dry if not mystic technology and make it relevant is a valuable tool in engaging people in the techniques of problem solving."
— Kathleen Bader, Former President & CEO, NatureWorks LLC, and Director, Textron, Inc.

"Our organization has benefited significantly from a relationship with Gregg Young. Gregg's approach to problem solving is unique, and his best practice tools provide a practical, yet powerful framework for solving real world problems."
— Mark Vrana, Vice President, Technology and Quality, Franklin International, Inc.

"Gregg makes a compelling case for the effectiveness of using the Best Practice tools to significantly reduce waste and cost. I really appreciate the tone of the book - the openness to share what he has learned to help anyone become successful without holding back anything."
—Randy Spitzer, Author, *Take Responsibility*

"Whether you're looking for a dynamic and engaging speaker, or a writer who takes quality and critical thinking processes from complex to simple, Gregg Young is your man! His Sherlock Holmes metaphor for critical thinking is both entertaining and thought provoking. His enthusiasm is contagious. Gregg transcends the norm, moves us beyond routine problem-solving, and leaves us ready to go out and tackle problems armed with both tools and confidence in using them."

—**Nancy L. Ohle, Managing Partner, HRPartner, LLC**

"Author Gregg Young pinpoints one of the most important skills anyone can master – how to identify and solve problems. The student who excels at those can write his or her own ticket."

—**Joseph G. Lehman, P.E., President**
Mackinac Center for Public Policy

"Young provides a fresh and insightful approach to problem solving that should significantly improve the effectiveness of most operations. As Sherlock Holmes, Young presents a witty, stimulating and thought provoking case for "reasoning backward" to solve problems. It's quite elementary, you know!"

—**Dr. Richard Dolinski, Former Vice President of Quality Performance at Dow Chemical; Founder and President, The Legacy Center for Community Success**

"The tools Gregg presents in this book give projects the starting jolt they need to be successful."

—**Carl Cordy, Six Sigma Master Black Belt, Visteon Corporation, and Author,** *Champions Practical Six Sigma Summary*

"The lessons from this book will open the eyes of every problem solver: you have to start at the effect-side of the problem and not just starting guessing about possible causes! It will help our engineers to become more effective *quality improvement sleuths*!"

—**Jo Mooren, Quality and Reliability Consultant, Philips Applied Technologies, Eindhoven, The Netherlands**

"Having been trained in DMAIC Six Sigma Processes, I was used to approach of testing the Xs to determine which ones are critical. However, I found your approach of comparing the best Ys to the worst Ys to find clues about the critical Xs to be quite intriguing. It enables you converge onto the problem much faster."

—**Ed King, Technical Specialist: Electronics & Instrumentation Engineering, Yazaki North America**

"For over 10 years the Author has been a mentor in the area of quality with excellent results. Mr. Young exudes quality in all he does. He is a true student of the quality process and his energies and knowledge have transferred to my team and organization."
—**Mike Shea, former President, Arnold Center, Inc.**

"I have known Gregg Young for almost twenty years and have always viewed him to be a leading edge thinker...This book will afford the reader a chance to get to know Gregg."
— **Dr. Timothy G. Nash, Vice President, Graduate and Specialty Programs, Northwood University**

"Gregg Young hit a home run with this book! It is the perfect handbook for any business student or person who desires to improve his or her abilities to think and solve problems. It is easy to understand, filled with every day work problems. I dare say the average person should be able to apply Young's techniques and improve his or her life! Sharpen your pencil and skills as you examine clues and work backward from effects to causes!"
—**Janie Guill**

"Problem solving is an essential skill to student success. Through descriptions and examples of best practice tools used successfully in industry, *Reasoning Backward* helps students *solve* problems rather than *guess* their way through problems."
—**Toni Krasnic, Author, *Concise Learning***

"Gregg provides the important best practice tools, the rest of the story on quality. Apply these lessons and prosper."
—**Mark McKinley, President, McKinley Technologies**

"This book is filled with excellent, practical, powerful tools that are sure to help individuals and enterprises achieve greater success."
—**John Miller, Adjunct Professor, Lawrence Technological University; Managing Partner, NuVu Data Services**

"Young provides a clear explanation for the different results that have been achieved when using different quality improvement processes, and more importantly he shows exactly how to get the results every leader was seeking in the first place when they launched these initiatives."
— **Eric Balinski, Managing Director, Goodrich Capital and Co-author, *Value Based Marketing for Bottom-line Success***

"We could do with a lot more high school students able to use and explain what is in this book. I like especially that it's improving my own thinking. Any teacher who applies even the basic ideas will find fresh ways to improve their instruction, and students mastering it will have a lifetime resource."
—**John Jensen, Ph. D.**

"I have been privileged to hear Mr. Young deliver his messages on several occasions. His depth of knowledge and his passion for the subject matter creates interest from the audiences."
—**Sharon Miller, President, ITH Staffing**

"Problem solving is a daily occurrence that few people have been trained to do well. As a result, they spend most of their time firefighting. They repeatedly deal with symptoms of the same issue with no success. Gregg Young's *Reasoning Backward* is an excellent guide to the person who wants end the firefighting cycle, get to the root cause and permanently eliminate problems. *Reasoning Backward* guides the reader on how to use Shainin Statistical Engineering to accomplish this. It presents lots of well-explained examples and is an excellent reference for the experienced problem solver or a person just being introduced to in using the Shainin techniques."
—**John Methot, ASQ CQE CSSBB, Kostal of America**

"Gregg Young has 25 years' history using Six Sigma and building upon the work of Dorian Shainin to drive improvements well beyond those that "traditional" Six Sigma achieves, and much more rapidly. Young has also developed a hybrid approach towards cycle time reduction melding Cost-Time Management and Theory of Constraints, and a "Planned Innovation" new product development process. The scope of Mr. Young's vision and creative ideas transcends the traditional Quality "box," and thus should be of special interest. I would urge your strong consideration of Mr. Young as a possible consultant."
—**William J. Murphy, former Associate Dean of the General Motors University Quality College, ASQ Six Sigma Green Belt, Six Sigma Black Belt, Quality Engineer, and Manager of Quality & Organizational Excellence**

"Gregg Young has given us all a shiny new tool for our Quality Tool Boxes. In *Reasoning Backward*, Gregg has brought forth not only a working description of various useful techniques, but also a framework for how and when to use them. His writing is clear and straightforward, as are his thoughts and methods. If you are looking for a book to support the unreasoned practices that many have been preaching and pursuing for years, this isn't it! If, on the other hand, you are looking for a source of clear presentation for usable problem solving tools and strategies, I highly recommend *Reasoning Backward*."
—**Michael L. Kendel, P.E.**

Reasoning Backward

How Sherlock Holmes
Can Make You
A Better Problem Solver

Gregg Young

© Copyright 2012 Gregg Young. Published in the United States of America. All rights reserved. No part of this book may be reproduced or transmitted in any manner whatsoever, except for the inclusion of brief quotations in a review, without the prior written permission of the publisher. For information, contact Young Associates, Inc., 2911 Highbrook Dr., Midland, MI 48642 (989) 492-2029, gregg@youngassocinc.com.

DISCLAIMER

This book includes information gathered from many sources and personal experiences. This general reference introduces and teaches techniques with a proven history of delivering superior results. These techniques are a stimulus for thought, not a substitute for it. Every problem is unique, so problem solvers must choose techniques and analyze the results carefully to achieve the desired outcomes. Although the author and publisher have prepared this book with utmost care and diligence and have made every effort to ensure the accuracy and completeness of the information contained within, we assume no responsibility for errors, inaccuracies, omissions, inconsistencies, or results obtained from the use of this book. No warranty may be created or extended by sales representatives or written sales materials. The publisher and author disclaim any personal liability for any loss or any other damages, direct or indirect, resulting from the advice and information presented within.

Publisher's Cataloging-in-Publication

Young, Gregg.
  Reasoning backward: how Sherlock Holmes can make you a better problem solver/ Gregg Young.
  p. cm.
  Includes index.
  Library of Congress Control Number: 2011934759
  ISBN-13: 978-0-9830113-0-9
  1. Problem Solving – Problem-based learning 2. Problem Solving I. Title
  LB1027.42   BF449   2010   153.4'3–dc22

QUANTITY DISCOUNTS ARE AVAILABLE TO YOUR SCHOOL, EDUCATIONAL INSTITUTION, ORGANIZATION OR COMPANY
for educational purposes, gifts, incentives, fundraising, or reselling.

For more information, please contact the publisher at
Young Associates, Inc., 2911 Highbrook Dr., Midland, MI 48642
(989) 492-2029 – gregg@youngassocinc.com
http://youngassocinc.com   http://reasoningbackward.com

DEDICATION

To **Dorian Shainin**, whose genius makes it possible for everyone to become an effective problem solver

ACKNOWLEDGEMENTS

This book would not be possible except for the genius of the late Dorian Shainin, who developed the 12 convergence tools presented in this book that are based on Sherlock Holmes' reasoning backward strategy. They are the foundation of all best practice problem solving operations. His work is a shining beacon in the darkness of divergent thinking. His teachings have changed my life.

I am deeply indebted to Keki R. Bhote, the former Director of Quality for Motorola's Automotive and Industrial Electronics Division, for first making Dorian Shainin's methods available to the public, and for many of the examples in this book. His books, *World Class Quality* (1991) and *World Class Quality, 2nd edition*, (2000) have provided much valuable guidance and inspiration.

Special thanks also go to Jack Fooks and Nick Siriani of Westinghouse for their contributions to Cost-Time Management, and to the late Eliyahu Goldratt, whose breakthrough, the Theory of Constraints, is revolutionizing management in the 21st century.

I am indebted to Frank R. Bacon, who created the Planned Innovation process that revolutionizes new product development, making success the norm and not the exception.

This book is only possible because Sir Arthur Conan Doyle left us his legacy, Sherlock Holmes, to provide the basic reasoning backward strategy that is the basis of all the methods in this book.

A NOTE TO STUDENTS

This book introduces problem-solving strategies and tools developed in industry and based on the methods of Sherlock Holmes. Experience has proven they are the most powerful methods available.

The strategies and principles presented in Chapter 1 have value for students immediately. For example, when taking tests, Holmes' strategies of "reasoning backward" and "first eliminating the impossible" help students see problems more clearly, which leads to the discovery of better solutions. The specific tools that follow beginning in Chapter 3 are proven best practices, but they are likely to have more long-term value than short-term value for students, simply because students may have less opportunity to use these tools in school. One of my goals is to make students aware of these techniques before they leave school, so they will already have access to best practices when they enter the workforce, better prepared to create value for themselves, their future employers, their communities, and society.

Students will learn convergent thinking skills based on making careful observations, not guesswork, as outlined in Sherlock Holmes' Reasoning Backward model. They will learn why divergent thinking (Reasoning Forward) is never the best way to approach a problem. Divergent thinking slows problem solving and leads to partial solutions, while convergent thinking develops complete solutions much more quickly. This book enables students to approach issues with powerful tools, so they are ready to solve problems effectively.

Discovering these best practices has changed my life profoundly. Until then, problem solving was always slow because my teams and I never knew where to start, so we usually developed partial solutions. The best practice tools have changed that situation forever. Now, my passion is to share these techniques, so everyone can become an effective problem solver. In today's world, who can accept anything less?

Gregg Young
Midland, Michigan

CONTENTS

Chapter 1 – Sherlock Holmes on Problem Solving **23**

Chapter 2 – The Best Practice Tools – An Overview **51**

Section 1 – "Eliminate the Impossible"
Clue Generation Tools

Chapter 3 – Multi-Vari **67**
    Patterns of variation provide clues about root causes
        Example 1 – Machining Operation
        Example 2 – Accounts Receivable
        Example 3 – Tile Adhesion
        Example 4 – Hotel Customer Service
        Example 5 – High Employee Turnover
        Multi-Vari Directions and Template

Chapter 4 – Concentration Chart **88**
    Find clues about root causes of Within-unit variation
        Example 1 – Paint Defects
        Example 2 – Massive Shorts in TV Sets
        Example 3 – Accounts Receivable
        Example 4 – Wave Solder Defects
        Example 5 – University Recruiting
        Concentration Chart Directions

Chapter 5 – Paired Comparisons™ **99**
    Universal tool for eliminating non-critical factors
        Example 1 – Noisy Micro-motors
        Example 2 – Turkeys
        Example 3 – Precipitate in a Dispersion
        Example 4 – Bacterial Contamination on Dairy Farms
        Example 5 – Detecting Heart Attacks
        Example 6 – Warped Grills
        Paired Comparisons Directions

Chapter 6 – Component Search™ **122**
    Powerful tool if the product can be disassembled and reassembled
        Example 1 – Non-Firing Burner
        Example 2 – Hourmeter
        Example 3 – Oscillator Time Delay
        Component Search Directions and Template

Section 2 – "Identify the Truth"
Identification & Validation Tools

Chapter 7 – Variable Search™ **147**
    Process-oriented version of Component Search™
        Example 1 – Press Brake
        Example 2 – Control Module
        Example 3 – Cracked Epoxy Adhesive
        Variable Search Directions and Template

Chapter 8 – Full Factorial **170**
    Used differently – Links to Variable Search™ and used only for 2-4 variables after screening is complete; Includes discussion of Classical Fractional Factorials and the Taguchi Methodology
        Example – Wave Soldering

Chapter 9 – B vs. C™ **181**
    Verifies root causes by turning the problem on and off
        Example 1 – Warped Grills Revisited
        Example 2 – Press Brake Revisited
        Example 3 – Cracked Epoxy Adhesive
        Example 4 – Wire Bond Strength
        Non-manufacturing Applications
        B vs. C Directions and Template

Section 3 – Set Limits for Flawless Performance
Optimization Tools

Chapter 10 – Scatter Plots and Simplex **197**
    Used differently to establish realistic specifications for critical factors
        Example 1 – Ignition Amplifier

Example 2 – Diode Baking Process
Scatter Plot Directions and Template

Section 4 – Maintain Control
Control Tools

Chapter 11 – Process Certification and Positrol 213
Assures process does not revert to making defects
Example 1 – Checklist
Example 2 – Plastic Injection Molding
Example 3 – Wave Solder Process

Chapter 12 – Pre-Control 221
More powerful, next generation of Statistical Process Control
Example – Wave Solder Process

Chapter 13 – Putting the Tools Together 227
A Best Practice Problem Solving Process Case Study – Use the tools in sequence to quickly solve any quality problem
Example – Wave Soldering

Section 5 – Cycle Time Reduction Tools

Chapter 14 – Cost-Time Management 249
Reduces cycle time to improve cash flow
Cost-Time Profile Directions

Chapter 15 – Theory of Constraints 262
Links company profit/year to product profit/hour

Chapter 16 – Solving Organizational Problems 272
Adapting the Tools to Solve Complex Problems Within and Between Organizations

Section 6 – Open-ended Problem Solving

Chapter 17 – Opportunity Analysis 294
Innovating with a 95% rate of success

Chapter 18 – TRIZ 312
    The Theory of Inventive Problem Solving

Chapter 19 – Poka-Yoke 328
    Mistake Proofing to achieve Zero Defects

Chapter 20 – Summary and Epilogue 333

Sherlock Holmes' Top 10 Tips 339

Other Relevant Sherlock Holmes Quotations 341

Index 347

The Best Practice Problem Solving Tools

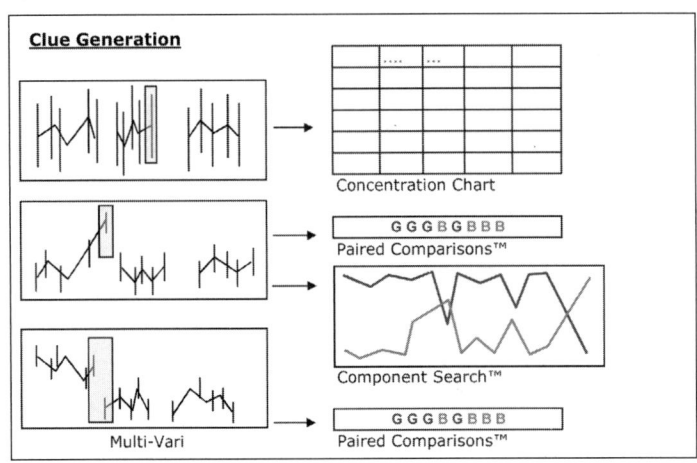

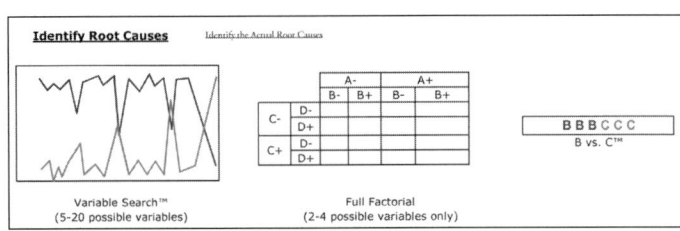

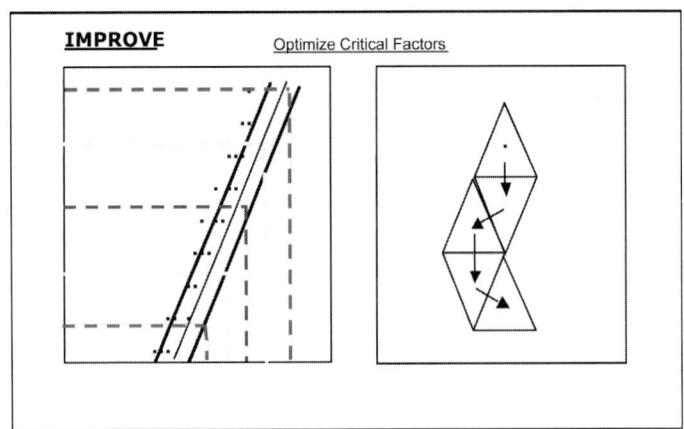

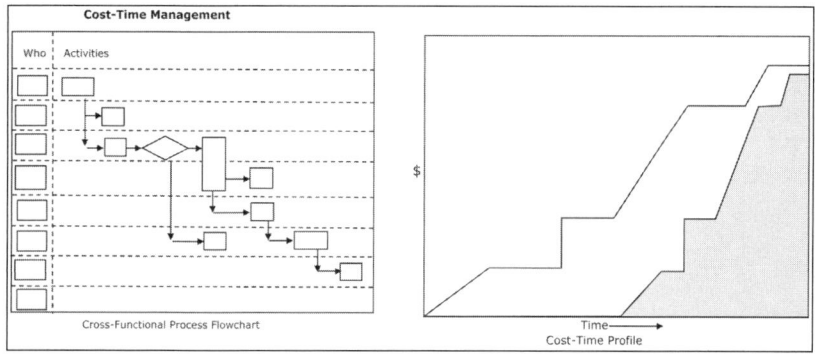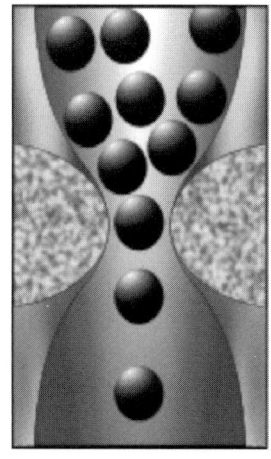

A problem is a situation that requires improvement.
Is it a Closed-end Problem or an Open-ended Problem?

Closed-end
(the best is good enough, but it is not achieved every time)

Principles
- If it ever works well, it is fundamentally sound – learn from it.
- Observe the current operation – never brainstorm.
- Compare extremes – best vs. worst – look for patterns and consistent differences.

Analytical Tools
- Multi-Vari to identify categories, patterns
- Paired Comparisons™ to compare extremes
- B vs. C™ to validate the solution
- Scatter Plots to set targets & tolerances
- Process Certification to remove noise
- Positrol to lock in improvement
- Reduce cycle time

Lesson for Students
In situations that are not perfect every time, ask "What's different when problems occur?" Patterns and consistent differences provide clues that lead to 90-100% improvement every time in just days to weeks.

Open-ended
(the best is not good enough; ideality is never achieved)

Formulate Hypotheses
- Unmet Need
- Winning Solution
- Value of the Winning Solution

Test the Hypotheses – Ask 4 Questions
- How is it done now?
- How much does it cost now?
- What (if anything) is wrong with how it is done now?
- What is the value of making improvements?

Take Appropriate Action
- Proceed with plan as is, or modify the initial plan
- Development tools may include TRIZ (apply solutions from similar problems in other areas) and Poka-Yoke (designs and operations that are mistake proof).

Lesson for Students
In any situation where the best performance never achieves ideality, this approach yields successful solutions over 95% of the time.

Reasoning Backward – 2nd Edition - Foreword

Remember reading all those detective stories in elementary and high school? We were taught to look for clues first and only then to draw deductions, just like Sherlock Holmes, and now just like Gregg Young is advocating in this book. We need to use the process of observation, deduction, and knowledge and make it available for everyone. Here are excellent real-world examples of these problem-solving practices applied in industry. The author has clearly explained the concepts. I read this book with great interest from cover to cover and immediately became a big fan. In this second revised edition, I found my head nodding up and down in agreement. I enjoyed the personal reflections on the great impact these concepts and experiences have had in Gregg's own life and share the same sentiment. Your own problem solving capability, success rate, speed, and confidence will increase tremendously by using these techniques. This book, and several copies, will accompany me in all of my consulting work. We owe a debt of gratitude to Dorian Shainin, Sir Arthur Conan Doyle, Francis Bacon, and now, Gregg Young.

Beyond variation reduction, this book incorporates all the Best Practices the author is familiar with, so it serves as a guide for more complete company-wide improvement. His definition, distinction, and use of different strategies for "open-ended" and "closed-end" type problems is excellent. In addition to the management levels in a company, there is an appeal to the "grassroots" of an organization. Many companies have missed opportunities to have these problem solving tools available and used by everyone. Some overly formalized problem solving systems have become elitist, and more about creating a lifelong career path for statisticians and quality professionals, than about improvement by getting everyone involved. Others have tried to keep this knowledge secret and proprietary in order to keep the benefits to themselves and their clients. These concepts should be used with no unnecessary barriers. The way to make giant strides is to get everyone involved, and have as many people as possible "reasoning backward". That's what this book and the Sherlock Holmes connection are all about. Young has taken this powerful knowledge and reduced it to a form where anyone can use it successfully. Everyone does not need to know why it works, or how it all came to be. They just need to know what to do to get results. This book helps people and businesses thrive. For this, I applaud Gregg Young and "Reasoning Backward".

Pete Peters
The Variation Specialists

> "The significant problems we face today cannot be solved at the same level of thinking we were at when we created them."
>
> **—Albert Einstein**

> "In solving a problem of this sort, the grand thing is to be able to reason backward. That is a very useful accomplishment, and a very easy one, but people do not practice it much. In the everyday affairs of life, it is more useful to reason forward, and so the other comes to be neglected. There are fifty who can reason synthetically for one who can reason analytically."
>
> "Always approach a case with an absolutely blank mind. Form no theories, just simply observe and draw inferences from your observations."
>
> "It is a capital mistake to theorize before one has data. Insensibly one begins to twist facts to suit theories, instead of theories to suit facts."
>
> "I never guess. It is a shocking habit – destructive to the logical faculty."
>
> "Once you eliminate the impossible, whatever remains, no matter how improbable, must be the truth."
>
> **— Sir Arthur Conan Doyle,**
> **Excerpts from *The Complete Sherlock Holmes***

Reasoning Backward

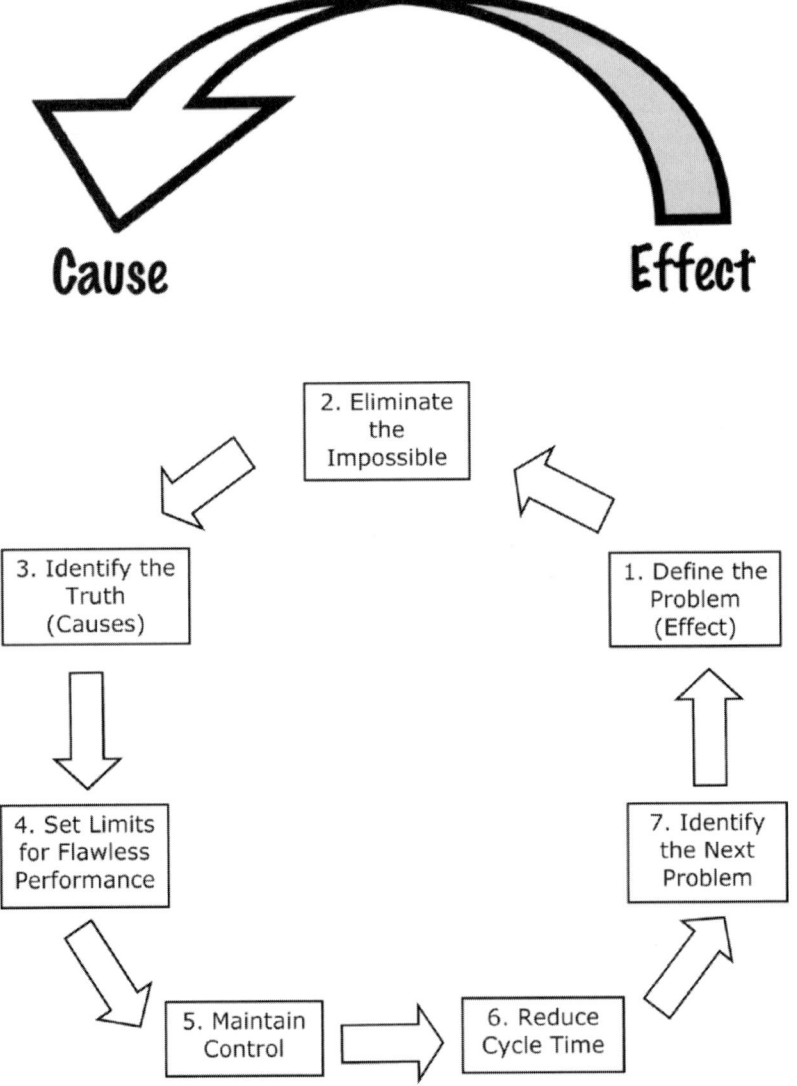

Sherlock Holmes' Top 10 Tips for Effective Problem Solving

1. "What is out of the common is usually a guide rather than a hindrance. In solving a problem of this sort, the grand thing is to be able to reason backward. That is a very useful accomplishment, and a very easy one, but people do not practice it much. In the everyday affairs of life, it is more useful to reason forward, and so the other comes to be neglected. There are fifty who can reason synthetically for one who can reason analytically ... Most people, if you describe a train of events to them, will tell you what the result would be. They can put those events together in their minds, and argue from them that something will come to pass. There are few people however, who, if you told them a result, would be able to evolve from their own inner consciousness what the steps were which led up to that result. This power is what I mean when I talk of reasoning backward, or analytically." – *A Study in Scarlet*

2. "When you have eliminated the impossible, whatever remains, no matter how improbable, must be the truth." – *The Sign of Four* (and several other stories)

3. "Always approach a case with an absolutely blank mind. It is always an advantage. Form no theories, just simply observe and draw inferences from your observations." – *The Adventure of the Cardboard Box*

   "It is a capital mistake to theorize before one has data. Insensibly one begins to twist facts to suit theories, instead of theories to suit facts." – *A Scandal in Bohemia*

4. "How dangerous it always is to reason from insufficient data." "Data! Data! Data!" he cried impatiently. "I can't make bricks without clay." – *The Adventure of the Speckled Band*

5. "It is of the highest importance in the art of detection to be able to recognize, out of a number of facts, which are incidental

and which vital. Otherwise, your energy and attention must be dissipated instead of being concentrated." – *The Reigate Puzzle*

6. "I can see nothing," said Watson. "On the contrary, Watson, you can see everything. You fail, however, to reason from what you see. You are too timid in drawing your inferences." – *The Adventure of the Blue Carbuncle*

7. "Detection is, or ought to be, an exact science, and should be treated in the same cold and unemotional manner. You have attempted to tinge it with romanticism, which produces much the same effect as if you worked a love story or an elopement into the fifth proposition of Euclid." – *The Sign of Four*

8. "I never guess. It is a shocking habit – destructive to the logical faculty." – *The Sign of Four*

9. "Nothing clears up a case so much as stating it to another person." – *Silver Blaze*

10. "You know my methods. Apply them." – *The Sign of Four*

Chapter 1

Sherlock Holmes on Problem Solving

The Problem with Problem Solving

Problem solving is a critical skill. We encounter problems almost everywhere, and our success depends on how we handle them. Some people solve problems very effectively by using Sherlock Holmes' logic and methods. They develop complete solutions to most problems very quickly. Most people are much less effective – they normally find partial solutions and much more slowly. The problem with problem solving is this inconsistency.

This difference in effectiveness is not a reflection of the people, but rather the problem solving strategies and tactics they use. With powerful Holmesian strategies and tactics, almost anyone can become an effective problem solver. With weak strategies and tactics, even the brightest and most experienced people have limited effectiveness. This book reveals the proven strategies and tactics that enable anyone – student or adult – to become an effective problem solver.

What is a problem? This book addresses two types of problems:

- **Closed-end Problems** – activities that work perfectly well most of the time, generating completely acceptable outcomes, but that generate unacceptable outcomes some of the time. These are "Fix What's Broken" situations.

- **Open-ended Problems** – situations where current performance is never acceptable, and where innovation is necessary to achieve a new level of performance.

Solving these different types of problems requires different skill sets. This book presents universal best practices for each type. These best practices were determined by evaluating dozens of different approaches according to the results they deliver. Many other books cover hundreds of problem solving tools and improvement methodologies, but this book is different in several ways.

− This book is comprehensive. It addresses both Closed-end Problems and Open-ended Problems, while other books address just one type or the other.
− This book is NOT a collection of hundreds of tools for problem solvers to consider. Such collections already exist, and they can easily overwhelm the reader. This book only presents those strategies, techniques, and tools that have consistently delivered superior results, that truly are best practices.
− This book targets adults and students. Today, students learn different subjects in school, but they don't learn how to use this knowledge to solve problems. They leave school with little or no insight about how to think analytically, so they are unable to solve problems quickly and completely. The same situation has traditionally existed everywhere, but in 2008, the Japanese government shifted its education focus from Memorization to Problem Solving. Fortunately, two opposite strategies are available for solving problems. Sherlock Holmes called them Reasoning Forward (divergent thinking) and Reasoning Backward (convergent thinking). Japan uses the more common but much weaker reasoning forward model. The reasoning backward approach has historically been 4X more effective, but it is not widely known in business and is virtually unknown in education.

This book introduces the reasoning backward tools to students for the first time, so they can leave school already prepared to become effective problem solvers.
- This is a handbook of the most effective choices, and only the most effective choices, for both Closed-end and Open-ended Problems.
- For Closed-end Problems, the most common reasoning forward approaches typically deliver partial solutions (20-50% improvement) after several months of effort. Conversely, the best practice reason backward approach delivers complete solutions, eliminating 90-100% of the problem in days to weeks. (The author's fastest experience was 100% elimination of a chronic problem in just 15 minutes.) The strategy behind this remarkable performance comes from *The Complete Sherlock Holmes* by Sir Arthur Conan Doyle. The problem solving tools based on Holmes' strategy were developed during the 20th century in manufacturing operations, but they have universal utility. Any reader can benefit from applying these methods. This book includes a variety of examples to demonstrate this versatility.
- For Open-end Problems that require innovation, conventional methods perform dismally. Historically, only 11% of all new products are successful. However, when development teams use the approach introduced here, the success rate jumps to 95%. While most people may never create a new product, the ways of thinking introduced here have utility in other situations. No list of best practice problem solving techniques would be complete without this method for successful innovation.

Strategy and Tactics for Closed-end Problems

Solving closed-end problems is detective work. Searching for the root causes of a problem is very much like searching for the perpetrator of a crime, so Sherlock Holmes' perspective is insightful.

Reasoning Backward

The first two Holmes stories include several short anecdotes that demonstrate the power of his method – Observation followed by Deduction.

The first comes from "A Study in Scarlet". Holmes is talking with Watson shortly after their first meeting.

> "The rules of deduction are invaluable to me in practical work. Observation with me is second nature. You appeared to be surprised when I told you, on our first meeting, that you had come from Afghanistan."
>
> "You were told, no doubt."
>
> "Nothing of the sort. I *knew* you came from Afghanistan. From long habit the train of thoughts ran so swiftly through my mind that I arrived at the conclusion without being conscious of intermediate steps. There were such steps, however. The train of reasoning ran, 'Here is a gentleman of medical type, but with the air of a military man. Clearly an army doctor, then. He has just come from the tropics, for his face is dark, and that is not the natural tint of his skin, for his wrists are fair. He has undergone hardship and sickness, as his haggard face says clearly. His left arm has been injured. He holds it in a stiff and unnatural manner. Where in the tropics could an English army doctor have seen much hardship and got his arm wounded? Clearly in Afghanistan.' The whole train of thought did not occupy a second. I then remarked that you came from Afghanistan, and you were astonished."
>
> "It is simple enough as you explain it," I said, smiling.

Later in the same conversation, Watson looks out the window and comments:

"I wonder what that fellow is looking for?" I asked, pointing to a stalwart, plainly dressed individual who was walking slowly down the other side of the street, looking anxiously at the number. He had a large blue envelope in his hand, and was evidently the bearer of a message.

"You mean the retired sergeant of Marines," said Sherlock Holmes.

"Brag and bounce!" thought I to myself. "He knows that I cannot verify his guess."

The thought had hardly passed through my mind when the man whom we were watching caught sight of the number on our door, and ran rapidly across the roadway. We heard a loud knock, a deep voice below, and heavy steps ascending the stair.

"For Mr. Sherlock Holmes," he said, stepping into the room and handing my friend the letter.

Here was an opportunity of taking the conceit out of him. He little thought of this when he made that random shot. "May I ask, my lad," I said, in the blandest voice, "what your trade may be?"

"Commissionaire, sir," he said, gruffly. "Uniform away for repairs."

"And your were?" I asked, with a slightly malicious glance at my companion.

"A sergeant, sir, Royal Marine Light Infantry, sir. No answer? Right, sir."

He clicked his heels together, raised his hand in salute, and was gone.

I confess that I was considerably startled by this fresh proof of the practical nature of my companion's theories.

My respect for his powers of analysis increased wondrously. There still remained some lurking suspicion in my mind, however, that the whole thing was a prearranged episode, intended to dazzle me, though what earthly object he could have in taking me in was past my comprehension. When I looked at him he had finished reading the note, and his eyes had assumed the vacant lack-luster expression which showed mental abstraction.

"How in the world did you deduce that?" I asked.

"Deduce what?" said he, petulantly.

"Why, that he was a retired sergeant of Marines."

"I have no time for trifles," he answered, brusquely; then with a smile, "Excuse my rudeness. You broke the thread of my thoughts; but perhaps it is as well. So you actually were not able to see that that man was a sergeant of Marines?"

"No, indeed."

"It was easier to know it than to explain why I know it. If you were asked to prove that two and two made four, you might find some difficulty, and yet you are quite sure of the fact. Even across the street I could see a great blue anchor tattooed on the back of the fellow's hand. That smacked of the sea. He had a military carriage, however, and regulation sidewhiskers. There we have the marine. He was a man with some amount of self-importance and a certain air of command. You must have observed the way in which he held his head and swung his cane. A steady, respectable, middle-aged man, too, on the face of him all facts which led me to believe that he had been a sergeant."

"Wonderful!" I exclaimed.

"Commonplace," said Holmes.

Sherlock Holmes on Problem Solving

The third anecdote comes from "The Sign of Four". Watson poses a problem to Holmes:

"I have heard you say it is difficult for a man to have any object in daily use without leaving the impress of his individuality upon it in such a way that a trained observer might read it. Now, I have here a watch which has recently come into my possession. Would you have the kindness to let me have an opinion upon the character or habits of the late owner?"

I handed him over the watch with some slight feeling of amusement in my heart, for the test was, as I thought, an impossible one, and I intended it as a lesson against the somewhat dogmatic tone which he occasionally assumed. He balanced the watch in his hand, gazed hard at the dial, opened the back, and examined the works, first with his naked eyes and then with a powerful convex lens. I could hardly keep from smiling at his crestfallen face when he finally snapped the case to and handed it back.

"There are hardly any data," he remarked. "The watch has been recently cleaned, which robs me of my most suggestive facts."

"You are right," I answered. "It was cleaned before being sent to me."

In my heart I accused my companion of putting forward a most lame and impotent excuse to cover his failure. What data could he expect from an uncleaned watch?

"Though unsatisfactory, my research has not been entirely barren," he observed, staring up at the ceiling with dreamy, lack-luster eyes. "Subject to your correction, I should judge that the watch belonged to your elder brother, who inherited it from your father."

"Quite so. The W. suggests your own name. The date of the watch is nearly fifty years back, and the initials are as old as the watch: so it was made for the last generation. Jewelry usually descends to the eldest son, and he is most likely to have the same name as the father. Your father has, if I remember right, been dead many years. It has, therefore, been in the hands of your eldest brother."

"Right, so far," said I. "Anything else?"

"He was a man of untidy habits – very untidy and careless. He was left with good prospects, but he threw away his chances, lived for some time in poverty with occasional short intervals of prosperity, and finally, taking to drink he died. That is all I can gather."

I sprang from my chair and limped impatiently about the room with considerable bitterness in my heart.

"This is unworthy of you, Holmes," I said. "I could not have believed that you would have descended to this. You have made inquiries into the history of my unhappy brother, and you now pretend to deduce this knowledge in some fanciful way. You cannot expect me to believe that you have read all this from his old watch! It is unkind and, to speak plainly, has a touch of charlatanism in it."

"My dear doctor, said he kindly, "pray accept my apologies. Viewing the matter as an abstract problem, I had forgotten how personal and painful a thing it might be to you. I assure you, however, that I never even knew that you had a brother until you handed me the watch."

"Then how in the name of all that is wonderful did you get these facts? They are absolutely correct in every particular."

"Ah, that is good luck. I could only say what was the balance of probability. I did not at all expect to be so accurate."

"But it was not mere guesswork?"

"No, no: I never guess. It is a shocking habit – destructive to the logical faculty. What seems strange to you is only so because you do not follow my train of thought or observe the small facts upon which large inferences may depend. For example, I began by stating that your brother was careless. When you observe the lower part of the watch-case you notice that it was not only dented in two places but it is cut and marked all over from the habit of keeping other hard objects, such as coins or keys, in the same pocket. Surely it is no great feat to assume that a man who treats a fifty-guinea watch so cavalierly must be a careless man. Neither is it a very far-fetched inference that a man who inherits one article of such value is pretty well provided for in other respects."

I nodded to show that I followed his reasoning.

"It is very customary for pawnbrokers in England, when they take a watch, to scratch the numbers of the ticket with a pin-point upon the inside of the case. It is more handy than a label as there is no risk of the number being lost or transposed. There are no less than four such numbers visible to my lens on the inside of this case. Inference – that your brother was often at low water. Secondary inference – that he had occasional bursts of prosperity, or he could not have redeemed the pledge. Finally, I ask you to look at the inner plate, which contains the keyhole. Look at the thousands of scratches all round the hole – marks where the key has slipped. What sober man's key could have scored those grooves? But you will never see a drunkard's watch without them. He winds it at night, and he leaves these traces of his unsteady hand. Where is the mystery in all this?"

"It is as clear as daylight," I answered. "I regret the injustice which I did you. I should have had more faith in your marvelous faculty."

Reasoning Backward

The following excerpts from *The Complete Sherlock Holmes* create a framework for readers to effectively attack closed-end problems. Consider them Holmes' Top 10 Tips.

Tip #1 "I have already explained to you that what is out of the common is usually a guide rather than a hindrance. In solving a problem of this sort, the grand thing is to be able to reason backward. That is a very useful accomplishment, and a very easy one, but people do not practice it much. In the everyday affairs of life, it is more useful to reason forward, and so the other comes to be neglected. There are fifty who can reason synthetically for one who can reason analytically."

"Most people, if you describe a train of events to them, will tell you what the result would be. They can put those events together in their minds, and argue from them that something will come to pass. There are few people however, who, if you told them a result, would be able to evolve from their own inner consciousness what the steps were which led up to that result. This power is what I mean when I talk of reasoning backward, or analytically."

— *A Study in Scarlet*

This quotation is the fundamental concept all effective problem solvers use. Everything derives from it.

Synthetic thought is the way we live life everyday. We reason forward from cause to effect. We generate a variety of possible options, and then decide which one or ones to pursue. During problem solving, this approach is inappropriate when searching for root causes because the root causes already exist and simply need to be discovered. It is ineffective because it guesses about root causes rather than systematically searching for them. Synthetic thinking is only appropriate for developing possible solutions to implement, after the searcher has identified the root causes analytically.

Sherlock Holmes on Problem Solving

Analytical thinking is convergent thinking. It reasons backward from effect to cause. It is the superior approach for identifying root causes because it quickly leads to complete solutions. Analytical thinkers systematically look for clues that will reveal all of the root causes. They use observation followed by deduction, the same technique used by Holmes. This straightforward approach has helped thousands of people become effective problem solvers.

> **Tip #2** "Once you eliminate the impossible, whatever remains, no matter how improbable, must be the truth."
> — *The Sign of Four*

This most famous tip from the Sherlock Holmes' stories perhaps best summarizes effective problem solving. Observe the situation. Look for patterns and consistent differences between the best performance and the worst performance. Eliminate all factors that are not consistently different. Any factors that remain, factors that are consistently different when a problem exists and when it doesn't, must be involved in some way. These are the clues that lead investigators to discover all the root causes and develop complete solutions.

Holmes' comment "no matter how improbable" is particularly relevant to effective problem solving. The most critical factor in most problems is something no one has ever suspected. No amount of hypothesizing root causes would ever have come up with it as a factor. The primary reason to "observe with an absolutely blank mind" and "never guess" is to capture the causes one would otherwise overlook.

> **Tip #3** "Always approach a case with an absolutely blank mind. It is always an advantage. Form no theories, just simply observe and draw inferences from your observations."
> —*The Adventure of the Cardboard Box*

Reasoning Backward

> "It is a capital mistake to theorize before one has data. Insensibly one begins to twist facts to suit theories, instead of theories to suit facts."
> —*A Scandal in Bohemia*

These comments highlight the critical weakness of reasoning forward when solving problems. People guess first, and then test their guesses, rather than simply observing and letting the situation reveal itself. Save all hypothesizing for identifying possible solutions after reasoning backward has identified the root causes.

Tip #4
> "How dangerous it is to reason from insufficient data."
>
> "Data, Data, Data! I can't make bricks without clay."
> —*The Adventure of the Speckled Band*

These comments elaborate on Tip #3. Observe carefully. Deduce carefully. Make sure your conclusions do not overreach your data.

Tip #5
> "It is of the highest importance in the art of detection to be able to recognize out of a number of facts which are incidental and which are vital."
> —*The Reigate Puzzle*

Invariably there are dozens, hundreds, or even thousands of possible causes for any problem, but just as certainly, no more than three factors are responsible for 90-100% of the problem. The most effective problem solvers use Holmes' "observation, deduction, knowledge" strategy and a few simple tools to eliminate the incidental and unimportant factors and focus on the vital few.

Sherlock Holmes on Problem Solving

Tip #6
"I can see nothing," said Watson, handing it back to Holmes.

"On the contrary, Watson, you can see everything. You fail, however, to reason from what you see. You are too timid in drawing your inferences."
—*The Adventure of the Blue Carbuncle*

This tip is the extension of Tip #4 to its natural conclusion. Tip #4 guides the investigator always to have adequate data to draw sound conclusions. Tip #6 challenges the investigator to use the data wisely and reason through the problem completely. A few simple tools make this a straightforward process.

Tip #7
"Detection is, or ought to be, an exact science, and should be treated in the same cold unemotional manner. When you attempt to tinge it with romanticism, you produce the same effect as if you worked a love story into the fifth proposition of Euclid."
—*The Sign of Four*

Tips #1 and #2 cautioned against speculation or guesswork when approaching a problem. Tip #7 goes a step further, cautioning against the introduction of emotion into the deductive process as well. It is easy, even natural, to let one's feelings get involved. Resist this temptation. Simply let the data reveal the answer.

Tip #8
"I never guess. It is a shocking habit -- destructive to the logical faculty."
—*The Sign of Four*

Hypotheses, theories, and guesses are never part of an effective problem solver's search for root causes. This philosophy goes back nearly 400 years to Sir Francis Bacon, the creator of the Scientific Method. In *Novum Organum*, published in 1620, Bacon wrote:

Reasoning Backward

> "Men have sought to make a world from their own conception and to draw from their own minds all the material which they employed, but if, instead of doing so, they had consulted experience and observation, they would have the facts and not opinions to reason about, and might have ultimately arrived at the knowledge of the laws which govern the material world."

He counsels us that man, lacking in complete knowledge and having natural biases, cannot consistently reason a solution without data. Bacon never guessed. He only observed and formulated hypotheses based upon his observations. He called his first hypothesis the "First Vintage", an interim conclusion, but not the final one. He then made further observations and refined his First Vintage to a "Second Vintage". In this way, he obtained the truth "by gradual degrees".

The basic outline of the Scientific Method today can be stated:
- State the Problem
- Conduct Research
- Formulate Hypotheses
- Test the Hypotheses
- Confirm Hypotheses, or Formulate New Hypotheses

The difference between reasoning forward and reasoning backward is the second step. Those who reason forward spend little or no time conducting research before starting to formulate hypotheses about possible root causes. These investigators develop a long list of possibilities, all of which require testing. By shortening or omitting the research/observation step and immediately formulating dozens or hundreds of root cause hypotheses to test, today's most common problem solving processes have strayed from the Scientific Method.

Sherlock Holmes on Problem Solving

The greater the number of hypotheses that must be tested, the longer it takes to find the first root cause and the lower the probability that an investigator will find all the root causes.

Holmes' method of reasoning backward is true to Bacon. It focuses on conducting research, observing and gathering data from the situation. Holmes' deductions, the conclusions based on his observations, are his hypotheses. His theories always fit the facts he has observed without any bias. Holmes' "Observation, then Deduction" methodology is the approach that remains true to the Scientific Method.

> **Tip #9** "Nothing clears up a case so much as stating it to another person."
> —*Silver Blaze*

Writing straightens thinking, and thinking straightens writing. Presenting a summary of the situation to another person, whether verbally or on paper, requires one to consolidate all the data, which leads to additional insights and better understanding.

> **Tip #10** "You know my methods. Apply them."
> —*The Sign of Four*

Observation, Deduction, Knowledge. Never guess. The natural tendency for most people is to brainstorm. Effective problem solvers resist this temptation. Apply Holmes' simple strategy to dramatically improve problem-solving skills. Observe what's different when the problem occurs, and when it doesn't. Look for consistent differences. Factors that aren't consistently different aren't involved in the problem. Ignore them. Anything that is consistently different is involved in the problem in some way. It is a clue – pursue it. Use the clues to deduce the root cause or causes of the problem.

This guideline leads to a basic procedure for approaching any problem. Sir Francis Bacon and Sherlock Holmes used a simple, three-step method: Observation – Deduction – Knowledge. Effective problem solvers use the same approach. They observe carefully to discover clues, so they can eliminate the impossible. Then, they deduce the causes and implement the solution. The following steps are a tactical outline for implementing Holmes' strategy.

1. Define the problem precisely. Identify what it is, and what it isn't. Create a Decision Tree to capture this problem definition in a box at the top of the tree. Record progress on this tree. This technique originates with Bacon. He described making a list of all things in which the phenomenon in question occurs, a list of all things where it never occurs, and then considering factors by the degree to which they correlate to the presence or absence of the phenomenon. He would then look for consistencies within the lists and consistent differences between the lists. This would lead to his First Vintage hypotheses, his initial (but not final) conclusions.

2. Identify what makes the outcome of the activity good or bad. Describe the outcome when everything performs correctly. Identify the acceptability limits for this outcome.

3. Track performance with a Histogram or recent history.

4. Eliminate poor housekeeping and background noise as possible causes of the problem. This may resolve the problem immediately with no further study. It assures that all subsequent observations generate solid clues.

5. Identify categories to explore when searching for the most critical factor, the one responsible for 50-100% of all bad outcomes. Use the Multi-Vari tool described in Chapter 3. The category that contains the most critical factor will have the largest range of variation. Multi-Vari also reveals non-random patterns that provide additional clues about the root causes.

6. Compare performance extremes, the best versus the worst, to identify patterns and consistent differences. The root

causes will vary most when outcome performance varies most. Non-random patterns and consistent differences are clues that lead to the critical factors – pursue them. Factors that don't change are not critical – ignore them. This simple comparison of best and worst eliminates 95-100% of the non-critical factors immediately.

7. Confirm that the identified critical factors really are root causes by varying them intentionally to turn the problem on and off.

8. Establish limits for the critical factors that will generate flawless outcomes.

9. Develop the best solution to deliver flawless performance. This is the only place in the problem solving process where brainstorming or other forms of divergent thinking are appropriate.

10. Implement the best solution along with controls so the outcomes remain flawless.

11. Track the activity to maintain flawless performance.

Holmes' reasoning backward strategy and all of the best practice tools in this book have delivered superior problem solving results for many years. This approach derives from the following universal principles.

The Universal Principles

Effects have causes. Whenever any activity generates a good outcome, it is because every aspect of the activity is correct. Such an activity does not randomly start generating bad outcomes. Whenever it generates bad outcomes, something has changed. Problem solving is the search for what has changed. Problem solvers who use Holmes' reasoning backward model start with the unacceptable effect and work backward to discover its root causes. As long as the activity delivers both good and bad outcomes, it is always possible to find the root causes by using the reasoning backward model.

Pareto's Law is universal. (The 80/20 Rule) As it applies to problem solving, this principle becomes, "Whenever an activity that is capable of generating good outcomes makes a bad outcome, no more than three root causes are responsible." The primary root cause is always responsible for at least 50%, and sometimes 100% of all bad outcomes. If a second root cause exists, it is usually responsible for about 15-25% of the problem. If there is a third root cause, it creates 10-15% of the defects. The challenge for problem solvers has always been to discover these 1-3 critical factors in the presence of dozens or hundreds of non-critical factors. Observant investigators pursue the clues generated by the critical factors and ignore everything else. They make Pareto's Law work for them, not against them.

If an activity EVER generates good outcomes, the activity is fundamentally sound. Whenever good outcomes occur, every input and condition is correct. Conversely, whenever a bad outcome occurs, something has changed. Once one set of conditions exists that works well, the process is fundamentally sound, even if these conditions occur only 1% of the time. Once one set of conditions works, the goal of problem solving is to discover which conditions are critical. For example, when Edison first discovered a filament that did not burn up in the light bulb after trying thousands that failed, he knew one set of conditions that worked. He finally knew where to start to make the bulb more robust because he finally knew one set of conditions that was fundamentally sound.

Compare performance extremes to identify non-random patterns and consistent differences. This concept is the central idea behind all the reasoning backward methods, building off the previous three principles. For any activity that sometimes produces good outcomes and sometimes produces bad, no more than three critical factors (out of dozens or hundreds of possible factors) are responsible for nearly 100% of the problem. Therefore, effective problem solvers directly compare the very best outcomes to the very worst outcomes. The 1-3 critical factors, the root causes of the problem, are certain to show maximum variation in these extremes. Any factor that is consistently different when the problem occurs is critical, and they pursue it. Any factor that is not consistently different when the problem occurs is non-critical, so they ignore it. This simple concept allows problem solvers to eliminate hundreds of non-critical factors immediately and focus on the critical factors right away.

The guidelines for the best practice approach appear in the Table. This approach eliminates bad outcomes by reducing variation of the critical factors in any activity, but it doesn't address the cycle time at all. To be a complete improvement process, one must also address cycle time, so two cycle time reduction methods are included in this book as well. Problem solvers usually eliminate bad outcomes first before addressing cycle time. If they reduce cycle time first, the activity will simply create more bad outcomes faster.

The Best Practice Approach
Never hypothesize the root causes of problems. Non-invasively observe the activity to discover clues that will identify the critical factors.
If an activity usually works well, but occasionally generates a bad outcome, it is fundamentally sound. When it creates good outcomes, every condition is set correctly. When it creates a bad outcome, some condition or conditions have changed.
No more than 3 critical factors are responsible for 90-100% of all bad outcomes.
One factor is always responsible for at least 50% of bad outcomes.
Compare performance extremes to discover patterns and consistent differences, which always relate to the 1, 2, or 3 critical factors.
The solution is tighter control of the critical factors.

Examples of Reasoning Backward

Reasoning backward observes first to find clues that reveal the root causes. Reasoning forward hypothesizes root causes first without any data. The following examples compare these two approaches directly to demonstrate the power of reasoning backward.

The reasoning backward tools use categories, non-random patterns, and consistent differences between good and bad outcomes to provide clues about the root causes of a problem. The patterns indicate where to look for root causes, and just as important, where not to look. The first two examples use patterns. The next two examples use consistent differences. The last example uses both concepts together.

Example 1: The Dictionary Challenge

The challenge is to find any word in a dictionary by asking up to 20 Yes/No questions. It uses Holmes' "eliminate the impossible" logic repeatedly to find the chosen word.

Someone using the "hypothesize and test" reasoning forward approach will guess words with a one-in-tens-of-thousands chance of success. Twenty questions are not even enough to try each letter once.

The reasoning backward approach starts by breaking the dictionary into two halves. It uses the first question to determine which half contains the mystery word. Assume the dictionary has about 1000 pages, and that the word is "fortify", found on page 329 of the dictionary. The first question eliminates half the words in the dictionary by determining that the mystery word comes on or before page 500. The questioner uses the strategy of eliminating half the remaining words with each question, as shown below.

Sherlock Holmes on Problem Solving

1. Is the word found beyond page 500?	No
2. Is it beyond page 250?	Yes
3. Is it beyond page 375?	No
4. Is it beyond page 312?	Yes
5. Is it beyond page 343?	No
6. Is it beyond page 327?	Yes
7. Is it beyond page 335?	No
8. Is it beyond page 331?	No
9. Is it beyond page 329?	No
10. Is it page 328?	No
11. Is it in the left column?	No
12. Is it in the top half of the right column?	Yes
13. Is it in the top quarter of the column?	No
14. Is it between 1/4 and 3/8 down the column?	No
15. Is it between 3/8 and 7/16 down the column?	No
16. Only three words remain. Is it "fortification"?	No
17. Is it "fortifier"?	No

After 10 questions, the investigator knows the word is on page 329. (Beyond 327, not beyond 329, and not 328)

Next, the questioner attacks page 329 in the same way, as shown. After 17 binary split questions, the questioner knows the word is "fortify" by process of elimination.

This approach creates "categories" by splitting the total into two halves, and observing which half contains the word, and which half doesn't. The next example uses the same concept, but with three categories instead of two.

Example 2: Pick a Card, Any Card...

This simple example with playing cards demonstrates the "category strategy" in action, as shown in the following figure. This powerful strategy assures the problem solver can identify an unknown card from a set of 27 cards by examining categories just 3 times.

The dealer lays out the 27 cards in 3 columns of 9 cards each as shown in A, and then asks someone to select one card and keep its identity secret, but to identify which column it is in. In this example, the person selected the 5 of clubs (shaded) from the left column. The dealer then picks up the three columns of cards, putting the selected column in the middle, and deals them out as shown in B. Once again, he/she asks the other person to identify the column that contains the selected card. As before, the dealer picks up the columns with the selected column in the middle, and deals them out as shown in C. Finally, he/she asks the other person to select the column with the chosen card one more time. The chosen card will always be the one in the center row of the selected column.

Sherlock Holmes on Problem Solving

When the person selects a column in Step A, it eliminates the other two columns. These 18 cards form the top three and bottom three rows of B. The chosen card is in row 4, 5, or 6. The selection in B removes 6 of these 9 cards, leaving only the 5, 6, and 2 of clubs. These three appear in the middle row in C, so the choice of column in the third step identifies the specific card every time.

The Multi-Vari tool in Chapter 3 uses the same principle. First, the problem solver selects the categories to consider. The most critical factor always causes the greatest variation in results, so whichever category has the greatest range of variation must be the category with the most critical factor. Every other category is eliminated.

Contrast this convergent strategy with the divergent strategy of reasoning forward. The dealer would simply be guessing cards, beginning with a 1-in-27 chance of guessing correctly. After three guesses, his odds have only increased to 3-in-27, 11%. It would take 14 guesses before the probability of success would reach 50%.

This category strategy provides three valuable insights.
1. It shows where to look for the most critical factor.
2. At least as important, it shows where not to look for the most critical factor.
3. It may reveal non-random patterns that provide additional clues and insights about other critical factors.

Example 3: Finding Three Needles in a Haystack

The contrast between reasoning forward and reasoning backward is dramatic in this classic problem. The search for needles in a haystack is an analogy for finding the few critical factors among hundreds of non-critical factors.

The "hypothesize root causes first, then test the hypotheses" approach is like adding more hay to the pile before starting to search for the needles by hand. It takes a long time to find the first needle, and an exhaustively long time to persevere and find them all.

Bacon and Holmes' direction to "observe first" is smarter. The searcher focuses on the consistent differences between needles and hay. After noting that needles are metal and magnetic, and that hay is neither, the searcher can use a metal detector to discover where to look, and then use a powerful magnet to attract all the needles quickly.

Note that burning the haystack or throwing it into a swimming pool would also address the consistent differences between needles and hay, but they are not attractive choices since they destroy the hay.

Example 4: M&M'S® Brand Chocolate Candies

Another analogy is looking for 3 M&M'S® Peanut Chocolate Candies in a large pile of M&M'S® Milk Chocolate Candies (Plain).

When one brainstorms possible root causes and then starts testing the hypotheses, it is like adding more unfilled candies to the pile and then dipping into the pile with a spoon, hoping to capture the peanut-filled candies. It usually takes many spoonfuls to find the first peanut candy, and an exhaustive number of spoonfuls to find all three.

The smarter approach focuses on the consistent differences between the unfilled and the peanut-filled candies. The peanut-filled candies are nearly spherical or oblong and the shortest dimension is about .375", while the unfilled candies are disks less than 0.25" thick. This leads to at least two possible search strategies that take advantage of this consistent difference. One option is to pour all the candies out onto a flat surface. The three peanut-filled candies will stand out when viewed from the side because they are all 2-6 times thicker than the unfilled candies. A second option is to slide all the candies down a ramp with a vertical gap of 0.25". All the unfilled candies will pass under the bar, while the peanut-filled candies stop at the bar, as shown.

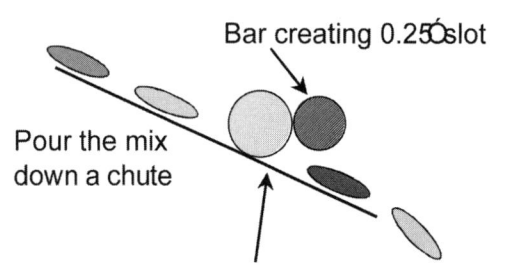

Bar creating 0.250" slot

Pour the mix down a chute

Trap all the Peanut-filled candies.
Ignore all the Unfilled candies.

Consistent differences provide powerful clues. Effective problem solvers observe the differences carefully, so they find complete solutions quickly.

Example 5: Find the Light Ball

This last example uses both categories and consistent differences to solve a problem. It uses 80 steel balls that all appear to be identical. However, one ball is lighter than the others are because it is hollow. The problem solver has a two-pan balance that only shows which side has the heavier load. The challenge is to identify the lighter ball by using the scale just 4 times.

When reasoning forward, one guesses which balls to weigh, either alone on in groups, and gets to the answer eventually, but the probability of finding the light ball in just 4 measurements is low.

Reasoning backward finds the light ball in exactly 4 readings. One first divides the balls into 3 groups – two groups of 27 balls and one group of 26. The first reading measures the two groups of 27 against each other, resulting in one of two outcomes. If one group is lighter, it contains the light ball, which eliminates the heavier 27 and the other 26 balls immediately. If the scale balances, then all 54 balls on the scale are eliminated – the light ball is among the other 26.

Next, one divides the remaining balls into thirds again. (Three groups of 9 if there are 27, or 9, 9, and 8 if 26 are left.) The second weighing is 9 vs. 9. As before, if one group is lighter, it contains the light ball. If they are equal, then the light ball is one of the 8 balls that was not weighed. This leaves either 8 or 9 balls left that contain the light ball.

The third step repeats this process. The remaining balls are divided into 3 groups of 3 (or 3, 3, and 2 if 8 remain), and one weighs 3 vs. 3. Once again, this eliminates two groups of balls, leaving either 2 or 3 balls, one of which is lighter.

The final weighing is 1 vs. 1. If there were just 2 balls left, one will be lighter. If there were 3 balls left, then one of the balls on the balance might be lighter, or if the 2 balls on the balance are equal, then the unweighed ball is the lighter one.

In this example, using groupings and consistent differences together solves the problem in exactly four steps with 100% certainty.

Summary:

This chapter introduced Sir Francis Bacon and Sherlock Holmes' approach.
- **Observe patterns and consistent differences** to identify every root cause and solve problems quickly and completely.
- It included the universal principles that make this approach so effective.
  ⇒ **Effects have causes.**
  ⇒ **Pareto's Law is universal.**
  ⇒ **If an activity EVER generates good outcomes, the activity is fundamentally sound.**
  ⇒ **Compare performance extremes to identify non-random patterns and consistent differences.**

The five examples illustrate why reasoning backward is so much more effective than reasoning forward.

Chapter 2 builds on this foundation. It includes strategies and tactics for implementing this approach. It first introduces a set of strategies designed to help students solve problems in school. Then, it introduces the set of tools based on Bacon and Holmes' methods that has been remarkably successful in solving problems in the workplace. Finally, Chapter 2 shows the linkage between the school strategies and the workplace tools that reduce these strategies to practice, so anyone can become an effective problem solver.

The rest of the book presents these powerful tools in detail. Each chapter presents one tool and includes several examples that demonstrate its use. The examples come from a variety of situations to demonstrate the universal utility of the observation-based approach.

Chapter 2

Today's Best Practice Tools For Solving Closed-end Problems

An Overview of Strategies and Tactics

After deciding to use Holmes' Reasoning Backward method of Observation followed by Deduction, the next question is how to do it. This chapter introduces the specific tools anyone can use to think analytically and solve problems quickly and completely.

Ten Universal Strategies

Schools today rarely address problem-solving strategies in detail. Teachers may discuss it briefly when covering the Scientific Method in science classes, or it may be mentioned in a mathematics class. Several useful strategies for students exist, but most curricula do not spend time covering them. In their book, *Problem-Solving Strategies for Efficient and Elegant Solution, Grades 6-12: A Resource for the Mathematics Teacher*, Alfred S. Posamentier and Stephen Krulik lay out ten powerful strategies for solving mathematics problems and problems in everyday life. These ten strategies are the core concepts behind the reasoning backward tools covered in the rest of this book.

Strategy #1: **Work backward**. In math problems that require a proof, this method is obvious, but it also has broader utility. Beginning with the end in mind is always sound strategy. People live their lives by working forward, but when problems occur, working backward from the effect to the causes is most effective. Working backward is the preferred method when developing time schedules, analyzing traffic accidents and criminal investigations, mapping out a route for a trip, scheduling airplane flights, students planning their courses in high school in preparation for college, and in many games driven by endgame strategies. Of all ten strategies, working backward is the most powerful (hence it being #1 on the list), and also the most unnatural. Effective problem solvers take Sherlock Holmes' advice and always start by working backward. The clues uncovered by working backward dictate what strategy to apply next.

Strategy #2: **Find a pattern**. In math problems, the search for repeating patterns provides clues and often leads to solutions. In everyday life, people use patterns to remember numbers, addresses, to solve crimes, and in medical research. Police officers use this approach to observe recurring patterns when monitoring crowd behavior.

Strategy #3: **Adopt a different point of view**. This can also mean **act out the problem** or **model it using objects**. This approach is very common in geometry problems, but it applies in many other types of problems as well. In everyday life, working backward always provides a different point of view. Other examples include searching for someone in a crowd by finding a high point above everyone, a presenter looking at the presentation from the audience's view, sports teams developing plans built around their opponent's strengths and weaknesses rather than their own, and during negotiations.

Strategy #4: **Solve a simpler problem**. This is an excellent strategy in many situations. Examine the given data and look for an analogous problem that is easier to solve. An everyday example is when someone starts using new computer software. They will often begin by using part of its functionality rather than trying to master everything up front. In many complex operations, it may be very difficult to analyze the finished output. It is often much simpler to study an earlier point in the operation.

Strategy #5: **Consider extreme cases**. This can also mean **search for highlights and copy shining successes**. This often works well in math problems, especially geometry problems. In everyday situations, this is perhaps the most powerful strategy when reasoning backward. Consider the activity when it works perfectly, and when it is at its worst. Look for consistent differences. They are the clues that lead to the root causes. People also use this strategy when considering best case and worst-case scenarios, special cases, strategies for large purchases and garage sales, budgeting time, and new product testing.

Strategy #6: **Make a drawing, picture, or diagram**. Many math problems benefit from this technique, and it is widely used in everyday life as well. Consider maps, graphs, instruction manuals, accident reports, home décor layouts, sports plays, and note taking.

Strategy #7: **Guess intelligently and check, including approximations**. In math problems, one can make an estimate of the answer and test it to approach the answer in a series of steps. In everyday life one uses this technique when testing the doneness of a roast in the oven, when a carpenter tests the fit of an odd-shaped piece of wood into a specific place, and when a lawyer tests questions before an interview to establish which ones are most effective.

Strategy #8: **Account for all possibilities**, or **make an organized or exhaustive list**. This works well in many math problems, and it is widely used to decide the mode of transportation and route for a trip, to diagnose computer malfunctions or why a lamp doesn't work, to study a menu or choose a TV program. It is a good choice in everyday life when the list of possibilities is finite and manageable. It is less useful in many chronic problem situations because the number of possible causes is too large, and the most critical factor is often something that no one would ever consider. In these cases, this technique leads to frustration rather than to a root complete solution.

Strategy #9: **Organize data**, or **make a table or graph**. The key to solving many math problems is to organize the given information

Reasoning Backward

in a different way. It might be visual, tabular, or simply another way of looking at the data. One uses the same approach in many situations, such as organizing bills by category, budgeting, planning a shopping or sightseeing trip, preparing records for filing income tax forms, studying for tests, analyzing surveys, organizing closets, rooms, workplaces, and data mining activities.

Strategy #10: **Reason logically**. Most math problems use this principle without ever mentioning it, and it is fundamental in much of everyday life. One uses logical reasoning in conversation, negotiation, problem prevention, planning work strategies, determining the strength of an argument, planning a court case, and in achieving success or advancement on the job.

Each of the tools presented in this book uses several of these strategies at once to make it easy for anyone to become an effective problem solver. The reasoning backward method includes four phases of tools. A table follows the discussion of each phase showing which strategies are Always (***), Usually (**), Sometimes (*), and Rarely or Never ( ) as part of using each specific tool.

First, Clue Generation (Eliminate the Impossible) uses the process of elimination to discover clues about the critical factors. The clue generation tools eliminate non-critical factors, so the few factors that remain are involved in some way. They put into practice Holmes' basic strategy, "Once you eliminate the impossible, whatever remains, no matter how improbable, must be the truth." Clue Generation eliminates 95-100% of the non-critical factors, so only a few candidates remain.

The second phase, Identification and Validation (Identify the Truth), examines the few remaining factors still left after Clue Generation and determines which ones actually are critical. Validation confirms the critical factors by varying them intentionally to turn the problem on and off.

Next, Optimization establishes the right values for the critical factors, so the activity can operate flawlessly.

Finally, the Control phase prevents the problem from recurring.

Today's Best Practice Tools For Solving Closed-end Problems

After the reasoning backward tools have eliminated the problem, investigators can work to shorten the cycle time of the activity.

Problem solving is straightforward when one reasons backward, but most situations require a series of tools to solve the problem completely. The power of reasoning backward is the organized structure it provides. Complete solutions become the expected outcomes, while approaches that reason forward usually generate partial solutions and frustration.

A useful analogy comes from golf. A new problem is a new hole to play. Reasoning backward means choosing each shot based on the location of the hole. The tools are the different clubs in a player's golf bag. Every situation calls for a different club. Golf success occurs when a series of shots puts the ball in the cup. A hole-in-one can happen, and one tool can sometimes solve a problem completely, but that is not the norm. Investigators should always expect to use a series of tools to solve a problem.

Eliminate the Impossible – Clue Generation

Clue generation tools are the first choice when starting on any closed-end problem. These non-invasive tools are observation techniques in line with Holmes' approach to solving crimes and are useful in any situation. They sample finished outcomes looking for clues about the causes of bad outcomes. Historically, in about 75% of cases, people solve problems completely just by observing the activity with these non-invasive techniques and looking for patterns and consistent differences.

Clue Generation includes four techniques. Multi-Vari and Concentration Charts look for non-random patterns when bad outcomes occur. Paired Comparisons™ and Component Search™ look for consistent differences between the best and worst outcomes.

Multi-Vari is usually the first tool chosen. It periodically samples outcomes from the activity looking for non-random patterns that provide clues about the critical factors. First create categories or families of variation to study. Then, observe which category contains the widest range of outcomes because it contains the most critical factor. Multi-Vari can also reveal non-random variation patterns that provide additional clues about the critical factors. These simple data tell an investigator where look for the most critical factor, where not to look, and what tool to select for the next step in the search.

A **Concentration Chart** is the next tool when searching for recurring, non-random patterns of defects. It might be a list, or it could be a diagram of an object showing the location, nature, frequency, and severity of the problem. Pareto's Law assures that the flaws will not be random – there will be repetitive patterns that will provide clues about the root causes.

Paired Comparisons™ looks for consistent differences between multiple samples of the very best outcomes from an activity and an equal number of the very worst outcomes. In the first variation of this tool, compare a best sample and a worst sample directly, head-to-head, and look for consistent differences. In a second variation, collect all the information that exists on each of several best and worst samples and then rank all the samples according to each factor. Factors that are consistently different between best and worst are involved in the creation of the defects in some way. Factors that are not consistently different are non-critical. By using this tool early, investigators quickly identify a handful of possible candidates, which is essential to solving problems quickly and completely.

The first recorded use of the Paired Comparisons approach is in Sir Francis Bacon's *Novum Organum* in 1620. He listed things always associated with a phenomenon and things never associated with the phenomenon. Then, he identified consistencies within each list, and consistent differences between each list. These observations led him to his First Vintage, his initial clues and conclusions that would gradually lead him to the solution. This simple approach is the foundation of the Scientific Method.

Today's Best Practice ToolsFor Solving Closed-end Problems

	Multi-Vari	Concentration Chart	Paired Comparisons™	Component Search™
Work Backwards	***	***	***	***
Find a Pattern	***	***	***	***
Adopt a Different Point of View Act it out/Use Objects	**	***	*	***
Solve a Simpler Problem	*	**	**	***
Consider Extreme Cases	**	***	***	***
Make Drawing	**	***		
Intelligent Guess & Test				
Make an Organized List / Account for all possibilities			*	***
Organize Data / Use a Table or Graph	***	***	***	***
Logical Reasoning	***	***	***	***
Effective Strategies Used (out of 10)	8	8	8	8

Component Search™ is the last of the Clue Generation tools. It comes from assembly operations where one can disassemble and reassemble a finished unit, and it still works. This tool directly compares one very good finished unit to one very bad unit. The investigator switches components between the two units, one at a time, and measures the performance each time, until the performance changes. While many people are not involved in manufacturing operations and may not have occasion to use this tool, it uses a critical thinking skill that has broad utility. It is included here to raise awareness of the concept.

Identify the Truth – Identification and Validation Tools

In 75% of problems, combinations of the clue generation tools completely solve the problem. In the remaining 25% of cases, the clues from these tools eliminate dozens to hundreds of possible factors, leaving fewer than a dozen or so candidates to investigate further. These problems require some intervention in the activity to solve the problem. For problems with 5 or more candidates to evaluate, Variable Search™ is the tool of choice. Full Factorials are only practical in situations where clue generation has narrowed the number of possibly critical factors to just 2, 3, or 4. The final tool in this phase of problem solving, B vs. C™, validates the correct identification of critical factors by turning the problem on and off intentionally.

Just like Component Search™, both Variable Search™ and Full Factorials are primarily manufacturing tools. They are included here to create awareness and as a reference to demonstrate a critical thinking strategy, even though some readers may never have the opportunity to use the specific tools.

Variable Search™ uses the same methodology as Component Search™, except one switches process conditions instead of components. First, one selects a best value and a marginal value for each of the possible factors, and then switches the conditions from best to marginal and vice versa, one at a time, looking for changes in the outcomes. As before, factors that create changes when they are switched are critical. Factors that don't create change are non-critical. Variable Search™ quickly identifies all the critical factors whenever there are 5 to about 12 possible factors left after Clue Generation.

The classical **Full Factorial** tool is only practical when there are 4 or fewer factors to study. Variable Search™ switches every factor with every other factor for 5 or more factors without requiring excessive numbers of experiments. For 4 or fewer factors, the traditional Full Factorial design is completely manageable. It identifies all the critical factors, their interactions, and their best settings.

B vs. C™ validates that all the critical factors have been found. Switch all the critical factors from their best settings to their marginal settings at the same time to turn the problem on and off intentionally. Then, one evaluates the results using Paired Comparisons™. When the activity responds as expected, it proves the problem has been solved.

Today's Best Practice ToolsFor Solving Closed-end Problems

	Variable Search™	Full Factorial	B vs. C™
Work Backwards	***	***	***
Find a Pattern	***	***	***
Adopt a Different Point of View Act it out/Use Objects	***		***
Solve a Simpler Problem	***		***
Consider Extreme Cases	***	***	***
Make Drawing			
Intelligent Guess & Test	**		
Make an Organized List / Account for all possibilities		***	***
Organize Data / Use a Table or Graph	***	***	***
Logical Reasoning	***	***	***
Effective Strategies Used (out of 10)	8	6	8

Set Limits for Flawless Performance – Optimization Tools

Once the critical factors are known, the problem solver must establish limits that will eliminate the problem. Use Scatter Plots (Tolerance Parallelograms) for non-interacting factors and Simplex for interacting factors.

	Scatter Plots	Simplex
Work Backwards	***	***
Find a Pattern	***	***
Adopt a Different Point of View Act it out/Use Objects	***	***
Solve a Simpler Problem	***	***
Consider Extreme Cases	***	***
Make Drawing		
Intelligent Guess & Test	***	***
Make an Organized List / Account for all possibilities	***	***
Organize Data / Use a Table or Graph	***	***
Logical Reasoning	***	***
Effective Strategies Used (out of 10)	9	9

Reasoning Backward

When factors do not interact (most of the time), a simple **Scatter Plot** is effective and straightforward. One selects 30 outcome data points from at least 10 different values of the critical factor from throughout its entire range of variation. The key measurement is the vertical separation of the data. The tighter the data are, the more critical the factor. By starting with the acceptable values for the outcomes, this tool determines the range of critical factor values that will create acceptable outcomes every time. The Scatter Plot is the easiest and fastest way to determine what a specification should be.

Whenever Variable Search™ indicates two critical factors interact to produce unacceptable outcomes **Simplex** varies both factors to determine the optimum setting for each. This technique is included here to create awareness, so readers will know what to do if they encounter interacting factors in the future.

Maintain Control – Control Tools

These three tools lock an activity into flawless performance, preventing the recurrence of bad outcomes over time. Process Certification identifies the external factors that could cause problems to recur, and it provides a checklist for maintaining the activity in top form. Positrol (an acronym for Positive Control) provides a regular schedule for checking settings of the critical factors to prevent drift. Pre-Control is the most advanced and easiest-to-use form of control chart because it monitors activities quickly and easily.

Process Certification uses five generic checklists of factors plus any other unique factors specific to the activity. It identifies the key issues that regular maintenance must address.

After identifying and optimizing the critical factors, a **Positrol** chart shows what to control, to what level, by whom, where, and how often. It also includes a tracking chart as a permanent record.

Today's Best Practice Tools For Solving Closed-end Problems

	Positrol	Process Certification	Pre-Control
Work Backwards	***	***	***
Find a Pattern		**	***
Adopt a Different Point of View Act it out/Use Objects		**	***
Solve a Simpler Problem	***		***
Consider Extreme Cases	***	**	***
Make Drawing			
Intelligent Guess & Test			
Make an Organized List / Account for all possibilities		***	*
Organize Data / Use a Table or Graph	***	***	***
Logical Reasoning	***	***	***
Effective Strategies Used (out of 10)	5	7	8

Pre-Control is the most advanced form of control chart. Its simplicity and its power make it the logical successor to traditional control charts. It is statistically more powerful and yet simple enough that anyone can use it to make good decisions in real time.

Cycle Time Reduction Tools

The previous methods focus exclusively on eliminating unacceptable outcomes by identifying and tightening control of the 1-3 critical factors that determine the performance of any activity. These methods do not address the other half of quality and productivity at all, cycle time. However, no set of tools is truly best practice if it does not address cycle time reduction. Therefore, Cost-Time Management and the Theory of Constraints are both included in this collection.

Westinghouse developed **Cost-Time Management** during the 1980s and won one of the initial Malcolm Baldrige National Quality

Awards for this development. Cost-Time Management is a visual way of measuring the cash flow of any activity. It starts by clearly showing all the dead time in the activity in a Cost-Time Profile. The easiest way to reduce cycle time is to eliminate dead time. Cost-Time Management effectively guides the elimination of dead time, and it is a helpful pre-cursor to other cycle time tools.

Theory of Constraints (TOC) was also developed during the 1980s. Its creator, the late Dr. Eliyahu Goldratt, introduced the Theory of Constraints in his groundbreaking book, *The Goal*, in 1984. TOC looks at the bottlenecks in any activity, the steps that limit its overall capacity.

Traditional accounting methods (and Cost-Time Management) try to optimize the unit costs of each step of the activity by running each step at capacity. Their fundamental premise is that one optimizes the total process by optimizing the individual steps in the process. However, if individual steps have different capacities and cycle times, then shortages and excess inventories result. These constraints reduce the productivity and profitability of the activity.

TOC overcomes this shortcoming. It optimizes the flow of the entire operation by managing the flow though the bottlenecks. It operates the bottlenecks at capacity, and all the other steps in the activity operate at reduced rates, which minimizes inventories and increases overall capacity.

The traditional method worked well one hundred years ago when direct labor was half the cost of a product. Direct labor was a variable cost, and overhead costs were small. Today direct labor is a fixed cost, and it is less than 10% of the total cost of a product, while overhead is 50% of the cost. This change has created the need for a different way of managing operations, which TOC provides.

Summary:

The beauty of all these best practice tools is their simplicity, power, and speed. Discovering them was a life-changing experience for me. Whenever my teams had tried to solve problems in the past,

Today's Best Practice Tools For Solving Closed-end Problems

we never knew where to start. We would try something, learn things, and try again. We usually needed several iterations to find an actual root cause. Upon discovering these best practices, my reaction was, "This is what we always needed – a reliable way to focus on the right factors right away!"

	Cost-Time Management	Theory of Constraints
Work Backwards	***	***
Find a Pattern	***	***
Adopt a Different Point of View / Act it out/Use Objects	***	***
Solve a Simpler Problem	***	***
Consider Extreme Cases	***	***
Make Drawing	***	***
Intelligent Guess & Test	***	***
Make an Organized List / Account for all possibilities	***	***
Organize Data / Use a Table or Graph	***	***
Logical Reasoning	***	***
Effective Strategies Used (out of 10)	10	10

Now, it hurts to see others struggle with this issue, when there is a much better way. This book shares the best practices with the world, so anyone can quickly learn how to apply these tools, and become a superior problem solver. In today's world who can afford to do anything less?

™ Paired Comparisons, Component Search, Variable Search, and B vs. C are service marks of Red X Holdings LLC.

Section 1
"Eliminate the Impossible"
Clue Generation Tools

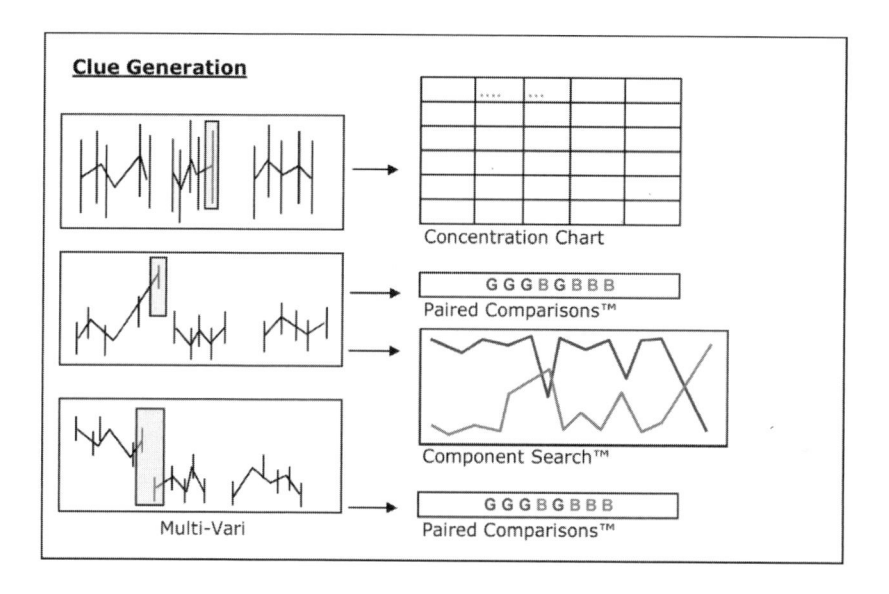

The first step in problem solving is Observation. These tools are non-invasive. They sample the operation and compare finished outcomes in order to discover patterns and consistent differences. These clues tell the investigator what to pursue and, more importantly, what to ignore. They identify the few critical factors to pursue further to discover all the root causes. By eliminating 95-100% of all non-critical factors immediately, these simple tools provide maximum advantage. In about 75% of cases, these few simple tools identify the critical factors and completely solve the problem without any invasive experimentation.

Use them well.

Multi-Vari

① Define the Problem (Effect)
② Eliminate the Impossible
③ Identify the Truth (Causes)
④ Set Limits for Flawless Performance
⑤ Maintain Control
⑥ Reduce Cycle Time
⑦ Identify the Next Problem

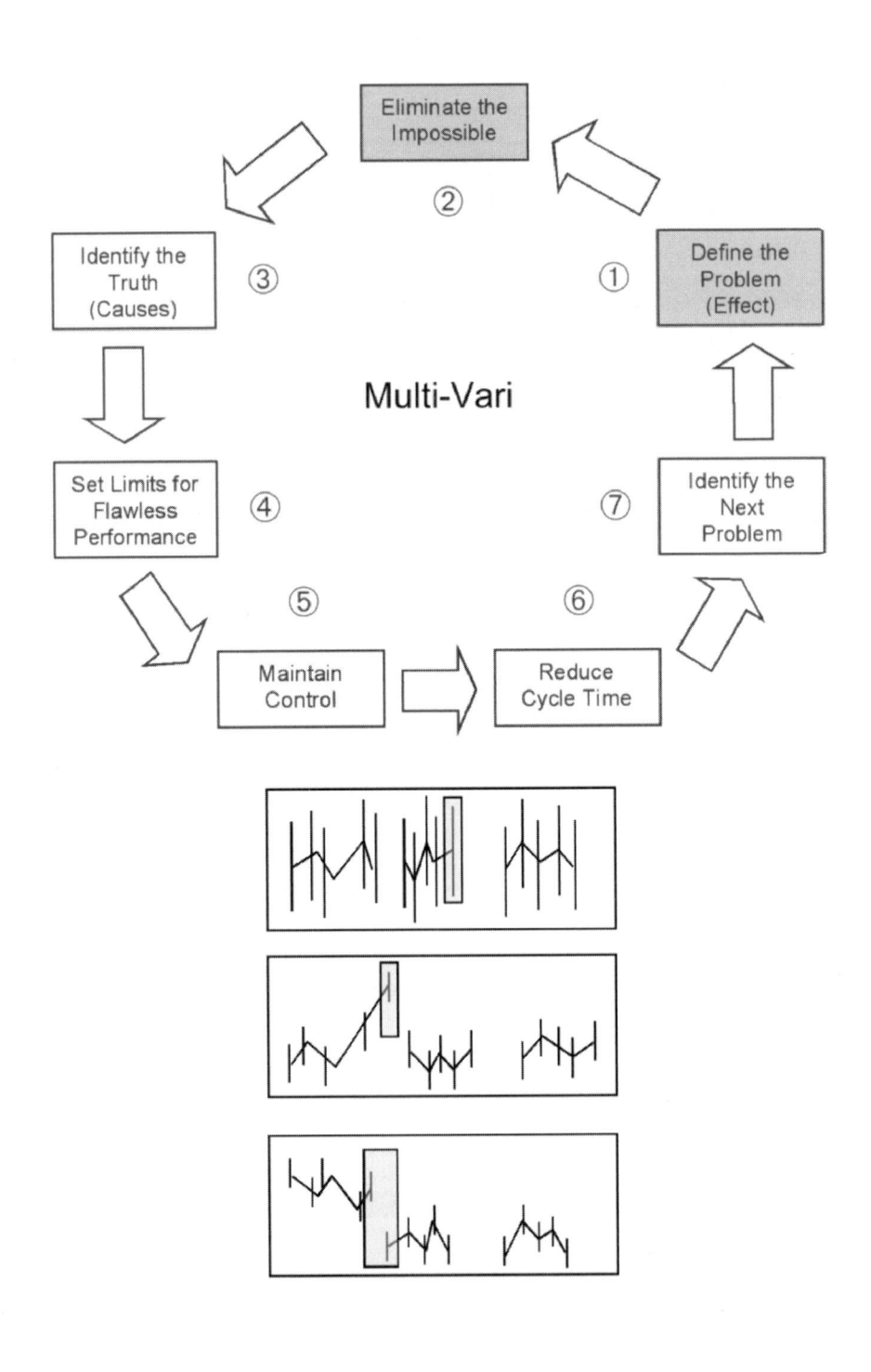

Chapter 3

The Multi-Vari Tool

Observe the activity. Let it show you where, and where not, to look for the most critical factor.

Concept and Expected Results:

Three of Holmes' Top 10 Tips are the basis for Multi-Vari.

"Once you eliminate the impossible, whatever remains, no matter how improbable, must be the truth."

"Always approach a case with an absolutely blank mind. Form no theories, just simply observe and draw inferences from your observations. It is a capital mistake to theorize before one has data. Insensibly one begins to twist facts to suit theories, instead of theories to suit facts."

"It is of the highest importance in the art of detection to be able to recognize out of a number of facts which are incidental and which are vital."

Multi-Vari puts these tips together into one simple technique that gets every problem solver off to a good start. It tells the investigator where to find the most critical factor, the one root cause responsible for at least 50% of the problem.

One starts by identifying possible categories that could contain the most critical factor. Then, one observes which category has the most variation – it contains the most critical factor. All other categories are eliminated. Multi-Vari is often the first tool to use because it tells one where to look, and just as importantly, where not to look.

In most manufacturing activities, there are three categories to consider – Within-unit variation (the same spot on every bad unit is flawed), Unit-to-unit variation (one unit is good, and the next is bad), and Time-to-time variation (performance drifts over time). Different categories are often appropriate for other types of activities, but the same principle always applies – the category with the widest range of variation is the home of the most critical factor.

In a typical problem, one uses four preliminary steps to assure people are solving the right problem. Before designing a Multi-Vari experiment, one must define the problem clearly, establish the measurement that distinguishes good performance from bad, track performance as a histogram or history, and complete a housekeeping check so Multi-Vari can generate good data.

General Description:

The first step in Multi-Vari is determining which categories to investigate. In most manufacturing operations the categories include:

- **Within-unit** – multiple performance readings on the same unit will have widely different values. For example, the paint thickness on a part may vary significantly at different locations on a surface. When rust appears on a car's body, different vehicles of the same design often have corrosion develop at the same spot. An investigation team would conclude, albeit long after the fact, that something was consistently different at that location, and they would know where to focus to improve the car's corrosion resistance.
- **Unit-to-unit** – an activity might create a good outcome followed by a bad one followed by several good ones, and so on in a random pattern. This type of pattern usually means one component or step in the activity is varying excessively.

The Multi-Vari Tool

- **Time-to-time** – the activity slowly drifts over time. Consider an automated machining operation. Cutting tools wear away over time. As the tool wears out, finished part dimensions can steadily increase as the smaller, worn tool cuts off less material.

In Multi-Vari, design a sampling plan that looks at all three categories. Examine 3-5 consecutive samples taken once per hour or at a few times during the day. This usually provides enough samples to find the pattern, but occasionally it may require more sampling, especially if the defect rate is very low. Continue sampling until the range of variation in all the samples is at least 80% of the historical range of variation. Choose the next experiment guided by the clues observed in Multi-Vari, including any non-random patterns in the data.

Once sampling has achieved the 80% threshold, simply measure the bad outcomes in each category. The category with the largest range of variation contains the most critical factor. Choose the next experiment accordingly. In manufacturing, if the factor is Within-unit variation, then a Concentration Chart is a common choice. If it is Unit-to-unit, then Paired Comparisons™ or Component Search™ are effective. If it is a Time-to-time issue, then Paired Comparisons™ is usually a good choice.

In other activities, different categories may be more effective, and the Multi-Vari process may change somewhat. First select the categories thought to be important and then examine a larger number of samples, dozens to perhaps a few hundred. This time only consider the bad samples, especially the very worst. Consider each sample relative to each category, and look for non-random patterns to appear. Multi-Vari indicates the policies or procedures that are the most critical factor for the operation.

Multi-Vari introduces Decision Trees as part of the problem-solving process. The Decision Tree starts with a statement of the problem and then branches into the categories that might contain the root causes. Use trees to track progress by identifying the category

Reasoning Backward

where the most critical factor is located and eliminating the other categories that do not contain critical factors. Each successive level of the tree branches further into sub-categories and eliminates factors until only the most critical factor is left. A Decision Tree provides a powerful visual summary of a project and is helpful when reporting on projects. Each case study in this book includes a Decision Tree to demonstrate the technique.

Examples of the Tool in Action:

Example 1 – A Machining Operation

Problem: An old lathe in a machining operation was not holding tolerance on the rotor shaft it machined. The company was considering purchasing a new lathe to replace the old one. Before making the purchase they ran a Multi-Vari experiment to search for the root cause, hoping to fix the problem rather than spend $70,000 for a new lathe.

The performance measurement was diameter of the shaft after machining. The investigator decided to measure both ends of each shaft he examined.

Performance History: The shaft diameter specification was 0.250" ± 0.001", a total acceptable variation range of 0.002". The company had previously measured the total range of variation of 0.0025", 25% too large. Now, the investigator was ready to design and run a Multi-Vari experiment to look for patterns and to find the category that contained the most critical factor.

He considered three categories: Within-unit (dimensional variation at each end of the shaft), Unit-to-unit (variation from one piece to the next), and Time-to-time (drift in

The Multi-Vari Tool

dimensions during the day). He sampled three consecutive pieces once per hour from 8:00 am until 12:00 pm, giving him 15 rotor shafts to measure.

As he measured the dimensions at each end of the shaft, he discovered every shaft was slightly out-of-round, so he measured the maximum and minimum diameter at each end of every shaft. He had 4 readings on each shaft, 60 readings in all, and he found three non-random patterns in the data, which provided all the clues he needed to identify 3 critical factors. He completely solved the problem in half a day using just this data.

Time	Sample No.	Left Max.	Left Min.	Right Max.	Right Min.	Mean	Hourly Mean
8:00	A	0.2509	0.2503	0.2506	0.2500	0.25045	
8:00	B	0.2510	0.2504	0.2506	0.2500	0.25050	**0.25044**
8:00	C	0.2508	0.2502	0.2506	0.2499	0.25038	
9:00	D	0.2505	0.2499	0.2501	0.2497	0.25005	
9:00	E	0.2504	0.2499	0.2500	0.2497	0.25000	**0.25007**
9:00	F	0.2506	0.2501	0.2501	0.2498	0.25015	
10:00	G	0.2498	0.2495	0.249	0.2488	0.24928	
10:00	H	0.2496	0.2493	0.2491	0.2490	0.24925	**0.24930**
10:00	I	0.2498	0.2494	0.2493	0.2490	0.24938	
11:00	J	0.2510	0.2505	0.2504	0.2500	0.25048	
11:00	K	0.2509	0.2505	0.2503	0.2499	0.25040	**0.25048**
11:00	L	0.2510	0.2506	0.2505	0.2501	0.25055	
12:00	M	0.2508	0.2504	0.2501	0.2500	0.25033	
12:00	N	0.2505	0.2501	0.2499	0.2496	0.25003	**0.25017**
12:00	O	0.2506	0.2502	0.2501	0.2497	0.25015	

USL	LSL	Target
0.2510	0.2490	0.2500

The largest range of variation was Time-to-time, so the most critical factor was a process condition that was changing over time, accounting for just over 50% of the variation. The dimensions started out at the high end of the specification at 8:00 am, drifted down at 9:00 am, and were out-of-spec low at 10:00 am. Then at 11:00 am, the readings were high again, and were drifting down again by noon.

The foreman (and team leader) was initially confused. His first idea for the most critical factor would have been the cutting tool wearing down, but the changes were going in the wrong direction. If the tool had been shrinking, then the parts would be getting larger, and they were getting smaller. Something else was happening consistently between 8:00 and 10:00, and then it was changing between 10:00 and 11:00.

The lathe operators took a coffee break at 10:00 everyday, which meant the lathe would cool down as it sat idle. This suggested that the time drift might be temperature related. As the machine warmed up, the part dimensions decreased. When the machine was cool, the dimensions were higher. He then wondered if the machine was running too hot, so he checked the coolant level in the unit and found it was only half full. He filled the coolant reservoir, the operating temperature dropped, and 50% of the variation went away.

The foreman also noticed two other patterns in the data, and both were Within-unit variations. The larger pattern was the out-of-round condition, accounting for about 30% of the variation. He checked the bearings in the lathe's chuck assembly, discovered they were worn, and installed new bearings at a cost of $200. The out-of-round condition disappeared.

The Multi-Vari Tool

Multi-Vari Decision Tree for the Rotor Shaft

```
Outcome: Rotor Diameter
    |
    ├── Time-to-time
    |     Hour-to-hour
    |     Factor #1 (50%)
    |     Tool wear? → No
    |     Temperature?
    |     Coolant raised to prescribed level
    |
    ├── Shaft-to-shaft
    |
    └── Within-shaft
          1. Out-of-round
          Factor #2 (30%)
          Worn bearings
          New bearings
          2. Taper
          Factor #3 (10%)
          Nonrandom taper
          Adjust guide
```

Rotor Shaft Multi-Vari Chart

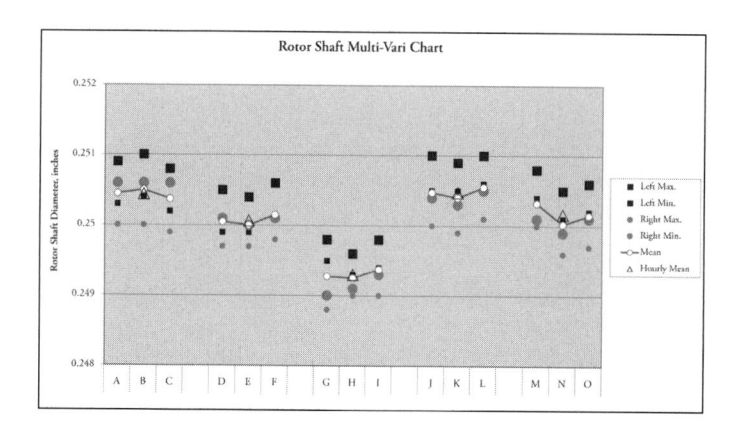

Finally, he observed that the left end of every shaft was always larger than the right end, creating a taper that accounted for about 10% of the variation. This meant the cutting tool was not moving parallel to the shaft as it moved from left to right. He checked the guide, found it was out of alignment, and reset it to parallel. Another 10% of the variation went away.

The initial range of variation had been about 125% of the acceptable tolerance. By eliminating 90% of the variation with three simple adjustments, the total range of variation dropped to less than 30% of the acceptable range. The old lathe was now performing defect-free with a C_{pk} of 6.7, or 20 σ. The company saved the $70,000 it did not have to spend on new equipment.

Example 2 – Accounts Receivable

Problem: A large hospital examined its billing operation and found that 30% of the bills it sent to patients contained errors. Performance measurements included patients being unhappy and accounts receivable averaging 65 days. To find the root causes, a team examined 300 recent invoices that were most in arrears and selected eight categories to consider initially, including:

- Length of a patient's stay in the hospital
- Patient's treatment – complex vs. simple
- Billing clerk
- Doctor-in-charge
- Nurse(s)
- Insurance company
- Billing dates
- Prescription drugs

The team found some variation in each category, but the overwhelming most critical factor was clear. Doctors-in-

The Multi-Vari Tool

charge were ordering tests that insurance companies were not covering. When the team discovered this situation, they also noted which tests caused the biggest problem. They resolved the situation by making doctors aware of the problem. The hospital established new policies that were fair to doctors and patients, and that addressed the insurance companies' need to put a cap on escalating costs.

Within a few months, average days outstanding had dropped below 60, and it continued to drop to 45 days after one year.

In another similar case, a different hospital started with receivables averaging over 45 days, which it dropped to 28 days in only 9 months. They reported generating $1.2 million in additional revenues due to better reimbursement for lab testing.

Problem Statement: 30% of all bills are going out incorrect, and Accounts Receivable average longer than 65 days.

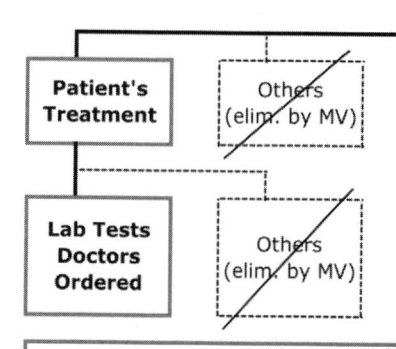

- Patient's Treatment
  - Others (elim. by MV)
- Lab Tests Doctors Ordered
  - Others (elim. by MV)

Action Taken: Established new policies that were fair to patients and physicians, and that addressed insurance companies' need to control costs.

Result: One year later, Accounts Receivable had dropped to < 45 days.

Reasoning Backward

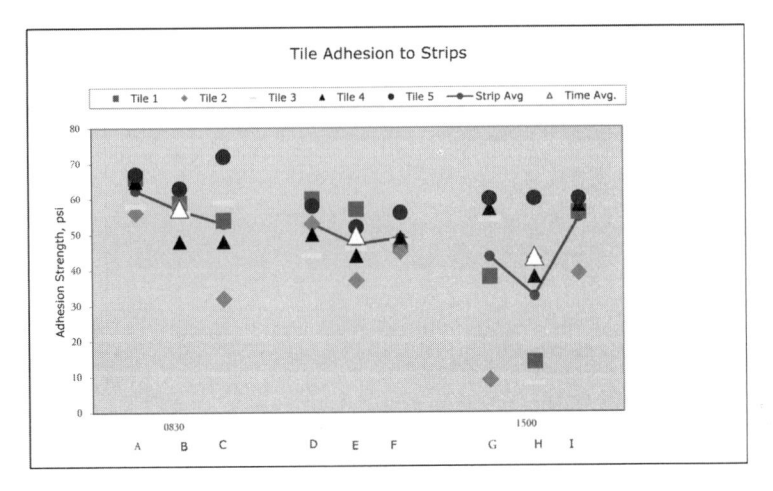

Example 3 – Tile Adhesion

In this problem, a company adheres tiles to strips of support material. Intermittent low bond strength has been a recurring problem. The strength of the adhesive bond is the performance measurement. The investigation team used Multi-Vari and sampled three consecutive strips at three times throughout the day. They tested five tiles on each strip, one in each corner, and one in the center. The resulting data appear in the following table and graph. Examine the data and identify as many non-random patterns and consistent differences (i.e., clues) as you can. What is the most critical factor? Are there other critical factors? If so, what are they? Compare your conclusions with the results shown in the Decision Tree.

Time	0830	0830	0830	1300	1300	1300	1500	1500	1500
Strip No.	A	B	C	D	E	F	G	H	I
Tile 1	66	59	54	60	57	47	38	14	56
Tile 2	56	58	32	53	37	45	9	43	39
Tile 3	58	56	59	44	46	48	54	8	60
Tile 4	65	48	48	50	44	49	57	38	58
Tile 5	67	63	72	58	52	56	60	60	60
Strip Avg.	62.4	56.8	53	53	47.2	49	43.6	32.6	54.6
Time Avg.		57.4			49.7			43.6	

Tile Adhesion to Strips

(Scatter plot showing Adhesion Strength, psi, vs. strips A–I across times 0830, 1300, 1500, with series for Tile 1–5, Strip Avg, and Time Avg.)

76

The Multi-Vari Tool

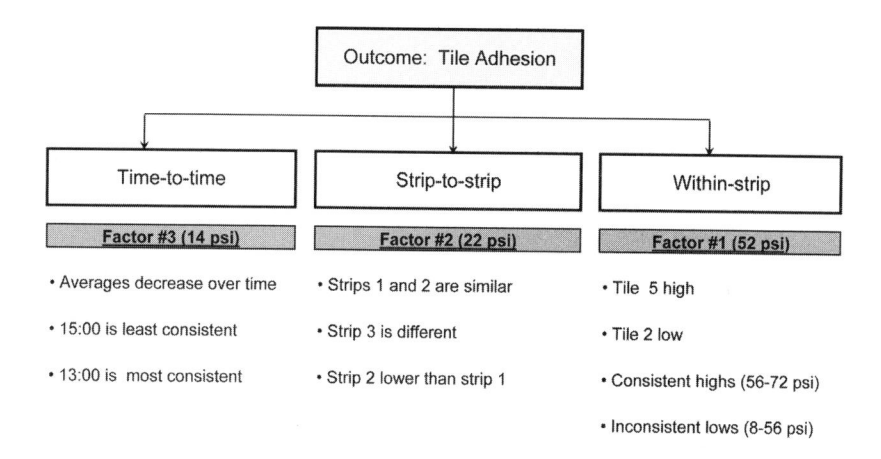

```
                    ┌─────────────────────────┐
                    │ Outcome: Tile Adhesion  │
                    └─────────────────────────┘
              ┌──────────────┼──────────────┐
              ▼              ▼              ▼
      ┌──────────────┐ ┌──────────────┐ ┌──────────────┐
      │ Time-to-time │ │ Strip-to-strip│ │ Within-strip │
      └──────────────┘ └──────────────┘ └──────────────┘
```

Factor #3 (14 psi) | **Factor #2 (22 psi)** | **Factor #1 (52 psi)**

- Averages decrease over time
- 15:00 is least consistent
- 13:00 is most consistent

- Strips 1 and 2 are similar
- Strip 3 is different
- Strip 2 lower than strip 1

- Tile 5 high
- Tile 2 low
- Consistent highs (56-72 psi)
- Inconsistent lows (8-56 psi)

Example 4 – Hotel Customer Service

A large hotel had been using in-room surveys of its guests for some time, but the results were poor, with less than 10% returned. In order to improve the quality of the feedback, hotel managers personally conducted interviews with 200 guests and collected feedback on 10 categories.

1. Parking and accessibility of the hotel
2. Front desk
3. Concierge
4. Housekeeping and room amenities
5. Room service (food and beverages)
6. Restaurants
7. Hotel facilities (including entertainment)
8. Business services
9. Climate of caring
10. Unexpected/unanticipated experiences

They rated the input for Importance on a 1-3 scale and then evaluated their Performance from 1-5 in each category.

Two categories scored well above the rest, in both Importance and Performance – Climate of caring and Unexpected/unanticipated experiences. The act of conducting the interviews scored highly in both categories. In addition, the front desk had a policy to call the room 10 minutes after the guest had checked in, to see if everything in the room was acceptable. This policy also scored highly in both categories. Guests also appreciated the hotel staff's willingness to bend the normal rules to accommodate guests' needs.

The hotel increased its focus on caring and unexpected experiences, and, not surprisingly, it experienced higher occupancy rates and increased repeat business.

Example 5 – High Employee Turnover

A company was frustrated with the high turnover rate of new hires, especially temporary employees. They used two modifications of Multi-Vari to understand this situation better, searching for ways to reduce turnover.

Its first effort focused on employees who had departed. It created eight categories.
1. Age
2. Marital status
3. Commuting distance to work
4. Length of service
5. Stated reason for leaving
6. Pay grade
7. Shift
8. Department

The Multi-Vari Tool

The results showed one clear factor that the company could address immediately. One department, the paint shop, had poor working conditions and health problems. The company took immediate action to improve housekeeping, environmental conditions, and morale.

The second effort compared temporary employees who turned over quickly to temporary employees who stayed with the company for over two years. In this case, it also compared eight parameters.
1. Commuting distance
2. Driver's license
3. Level of education
4. History of turnover at other companies
5. Perceived quality of supervision
6. Convenience of work schedule
7. Perception of relative pay
8. Perception of treatment relative to permanent employees.

The greatest range of variation occurred in three categories. The most significant was the perception of treatment of temporary employees relative to permanent employees. The company's Human Resources team could and did address this issue directly. The other two lesser issues – commuting distance (not surprisingly, the longer the commute, the more likely the employee was to leave) and level of education (employees with higher levels of education were more likely to leave for better opportunities) – were not issues the company could address directly in its hiring practices.

Multi-Vari Summary:

- Often the best first experiment to run
- Non-invasive

- Only requires a few small, well-planned samples gathered periodically (typically 3-5 consecutive samples gathered hourly)
- Identifies the category that contains the most critical factor
- Reveals non-random patterns that provide considerable additional information
- Occasionally solves a problem completely, but normally simply identifies where to find the most critical factor
- Dictates which experiment to run next
- Contributes significantly to solving problems in days to weeks
- Helps achieve $\geq$ 90% defect reduction every time
- Focuses on the most critical factor, the one responsible for at least 50% of the problem
- Takes the guesswork out of knowing where to start
- Tells exactly where to focus to develop complete solutions

Multi-Vari provides the framework for implementing Holmes' Tips 2, 5, 9. Approach the situation with a blank mind, with no pre-conceived theories that will get in the way. Identify relevant categories that could contain the most critical factor. Then simply observe where the greatest variation occurs. This quickly separates the vital category from the incidental ones. It eliminates the impossible so that whatever category remains must contain the most critical factor.

For students, the power of Multi-Vari is its different approach to critical thinking. The previous examples should help the student become an effective problem solver in whatever situations he or she may encounter now and in the future.

The first key learning is **never to approach a problem by brainstorming / guessing / hypothesizing what the root causes might be**. The effective problem solver **observes the situation first** to determine specifically where and how the problem is occurring, and where it is not occurring, in order to discover clues about its root causes. These clues will eliminate 95-100% of possible causes immediately and to focus on the few actual causes right away.

The second key learning is to **develop a trained eye for non-random patterns** in any situation to discover patterns that also provide clues about the root causes of the problem.

These are valuable life lessons for everyone.

Reasoning Backward

Multi-Vari
(The normal starting point)

Objective:
To determine in which category the greatest range of defects occurs. In production operations, these categories are usually Within-unit, Unit-to-unit, or Time-to-time. Other categories may be more appropriate in non-manufacturing activities.

Procedure:
(Note: This procedure uses manufacturing language. The reader must adapt the principles for other, non-manufacturing activities.)

- Select the outcome measurement
  - Select the outcome with the largest number of defects.
  - Select the defect mode with the largest number of defects.
  - Identify the problem. If the measurement is an attribute (a pass/fail feature), try to convert it to a variable with a graded severity scale.
  - Make sure the accuracy of the measurement is at least five times narrower than the allowed tolerances of the outcome.

- Design the Multi-Vari study
  - Determine the number of categories that exist within the activity. (Within-unit, Unit-to-unit, or Time-to-time in production operations)
  - Draw a Decision Tree showing these categories.
  - Determine the number of Time-to-time samples required. A suggestion is to start with just three time samples and continue further only if necessary.
  - Determine the number of consecutive Unit-to-unit samples required, usually 3-5.

The Multi-Vari Tool

- Determine the number of samples for each sub-category of Within-unit families (number of locations, machines, cavities, etc.)
- Multiply numbers of each type of sample together to determine the total number of samples needed.
- Create a table for this Multi-Vari data.

• Run the Multi-Vari study
  - Do not mix models within a given product. Run only the worst model.
  - Run the study by extending the Time-to-time samples until at least 80% of historic variation or specification tolerance is captured, whichever is less.
  - Minimize the number of adjustments made on the process during the study.
  - Pay particular attention to any discontinuities, such as coffee breaks, lunches, shift changes, operator changes, setup changes, tool changes, preventative maintenance, etc. that cannot be avoided during the run. In Time-to-time studies choose times before and after such discontinuities whenever possible.

• Interpret and Analyze the Data
  - Determine the category with the greatest variation. The most critical factor is in this category. Other critical factors may be in this category or in one of the other categories. Graph the data to facilitate the search for patterns in the data. The human eye can spot patterns and trends much more easily in a graph than from a table of numbers.
  - If the most critical factor is a Time-to-time shift, examine changes in temperature, humidity, tool wear, break and lunch periods, adjustments made to the process, and any parameter changes. Paired Comparisons™ may be appropriate as a follow-up.

Reasoning Backward

- If the most critical factor is Unit-to-unit, examine cyclical patterns, dust, dirt, housekeeping, etc. that might affect one unit but not another. A follow-up with Paired Comparisons™ may be appropriate.
- If the most critical factor is Within-unit, construct a Concentration Chart to determine repetitive locations of the defects.
- Look for non-random trends and other clues.
- Look for any samples that may exhibit unusual patterns. Unequal sensitivity may be an indication of interaction effects.
- On the Decision Tree, list all possible causes under each category to guide follow-up investigations.

The Multi-Vari Tool

Multi-Vari Template

Project: Date:
Team:
Outcome Measurement:
Defect Frequency and History:
Measurement (include target value and specification limits):
Accuracy of Measurement/Accuracy of Product Tolerance Ratio:
(If attribute, is a Likert severity scale possible?):
Decision Tree – Potential sources of variation:

```
                        ┌─────────────────┐
                        │ Outcome:        │
                        └─────────────────┘
┌──────────────┐   ┌─────────────────┐   ┌──────────────┐
│ Within-unit  │   │ Unit-to-unit    │   │ Time-to-time │
└──────────────┘   └─────────────────┘   └──────────────┘
   •                    •                    •
   •                    •                    •
   •                    •                    •
```

- Devise a Preliminary Sampling Plan. (Sampling from all machines, operators, stations, etc.) Is the number of samples excessive?

- Revise the Sampling Plan if necessary. (If any machines, operators, stations, etc. are historically believed to be best or worst, use them, and one from in the middle.)

- Create a table to record the gathered data. Identify the data clearly and group it according to category, family, and sub-family.

- 80% Rule Test: After collecting three different time samples, variation must be at least 80% of historic defect frequency or specification range. If not, continue to gather more samples over time until the range of data reaches the 80% level.

- Chart the data in a way that facilitates the search for clues, trends, and non-random patterns.

Conclusions: Can you identify the category that contains the most critical factor? Did you find any other critical factors?

How much does each contribute to the total number of defects?

Do you know enough yet to take action to eliminate the causes of bad outcomes? If so, what actions are appropriate? What are their effects?

If you have not identified any critical factors yet, what subsequent techniques will you try next? Why?

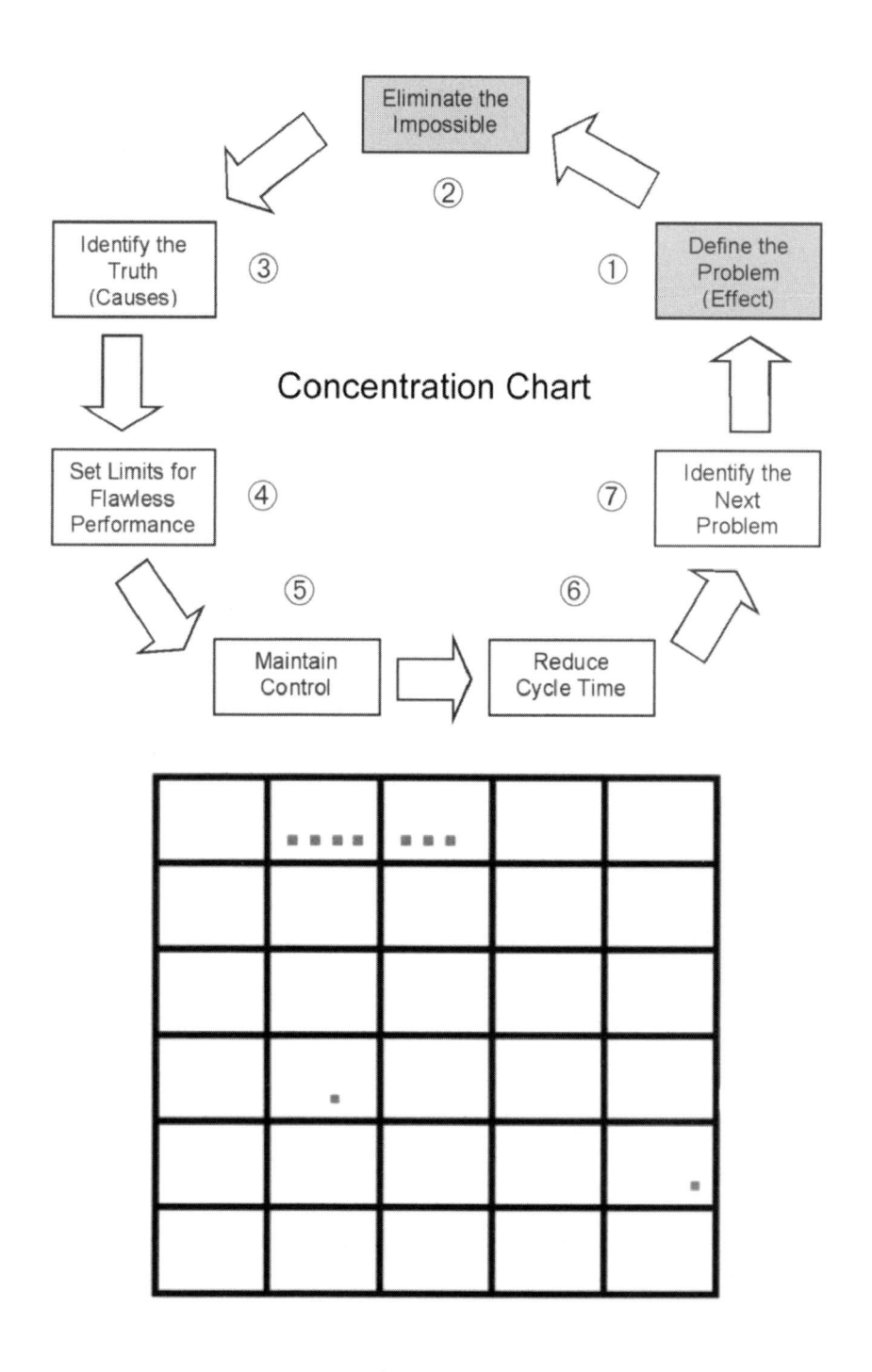

Concentration Chart

① Define the Problem (Effect)
② Eliminate the Impossible
③ Identify the Truth (Causes)
④ Set Limits for Flawless Performance
⑤ Maintain Control
⑥ Reduce Cycle Time
⑦ Identify the Next Problem

Chapter 4

The Concentration Chart

Bad outcomes are not random events;
look for repetitive patterns to provide clues

Concept and Expected Results:

Holmes' third tip best captures the logic of the Concentration Chart.

"Always approach a case with an absolutely blank mind. Form no theories, just simply observe and draw inferences from your observations. It is a capital mistake to theorize before one has data. Insensibly one begins to twist facts to suit theories, instead of theories to suit facts."

When the outcome is a physical object, a Concentration Chart is a graphical representation of the outcome marked to show where defects occur, their frequency, and their severity. In other situations, it might be a flow chart that shows where problems occur or a list of the types of bad outcomes that exist. The expected results are clues about the identity of most critical factor causing most of the problem.

General Description:

A Concentration Chart starts with some type of representation of the finished outcome – a drawing, chart, picture, map, flowchart, or even a list of defects. Mark the "chart" with the location of every defect from a number of samples. Each notation should include the nature of the defect to help identify patterns, and it should use some sort of scale to indicate severity. Finally, look for non-random patterns to provide clues about the most critical factor.

Tip #2 is important. An open mind is essential to actively look for all the clues present in the chart, and then to be ready to draw inferences from these observations.

Examples of the Tool in Action:

Example 1 – Paint Defects

In this problem, a paint shop that coats metal panels had an excessive number of panels with defects (18%) that required rework. The performance measurement was paint defects.

			I:9	I:16	I:8				
									G:2
			G:2 O:2						
		Fe:1							
					G:1				
			O:2						
								Fe:1	

A previous Multi-Vari experiment showed the problem was not Time-to-time or Panel-to-panel, but Within-panel. They created a Concentration Chart of the defects, which appears below. They divided the panel into small areas and counted the number of defects in each area. They also noted the type of defect, as shown in the key.

Defect Code	Total Defects
I = Inconel defects	33
G = "Glass" defects	5
O = Organic defects	4
Fe = Iron defects	2

The Inconel defects accounted for 75% of all defects, and they all occurred in one small area at the top of the panel where an Inconel hook supports the panel as it goes through the paint oven. Bits of Inconel chipped off the hooks and created paint defects. The operators had been performing maintenance on the hooks once per quarter, so they shifted to a bi-weekly schedule, and the defect rate dropped by 75%. They also redesigned the Inconel hook to a smaller size, and discovered that the "glass" defects dropped as well. In the end, they dropped the defect rate by 90%, a 10:1 improvement, and generated $900,000 per year in savings.

Corrosion patterns on late model automobiles are a related example of a Concentration Chart that anyone can create. Find a vehicle with corrosion showing in just one or two locations. Then, look for other models of the same body style and look for similar corrosion patterns. This indicates the paint process has some consistent problem where it fails to cover those particular areas of body adequately.

The Concentration Chart

Automobile (and other consumer product) recalls are a different variation of a Concentration Chart. When a manufacturer gets repeated warranty complaints about the same feature of a product, they must investigate their manufacturing process to discover the source of the problem. Then, they issue a recall to correct the original problem, as in the next example.

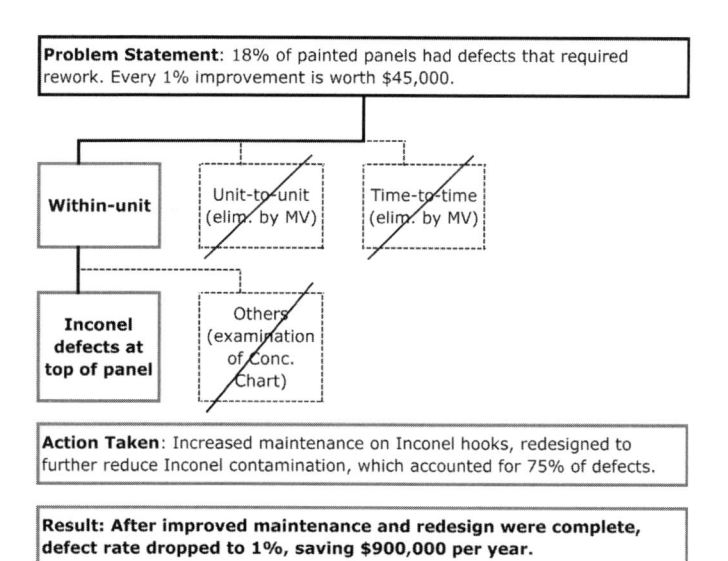

Problem Statement: 18% of painted panels had defects that required rework. Every 1% improvement is worth $45,000.

- Within-unit
  - Inconel defects at top of panel
  - Others (examination of Conc. Chart) [crossed out]
- Unit-to-unit (elim. by MV) [crossed out]
- Time-to-time (elim. by MV) [crossed out]

Action Taken: Increased maintenance on Inconel hooks, redesigned to further reduce Inconel contamination, which accounted for 75% of defects.

Result: After improved maintenance and redesign were complete, defect rate dropped to 1%, saving $900,000 per year.

Example 2 – Massive Shorts in Television Sets

A television manufacturer had excessive warranty claims for a new model that suffered massive shorts for some unexplained reason. Examination of the failed units using a Concentration Chart indicated the same part was shorting out every time. The company was unable to reproduce the failures in laboratory testing, so it did not know how to fix the problem.

Next, it created a different sort of Concentration Chart. It noted the location of each failure on a map of the United States. They quickly determined that most of the failures occurred in coastal areas, areas much more prone to lightning storms than interior regions of the country, as shown in the following Lightning Frequency Map. They redesigned the part that was failing to enable it to handle power surges without failing, which solved this warranty problem.

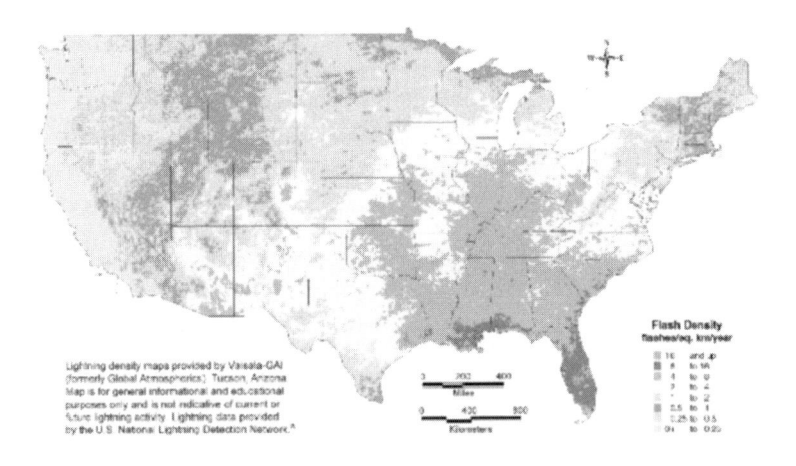

Example 3 – Accounts Receivable

The Accounts Receivable problem discussed in Chapter 3 is another example. Once the team had identified procedures ordered by the doctor-in-charge as the most critical issue, they listed the procedures that created the most problems. They measured both frequency and dollars involved, so

The Concentration Chart

they knew exactly which procedures were having the largest impact and needed immediate attention. This kind of list is a Concentration Chart for any administrative or transactional operation.

Example 4 – Wave Soldering

This problem was a wave soldering operation for printed circuit boards that experienced 1,500 ppm solder defects when the company specification at the time allowed a maximum of 500 ppm. The performance measurement was the number of solder joint defects. One day, the foreman ran a Multi-Vari experiment during the morning shift looking at Time-to-time, Board-to-board, and Within-board categories. He discovered the Within-board category contained the most critical factor.

Next, he created a Concentration Chart diagram of the board and found just two types of defects. Solder pinholes occasionally appeared along one edge of the board, but nowhere else, and one particular component had solder shorts at two different locations. The other 900+ connections on every board were perfect every time. The Concentration Chart for the pinholes appears below.

The location of the pinholes suggested the board tilted slightly during soldering, with the pinhole side a little too high, so the molten solder did not wet the board well. He adjusted the fixture at noon, and the defect rate dropped to 500 ppm that afternoon. Then, he addressed the solder shorts.

Reasoning Backward

Location of Solder Pinholes

Circuit Board

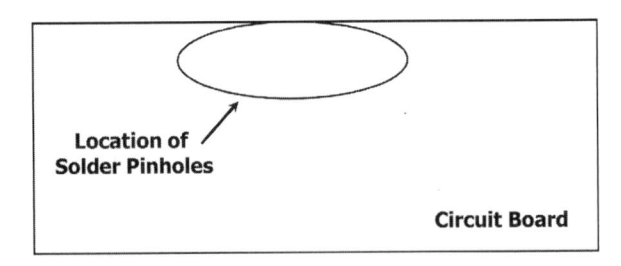

He first tried two pre-treatments on the component leads and the boards to improve the soldering surfaces, but neither had any effect. Then, he examined the size of the lead relative to the size of the hole into which it fit and determined the hole-to-lead ratio was higher than they would like. (Manufacturing liked a high ratio, so the mounting process is easier. Quality liked a low ratio because it gives a stronger connection.) They tried doubling over the lead to make it twice as wide and ran boards in this new configuration, as shown.

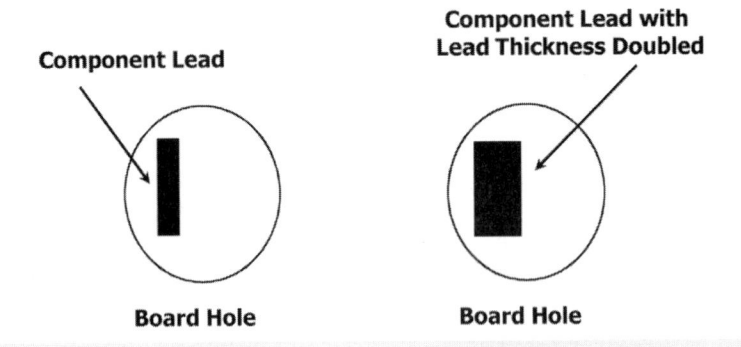

Component Lead

Component Lead with Lead Thickness Doubled

Board Hole   **Board Hole**

When they put these units through wave solder, the defect rate dropped to zero. They ran an additional Multi-Vari experiment after the change, and the defect rate stayed at zero. It took the foreman just 1.5 days to eliminate this chronic problem.

The Concentration Chart

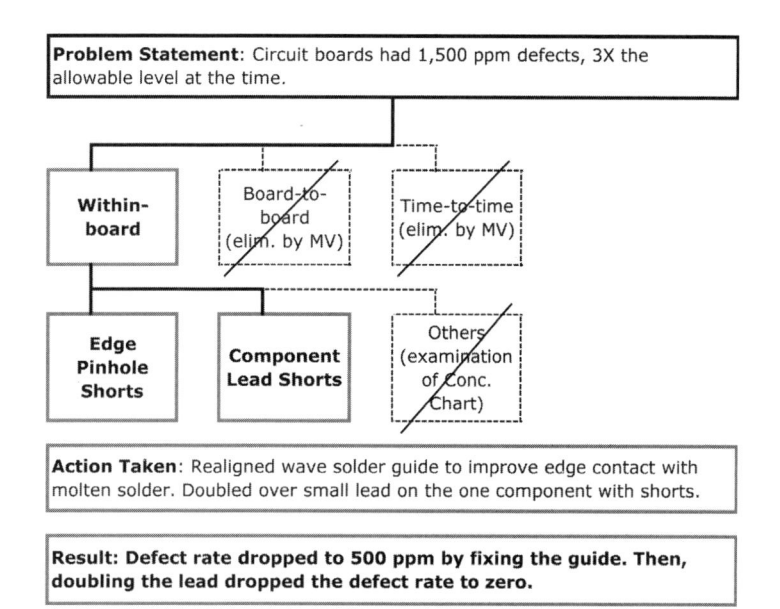

Problem Statement: Circuit boards had 1,500 ppm defects, 3X the allowable level at the time.

- Within-board
  - Board-to-board (elim. by MV) ~~crossed out~~
  - Time-to-time (elim. by MV) ~~crossed out~~
- Edge Pinhole Shorts
- Component Lead Shorts
- Others (examination of Conc. Chart) ~~crossed out~~

Action Taken: Realigned wave solder guide to improve edge contact with molten solder. Doubled over small lead on the one component with shorts.

Result: Defect rate dropped to 500 ppm by fixing the guide. Then, doubling the lead dropped the defect rate to zero.

Example 5 – University Recruiting

A small university wanted to increase the effectiveness of its recruiting efforts, so it started by using a map to understand where it was recruiting effectively, and where it wasn't. It divided the country into 20 geographic regions and discovered to its surprise that three of the regions where it was most successful were the furthest away.

The university then talked to some of the students from these three areas to discover why they had selected the university and learned two lessons. Several counselors in these regions recommended the school highly, and once students were attending the school and enjoying the experience, they influenced their friends.

Both these findings provided the school with actions they could take to improve their recruiting efforts.

Concentration Chart Summary:

- A universal tool
- A powerful way to discover clues about the most critical factor
- Improves both the speed and effectiveness of problem solving
- Used primarily on physical products, but recent applications include administrative, transactional, and service situations

The primary lesson is to **look for repetitive patterns whenever unacceptable results occur**. Problems occur for a reason. Whenever an activity usually performs well, but occasionally performs badly, three or fewer root causes are responsible for at least 90% of the failures. Simply observing which failure modes are most frequent will often reveal the most critical factor. Drawings, maps, lists, or flowcharts are all possible forms for a Concentration Chart, depending on the situation. This simple tool often provides very powerful insights that quickly lead to complete solutions.

The Concentration Chart

Concentration Chart – aka "Measles Chart"
(Use for Within-unit variation)

Objective: To plot the exact location(s) of the problem within the unit. The Concentration Chart will show a non-random concentration of defects in a particular location because Pareto's Law is universal.

Procedure:
- Make a drawing or template of the unit containing repetitive defects. (For transactional or administrative problems, this could simply be a flowchart or list.)
- Draw a grid, if necessary, to show the exact locations of the defects on the drawing.
- Mark the following as each unit is examined:
  ⇨ The location and severity of each defect type, with each defect type suitably noted.
  ⇨ The number of defects of each type in each location.
  ⇨ If a defect is an attribute, try to create a Likert scale to quantify severity.

- It is not necessary to note the time of each occurrence unless a Multi-Vari study showed a Time-to-time pattern of variation to be important.
- Study the non-random patterns of defects to discover clues to the identity of the most critical factor and any other factors that might be present.

Eliminate the Impossible	②

① Define the Problem (Effect)

③ Identify the Truth (Causes)

Paired Comparisons™

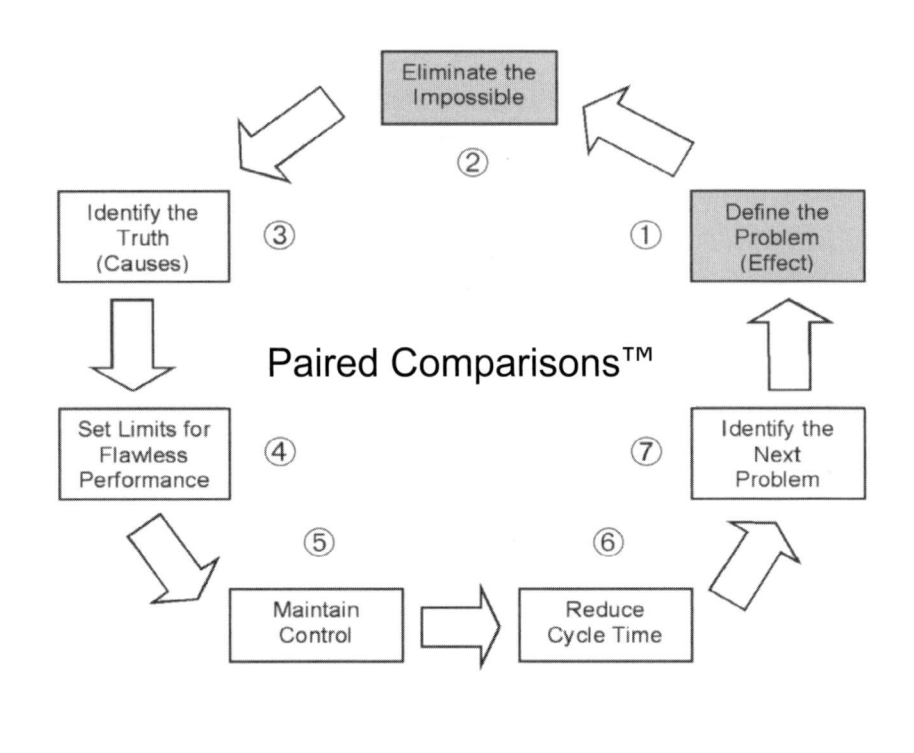

④ Set Limits for Flawless Performance

⑦ Identify the Next Problem

⑤ Maintain Control

⑥ Reduce Cycle Time

G G G B G B B B

Chapter 5

The Paired Comparisons™ Tool

Compare the best and worst outcomes directly;
Look for consistent differences between them

Concept and Expected Results:

Paired Comparisons™ is the oldest of all the convergent problem solving tools, going back long before Sherlock Holmes, all the way to Sir Francis Bacon. In *Novem Organum* (1620), he described drawing up two lists – one of all the things in which the phenomenon being investigated occurs, and one of all the things in which the phenomenon never occurs. Then, he ranked the lists according to the degree in which various factors occur in each entry. By observing which factors match the presence or absence of the phenomenon, he could deduce which ones were critical. Bacon says that by interpreting the results of these observations one can approximate the underlying cause of the phenomenon in question. He called this approximation the "First Vintage". It is not the final conclusion of the investigation, but simply the first hypothesis. Additional comparisons and hypotheses approach the truth "by gradual degrees".

The technique has changed only slightly in 400 years. This chapter introduces two versions of the method, one almost identical to Bacon's methodology, and a newer version that makes the process even easier.

Reasoning Backward

Paired Comparisons™ is a universal clue generation tool based on the concept "compare performance extremes to discover consistent differences." Select several examples of good and bad outcomes and compares them head-to-head. Look for factors that are consistently different. Any factor that is consistently different when an activity creates good outcomes and when it creates bad outcomes is critical. Pursue it. Any factor that is not consistently different is non-critical. Ignore it.

The purpose of Paired Comparisons™ is to identify and eliminate the non-critical factors without intervening in the activity, so subsequent activities can focus on the very few critical factors. This tool always narrows the focus to less than a dozen or so possibly critical factors, but usually it shortens the list to five or fewer factors. Occasionally Paired Comparisons™ will go further and solve the problem completely by identifying the 1-3 actual critical factors. Sometimes it will provide insight into their realistic specifications with no further work.

Paired Comparisons™ is often one in a series of experiments after Multi-Vari has identified the category that contains the most critical factor. However, sometimes it will be the first experiment chosen, as described by Bacon and in Example 2. An investigator can examine recent examples of best and worst outcomes and eliminate many non-critical factors immediately.

General Description:

Recall the key concepts of effective problem solving.

- Observe the activity first to remove all the factors that are not part of the problem, in order to focus on the 1-3 critical factors that are the causes of the problem. (Holmes' second tip counsels *"Once you have eliminated the impossible, whatever remains, no matter how improbable, must be the truth."*)

- Concentrate on the extremes – the best and the worst – to find clues because the critical factors will be most different and easiest to spot in the most extreme examples. (Holmes' stated, *"It is of highest importance in the art of detection*

The Paired Comparisons™ Tool

to be able to recognize out of a number of facts which are incidental and which are vital.")

- Don't guess what the critical factors might be. Let the activity show what they are. (In Holmes' words, *"I never guess. It is a shocking habit – destructive to the logical faculty."*)

Paired Comparisons™ extends these principles to practically any area of human endeavor with two variations of the tool. In the original version, select 6-8 samples of good outcomes from the activity and an equal number of samples of bad outcomes. Then compare one good sample to one of the bad samples head-to-head in every imaginable way, recording all differences. For physical products, this can be any observation or analytical test, or a comparison of any step in the manufacturing process. Next, select another good sample and compare it to another bad sample, looking for the same differences as in the first pair, plus any other differences. Repeat this process for a third pair and a fourth. By this time, some consistent differences should be apparent. If not, continue with the fifth, sixth, seventh and eighth pair, as necessary. The consistent differences that appear are clues to the identity of the critical factors.

The newer version begins with the same selection of 6-8 samples of the best outcomes and an equal number of worst outcomes, all taken as close together in time as possible. Gather all available process and performance data on these 12-16 samples and rank order the samples from best to worst according to each factor. Data should include everything that is known about each sample, including all data on the outcomes and all process data, including whatever analytical data exists.

The key to this newer version of Paired Comparisons™ is the Tukey Test, developed by the late John Tukey of Princeton University. This simple method determines the probability of there being a statistically significant difference between two or more different populations based on ranking a very small number of samples from each population, using the concept of End Counts.

Professor Tukey proved that by looking only at End Counts of the ranking (the consecutive samples from one population at the top of the ranking and from another population at the bottom of the ranking), one could conclude whether or not one population was significantly different from the other, to a given Confidence Level. This simple test is applicable anywhere, as shown in the following examples.

Examples of the Tool in Action:

Example 1 – Noisy Micro-motor (Using the original version of the tool)

This example involved a micro-motor for a vibrating pager. The manufacturer had been purchasing the motors from a foreign supplier whose consistency was poor. Most of the motors worked well, but some were excessively noisy. At the time, the company had 50,000 unacceptable motors in inventory. The project team selected eight of the best (quietest) motors and eight of the worst (noisiest) motors and compared them directly, looking for consistent differences. They selected eight parameters to measure on each motor in their search for significant differences. The first four parameters they measured showed no differences between the quiet and noisy motors. The fifth parameter they evaluated was Motor Speed. All eight quiet motors operated at 4800-5000 rpm. All eight noisy motors operated at 6900-7200 rpm. Clearly, motor speed was critical, so they took action to reduce the speed of the noisy motors.

Their solution to the problem was to add a small one-cent resistor to each noisy $5 motor, which reduced the speed of the motor to 4500-5000 rpm, and they all became quiet. This fix saved the company $248,000, and it established a new

The Paired Comparisons™ Tool

specification for the speed of the vibrating micro-motors. The problem never occurred again.

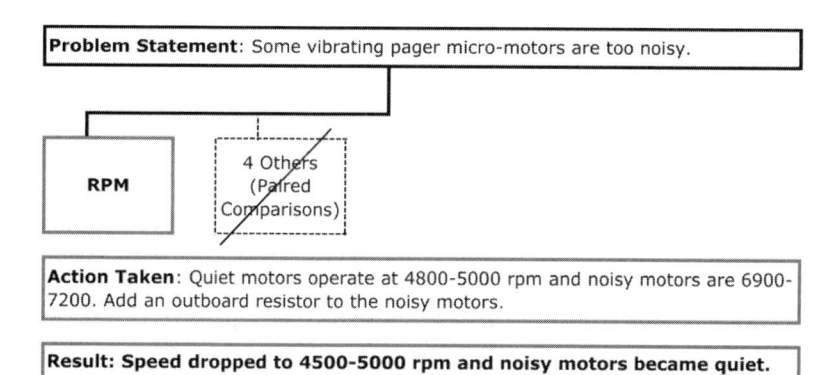

Problem Statement: Some vibrating pager micro-motors are too noisy.

RPM

4 Others (Paired Comparisons)

Action Taken: Quiet motors operate at 4800-5000 rpm and noisy motors are 6900-7200. Add an outboard resistor to the noisy motors.

Result: Speed dropped to 4500-5000 rpm and noisy motors became quiet.

Example 2 – Turkeys (Using the Tukey Test)

Reportedly, one of John Tukey's favorite examples used turkeys. Suppose two farmers are raising turkeys, and you want to know if one farmer's birds are heavier than the other farmer's birds. Weighing them all is highly impractical. Tukey determined that you could reasonably predict the answer by first selecting a small sample of birds from each flock (6 from Farmer A and 6 from Farmer B), and then weighing each bird. Then, rank order the birds' weights and label them as A or B. Suppose the ranking turned out as shown:

Heaviest A - A - A - A - B - B - A - B - A - B - B - B Lightest

In this example the Top End Count for A = 4 because the top four readings are birds from Flock A. The Bottom End Count for B = 3 because the bottom three readings are Flock B birds. The Total End Count = 4+3 = 7 because the Top End Count and the Bottom End Count come from different populations. The Tukey Test guidelines establish the Confidence Level that the populations are different with respect to the measured parameter based on the Total End Count, as shown in the Table. In the example, the Total End Count = 7, so the birds from Flock A are heavier at the 95% Confidence Level.

The Tukey Test is universal. Paired Comparisons™ applies it to find the root causes of differences between two populations of outcomes, the best and the worst. If the rank order from best to worst for a particular factor gives a Total End Count less than 6, then the factor is non-critical. If the Total End Count is 6 or more, then the factor is critical and is involved in the creation of bad outcomes in some way, to the indicated level of confidence. The higher the End Count and Level of Confidence are, the more critical the factor is.

Total End Count	Confidence Level that the Populations are Different
< 6	No Confidence
6	90%
7	95%
10	99%
13	99.9%

Example 3 – Precipitate in a Dispersion

In this problem, a chemical company makes a dispersion of a solid particles suspended in water. They manufacture the material in a large batch reactor using a series of chemical reactions. Usually they produce stable dispersions of the product with a very small particle size, but occasionally another precipitate with a much larger particle size forms as well. When this occurs, the company has to isolate and rework the batch to achieve the particle size and composition that customers require. The performance measurement is the presence or absence of the second precipitate.

The precipitate had appeared briefly at two separate times in the past and then mysteriously disappeared. The operation had been stable for about 18 months, but 3 months ago, the precipitate came back, worse than ever, and it persisted. Everyone is upset, and things are not getting better. Worst of all, no one can make changes to the process without a solid lead, and there is no agreement on how to intervene. People can only make measurements. The project team is under intense pressure to fix the problem before the division's profits are hurt too badly.

The chemical reactor has semi-automated control, like most modern chemical reactors. A computer controls reactant levels, temperature settings, and reaction conditions, but the operators have to intervene whenever something goes beyond the established limits. The computer automatically records 105 process conditions on every batch. (Unlike many operations where process data may be lacking, automated chemical reactors have the opposite problem – problem solvers are overwhelmed with data. Paired Comparisons™

cuts through the mass of non-critical data and gets to the critical data fast.)

In this case, Multi-Vari was not helpful because they make one batch per day, and the entire batch is homogeneous. Therefore, the team selected 8 of the best batches and 8 of the worst batches from recent production as its first experiment. The team ranked these 16 batches for each of the 105 readings from the controller and applied the Tukey Guidelines. It found that 104 factors had Total End Counts less than 6, so these factors were all non-critical. One surprising factor, Percent Non-Volatiles of the finished dispersion, had a Total End Count of 11.5, so it was involved in some way with a level of confidence greater than 99%. (The .5 count comes from a shared value at the transition point of the Bottom End Count, a best and a worst sample at 6.9% Non-Volatiles.)

It took the team just one day to collect and sort all the data and to identify the one measured factor that was involved in the problem. Unfortunately, this factor was a property of the finished product, and not a process setting they could immediately modify. The team's next step was to determine why the level of non-volatiles varied by hundreds of pounds, when the automated controller controlled all the reactants to within one pound.

It turned out that this reaction is done at low temperature, about 10°C. The reactor has a cooling jacket, but it does not provide adequate cooling. The operator has to manually add ice to the reactor to keep the temperature down. The level of ice addition determines the percent non-volatiles of the finished product. Whenever the ice level is low enough that the percent non-volatiles stays above 7.4%, the product is always good. Whenever the operators add extra ice to control

The Paired Comparisons™ Tool

the temperature, the non-volatiles level drops. If the non-volatiles level drops below 6.9%, the product is always bad.

After just one day, the team knew the first step to take to address the problem, but they still had questions that would require further analysis and testing. The ice is not just water ice; it is a brine solution so they can cool the ice to a lower temperature without having the system freeze up. They needed to discover if the problem was a chemical interaction with the excess amount of brine chemicals in the ice, or if it was just a mixing or shear problem due to the larger volume and different viscosity of the slurry. The answers to these questions are proprietary, but they dictated what other actions the company could take to assure the problem went away and did not return.

Unsorted Data	% Non-Volatiles
Good	6.9
Good	7.2
Good	7.4
Good	7.7
Good	7.6
Good	8
Good	7.8
Good	7.6
Bad	7
Bad	6.3
Bad	6.9
Bad	6.6
Bad	6.2
Bad	7.3
Bad	6.5
Bad	6.4

Sorted Data	% Non-Volatiles
Good	8
Good	7.8
Good	7.7
Good	7.6
Good	7.6
Good	7.4
Bad	7.3
Good	7.2
Bad	7
Good	6.9
Bad	6.9
Bad	6.6
Bad	6.5
Bad	6.4
Bad	6.3
Bad	6.2

Top EC	6
Bottom EC	5.5
TOTAL EC	**11.5**
% Confidence	> 99%

Paired Comparisons™ did not provide the ultimate solution to the problem in this example. Its purpose was simply to screen out the non-critical factors, so subsequent

Reasoning Backward

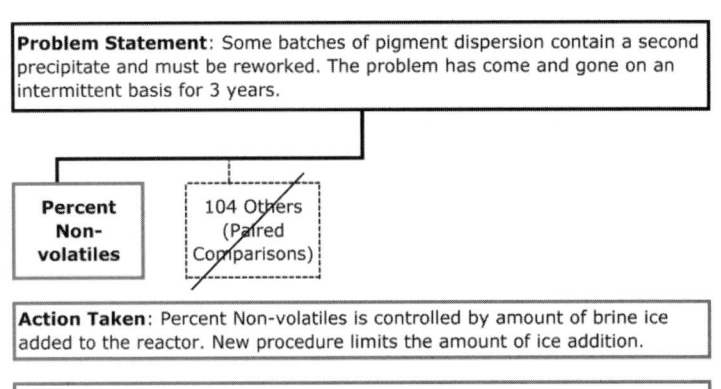

> **Problem Statement**: Some batches of pigment dispersion contain a second precipitate and must be reworked. The problem has come and gone on an intermittent basis for 3 years.

- **Percent Non-volatiles**
- ~~104 Others (Paired Comparisons)~~

> **Action Taken**: Percent Non-volatiles is controlled by amount of brine ice added to the reactor. New procedure limits the amount of ice addition.

> **Result**: Controlling the ice level prevented the undesired precipitate from forming.

experiments could focus on the correct factors, which it did flawlessly. In some cases, Paired Comparisons™ completely solves the problem, but that is a bonus. In this case, it performed remarkably well. It ended months of questions and finger pointing by eliminating 104 of 105 factors in just one day. It told management the one factor they absolutely had to control, which guided their future work. Even if the project team had never resolved what it was about low percent non-volatiles that made the product bad, they had already learned that they needed to limit the amount of ice they used. Paired Comparisons™ told them what levels of ice addition worked and didn't work, so it provided a first estimate of what the limit of ice addition should be. More experiments would be necessary to learn why the non-volatiles limit was what it was. (Note how well this example fits Bacon's concept of First Vintage, followed by subsequent experiments to achieve the complete truth by gradual degrees.)

Example 4 – Bacterial Contamination on Dairy Farms

This example demonstrates the utility of Paired Comparisons™ in biological environments. Paired Comparisons™ is universally applicable. It is never a bad place to start.

The company in this example makes chemicals for cleaning milking lines on dairy farms to prevent bacterial contamination of milk. The company was receiving complaints from some dairy farmers because their milk contained higher bacteria levels than desired. The levels were all within U.S. government guidelines, but the farmers' customers, the farm cooperatives, paid on a sliding scale based on contamination levels, so the higher levels were costing the dairy farmers money.

The company ran a Paired Comparisons™ test that compared 6 farms with no complaints to 6 farms that complained most frequently. It measured the contamination level at 22 common locations throughout each farm. With 12 readings at each location, the maximum possible Total End Count was 12. Two of the 22 factors had Total End Counts of 12, two more scored 10, and two more scored 9. The other factors were not important, including the company's chemicals.

To follow up on this study, the company contacted the six farms with the most complaints and showed them the changes they would need to make to improve performance. Four of them implemented the suggestions, contamination dropped, and complaints stopped. The other two farmers refused to change, and did not improve.

Reasoning Backward

The company took one further action to build on this new knowledge of the critical issues. They developed an audit service, offered it free to dairy farmers who purchased their equipment and chemicals, and dramatically increased their market share, displacing 60% of their competitors' business.

Example 5 – Detecting Heart Attacks

One of the most critical judgments an Emergency Room physician must make is when patients arrive complaining of chest pain. Has the patient suffered a heart attack, or is it something else that is not life threatening? The physician must gather data from the patient and make a decision – admit the patient to cardiac care or other treatment, or send the patient home. The amount of data can be overwhelming. The physician must evaluate all the available data and decide yes, this patient has, or no, the patient has not, had a heart attack. The list of possible factors physicians traditionally considered included chest pain severity, pain duration, pain location, blood pressure, breathing sounds, recent exercise, history of heart trouble, cholesterol level, drugs, diabetes, race, gender, age, smoker or not, diet, stress levels, weight, regular exercise, sweating, ECG results, and potentially, blood enzyme test results. Physicians were overwhelmed with data. The blood enzyme test was by far the most accurate predictor, but at the time of this study, it was slow and expensive. The patient had to be admitted for 6-8 hours, so it was impractical in almost all cases.

Studies of physician accuracy have historically shown that 2-8% of patients who have actually suffered a heart attack (myocardial infarction, or MI) have been mistakenly sent home from emergency rooms. Consequently, most physicians try to err on the side of caution (first, do no harm), so they admit patients who probably have not had heart attacks, just to be safe. In fact, only 10% of those admitted actually had suffered a heart attack; 90% could have gone home safely.

Dr. Lee Goldman, a cardiologist, set out to improve this situation. He used a computer to study hundreds of records over several years to look for consistencies in MI cases and non-MI cases, searching for an algorithm that could predict more effectively. (In effect, he was using the principles of Paired Comparisons™ – looking for consistent differences between two populations – patients who had and who had not suffered MI.) He succeeded in finding an algorithm that used just four of the nearly two-dozen possible factors, and he created a decision tree based on just those four factors. The four factors included:

- the electrocardiogram (ECG) results,
- whether or not the pain was unstable angina,
- the presence or absence of fluid in the lungs, which presented as crinkling breathing sounds in the stethoscope,
- systolic blood pressure <100.

The algorithm directed patients to the appropriate level of care based solely on these four conditions. For example, a patient with a clear ECG, but with unstable angina, fluid in the lungs, and blood pressure below 100 would be admitted to the intermediate care unit. Someone with an ECG abnormality but no other symptoms would get short-term care. A patient with an abnormal ECG and either two or all three of the other factors indicating a problem would be admitted to the cardiac care unit. None of the other potential factors was considered. The other factors were useful in predicting whether the patient might suffer a heart attack in the next few years, but they only complicated the diagnosis of whether or not an infarction had already occurred.

The Emergency Room at Cook County Hospital in Chicago conducted a two-year trial to compare the accuracy of the algorithm vs. physician diagnoses. (Understandably, there was a lot of resistance from the physicians, but they had to try something because of the chaos and skyrocketing costs from being overly cautious and admitting 9 non-MI cases for every 1 MI.) For the duration of the trial, every chest pain patient was first diagnosed by the ER physician, and then evaluated using the Goldman algorithm. The results were stunning – it was not even close.

Of the patients who were not seriously ill, the algorithm was 70% better at recognizing the non-MI situations than the physicians were. For patients who were suffering from MI, physicians were correct between 75 and 89% of the time. The algorithm was correct over 95% of the time. The Decision Tree from the Goldman algorithm became the standard for treatment at Cook County, and subsequently at other emergency rooms across the country.

Even in organisms as complex as human beings, and in such life-and-death situations as heart attacks, just four factors could quickly and accurately diagnose MI over 95% of the time.

One final note: this case study occurred several years ago. In the intervening years, the blood enzyme test has become both faster and less expensive. Today it is part of the screening protocol, along with breathing sounds, ECG, and blood pressure, and the results are even more accurate.

The Paired Comparisons™ Tool

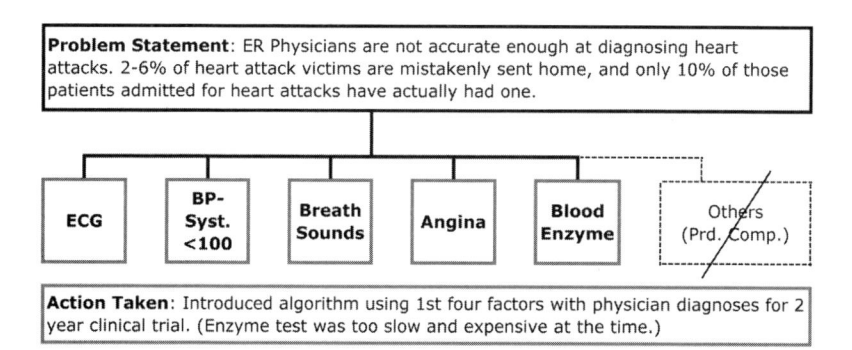

Problem Statement: ER Physicians are not accurate enough at diagnosing heart attacks. 2-6% of heart attack victims are mistakenly sent home, and only 10% of those patients admitted for heart attacks have actually had one.

- ECG
- BP-Syst. <100
- Breath Sounds
- Angina
- Blood Enzyme
- Others (Prd. Comp.)

Action Taken: Introduced algorithm using 1st four factors with physician diagnoses for 2 year clinical trial. (Enzyme test was too slow and expensive at the time.)

Result: Physicians were correct 79-85% of the time. Algorithm was correct over 95% of the time. New protocol used the algorithm. Several years later the enzyme test dropped in cost and time, and was added to the algorithm.

Example 6 – Warped Grills

The company was an appliance manufacturer in Mexico that made cooking grills for barbecues. The grills are made from spools of heavy wire that are straightened, cut to length, bent to shape, and welded together.

In this case, the grills usually came out square and flat, but occasionally, randomly, they were out-of-square and warped. The problem had existed for 7 years. Company engineers had studied the problem repeatedly but had never been able to solve it. The performance measurement that defined the two populations was Good (square and flat) vs. Bad (out-of-square and warped).

The front-line workers who made the grills learned the Paired Comparisons™ technique in a 1-day workshop. They barely spoke English, and the instructor did not speak Spanish. They applied Paired Comparisons™ by taking 6 of the best, square, flat grills and 6 of the worst, out-of-square, warped grills and making 17 different measurements on each one. They measured angles, side lengths, and the straightness

Reasoning Backward

of the 12 pieces. The data follow. To practice using this tool, examine the Sorted Data Tables before reading ahead.

When they sorted the data, they discovered straightness was the critical factor. With only this data, the line workers solved the problem completely in just one week.

The vital clue was straightness. All the heavy wire comes on spools and goes through a straightener. At the beginning

Sorted Data

	Out-of-Sq., C vs. D		Left Hook Dist		Right Hook Dist		Front Cross Length		Center Cross Length		Back Cross Length
Good	-1	Good	25	Bad	20	Good	216	Good	215	Bad	215
Good	0	Good	26	Bad	21	Bad	216	Good	215	Bad	215
Good	0	Good	28	Bad	23	Bad	216	Good	215	Bad	215
Good	0	Good	28	Good	27	Bad	216	Bad	215	Good	216
Good	0	Bad	41	Good	28	Good	216.5	Bad	215	Good	216
Good	1	Good	45	Good	30	Good	216.5	Bad	215	Good	216
Bad	8	Good	50	Good	45	Good	217	Good	216	Good	216
Bad	8	Bad	50	Bad	45	Good	217	Good	216	Good	216
Bad	9	Bad	56	Bad	45	Bad	217	Good	216	Bad	216
Bad	9	Bad	83	Bad	55	Bad	217	Bad	216	Bad	216
Bad	10	Bad	85	Good	60	Good	217.5	Bad	216	Bad	216
Bad	10	Bad	90	Good	60	Bad	218	Bad	216	Good	216.5
Top EC			4		3		0		0		3
Bot EC			4.5		2		1		0		1
TOT EC			8.5		5		1		0		4
% Conf			>95%		None		None		None		None

	Total Left Long. Length		Total Center Long. Length		Total Rt. Long. Length		Short Side Front Straight?		Short Side Back Straight?
Bad	483	Good	484	Good	484	Bad	V	Good	V
Good	484	Good	484	Good	484	Bad	V	Good	V
Good	484	Good	484	Good	484	Bad	V	Good	V
Good	484	Bad	484	Good	484	Bad	V	Good	V
Good	484	Bad	484	Good	484	Bad	V	Good	V
Good	484	Good	485	Bad	484	Good	X	Bad	X
Good	484	Good	485	Bad	484	Good	X	Bad	X
Bad	484	Good	485	Good	485	Good	X	Bad	X
Bad	484	Bad	485	Bad	485	Good	X	Bad	X
Bad	484	Bad	485	Bad	485	Good	X	Bad	X
Bad	484	Bad	485	Bad	486	Good	X	Bad	X
Bad	484	Bad	486	Bad	486	Good	X	Bad	X
	1		0	Top EC	0	TEC	6		6
	0		1	Bot EC	2	BEC	6		6
	1		1	TOT EC	2	TotEC	12		12
	None		None	% Conf	None	%Conf	>99%		>99%

114

The Paired Comparisons™ Tool

	Long Side Left Straightness		Long Side Right Straightness		Bowed Y/N - Direction		Angle Corner 1, diff from 90°		Angle Corner 3, diff from 90°
Good	S	Good	S	Good	N	Good	0	Good	0
Good	S	Good	S	Good	N	Good	0.5	Good	0
Good	S	Good	S	Good	N	Good	0.5	Good	0
Good	S	Good	S	Good	N	Good	0.5	Good	0.5
Good	S	Good	S	Good	N	Good	0.5	Good	0.5
Good	S	Good	S	Good	N	Good	0.5	Good	0.5
Bad	S	Bad	S	Bad	Y-L	Bad	1	Bad	0.5
Bad	S	Bad	V	Bad	Y-L	Bad	1	Bad	0.5
Bad	V	Bad	V	Bad	Y-L	Bad	1.5	Bad	1
Bad	X	Bad	V	Bad	Y-L	Bad	1.5	Bad	1.5
Bad	X	Bad	V	Bad	Y-L	Bad	1.5	Bad	2
Bad	X	Bad	V	Bad	Y-R	Bad	2	Bad	2.5
	5.5		5.5		6		6		3
	4		5		6		6		4
	9.5		10.5		12		12		7
	>95%		>99%		>99%		>99%		95%

of the spool, the arc of the wire is large (closer to straight), so the straightener succeeds in making the pieces straight. At the tail end of the spool, the arc of the wire is much tighter, and after one pass through the straightener, the pieces still have a small amount of residual curvature.

Workers cut all the pieces to length and put them into bundles for the grill assemblers to use. Assemblers take random pieces out of the bundle, put them into a fixture, and weld them in place. This explains why the problem was sporadic. When the assembler selected straight pieces, the grill was good, but if he used a curved piece, the grill was warped. Everyone had assumed that fixturing and welding would straighten the slightly curved pieces, but the opposite was happening – the curved pieces were bending the straight ones.

The line workers successfully solved this 7-year-old problem in just one week just by using Paired Comparisons™. The solution was always to check the straightness of the pieces when they leave the straightener. If the pieces have a residual curve, they go through the straightener again. From this point on, this plant never made another warped, out-of-square grill.

In addition to solving this chronic problem, the other powerful outcome of this example was showing that problem solving should not be limited to engineers. Line workers understand their day-to-day problems better than anyone else does. By giving them powerful tools, they become productive problem solvers. The best results occur when everyone is involved in solving problems. A pleasant side effect is the boost in employee morale, involvement, and commitment that occurs when people become effective problem solvers.

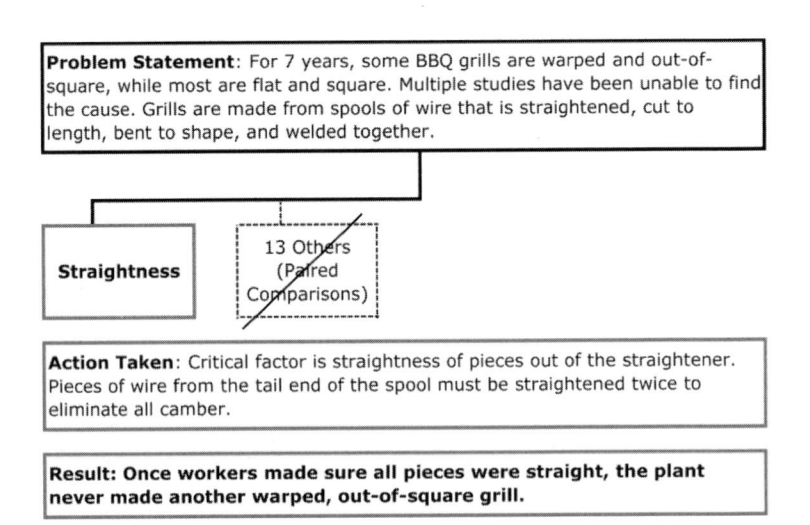

Problem Statement: For 7 years, some BBQ grills are warped and out-of-square, while most are flat and square. Multiple studies have been unable to find the cause. Grills are made from spools of wire that is straightened, cut to length, bent to shape, and welded together.

- Straightness
- 13 Others (Paired Comparisons)

Action Taken: Critical factor is straightness of pieces out of the straightener. Pieces of wire from the tail end of the spool must be straightened twice to eliminate all camber.

Result: Once workers made sure all pieces were straight, the plant never made another warped, out-of-square grill.

Paired Comparisons™ Summary:

- Universally applicable
- Demonstrated utility in sales and marketing, research and development, administrative operations, and a wide variety of production operations

The Paired Comparisons™ Tool

- Quickly narrows the focus of any project to a small number of possibly critical factors
- Accelerates subsequent problem-solving activities by eliminating false starts and blind alleys
- Never a bad place to start.

The primary lesson is to make the fundamental principle of Paired Comparisons™ the basis of all problem solving: **compare performance extremes to identify consistent differences**. This is the most critical principle to becoming an effective problem solver. Sir Francis Bacon spelled it out 400 years ago, Sherlock Holmes used it exhaustively 100 years ago, and it is still true.

Reasoning Backward

Paired Comparisons™
(For Unit-to-unit comparison of Good & Bad units of anything, a versatile tool for almost any area of human endeavor)

Objective:

To compare a series of good and bad units and search them systematically for differences that will provide clues about what is causing the variation in performance. Paired Comparisons™ is so versatile that it has been used in new product and process designs, production, field, support services, transactional and administrative work, farms, hospitals, and schools.

Prerequisites:
- Performance must be measurable, and the measurement accuracy must be at least five times narrower than the specification tolerance or product spread.
- Make every attempt to select the best and the worst examples within a more or less constant timeframe.
- If the performance measurement is an attribute, make every effort to convert it to a measurable variable with a Likert scale.

Procedure:
- Select six or eight best samples and an equal number of worst samples. They should be as far apart as possible with respect to the performance measurement under investigation.
- Consider all the process parameters and quality characteristics that are currently being measured. Their variation might explain the observed differences in performance. Something is causing the bad units to be bad. Consider everything – all process parameters, physical properties of the final outcomes, any analytical results, anything. Prioritize the list in descending order of likelihood of being a cause of the difference.

The Paired Comparisons™ Tool

- Make readings of each parameter for all the 12 or 16 selected units. Arrange them in rank order from the smallest reading to the largest reading (or vice versa), regardless of whether they are best or worst samples.
- Apply the Tukey Test, explained below.
- If the Total End Count is 6 or more, there is 90% or greater confidence that the particular parameter is important in explaining the difference between good and bad units.
- If the Total End Count is less than 6, there is not enough confidence that this parameter is important in explaining the performance differences.

The Tukey Test:
- Rank a group of readings of a specific quality characteristic or process parameter from lowest to highest, or vice versa, regardless of whether they are a best or a worst sample.
- Designate each of the 12 or 16 ranked readings as either good (G) or bad (B) from the original data.
- Draw a line starting from the top of these readings, when the "all bad" change to "good" for the first time (or vice versa). This is the Top End Count.
- Similarly, draw a line starting from the bottom where the readings change from "all good" to "bad" for the first time (or vice versa). This is the Bottom End Count.
- Add the Top and Bottom End Counts to determine the Total End Count. If the Top End Count is "all good", then the Bottom End Count must be "all bad" (or vice versa), or the Total End Count becomes zero.
- If a "good" and "bad" sample have the same reading at the point of transition from end count region to overlap region, then the end count is increased by only 1/2 instead of 1.
- The relationship between Confidence Level and Total End Count is as follows.

Total End Count	Confidence Level
6	90%
7	95%
10	99%
13	99.9%

This version of the Tukey Test assumes a scale where high is good and low is bad, or vice versa. A different variation is useful when the center readings are good, but readings that vary either high or low are bad. In that situation, report the readings for the good and bad units as the deviation from the target value rather than the actual readings. The good readings near the center of the distribution will show small deviations, while both tails of the distribution will show large deviations, and the Tukey Test will work as described previously.

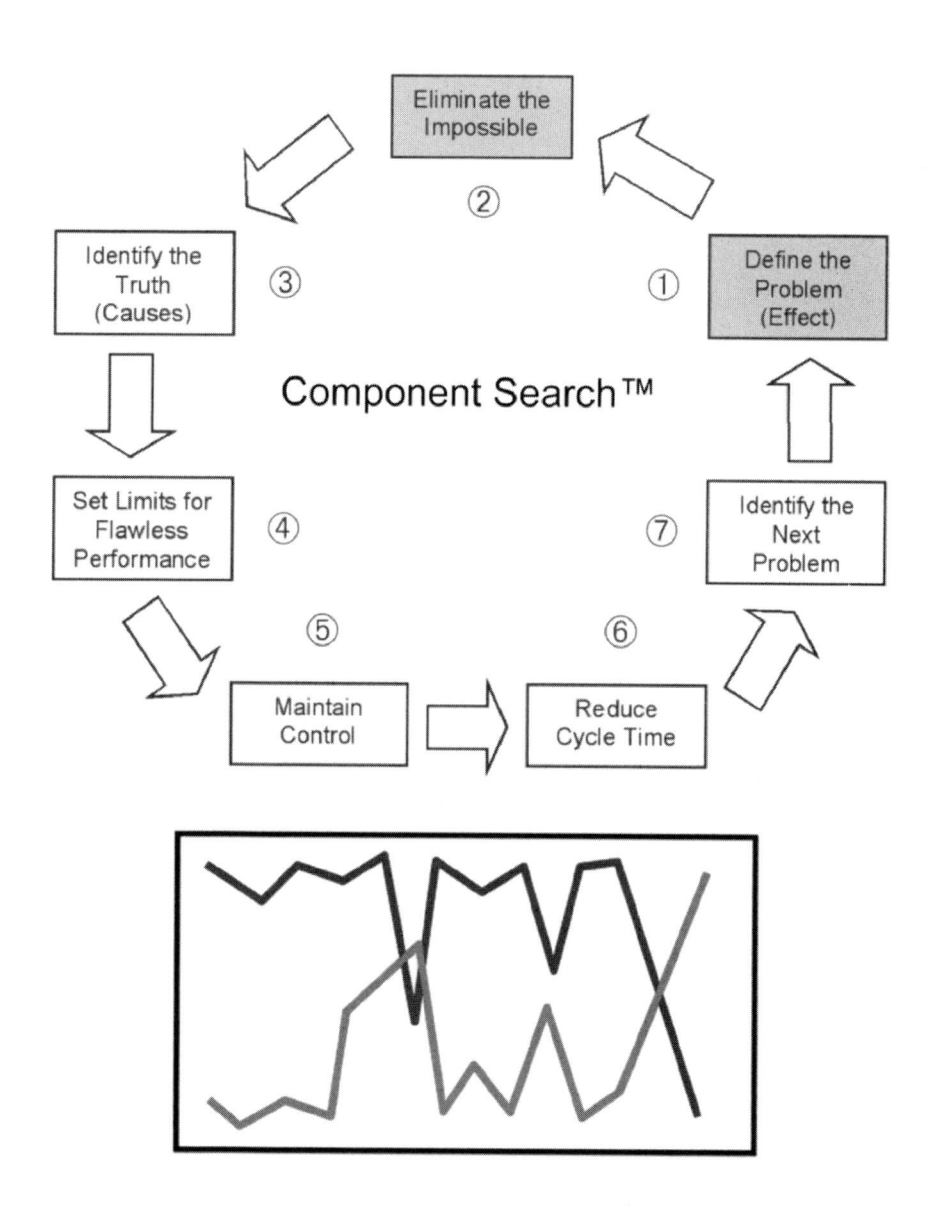

Component Search™

1. Define the Problem (Effect)
2. Eliminate the Impossible
3. Identify the Truth (Causes)
4. Set Limits for Flawless Performance
5. Maintain Control
6. Reduce Cycle Time
7. Identify the Next Problem

Chapter 6

The Component Search™ Tool

[**A Note to Readers:** This tool and the next two, Variable Search™ and Full Factorial, are primarily used in manufacturing operations. They are important parts of the complete set of best practice tools, but these tools may have not been directly applicable for many readers. They are included here to raise awareness of a different, powerful way of thinking and as a reference for the future.]

Concept and Expected Results:

Component Search™ derives from the same three Holmes' tips as the other Clue Generation Tools.

"Once you have eliminated the impossible, whatever remains, no matter how improbable, must be the truth."

"Always approach a case with an absolutely blank mind. Form no theories, just simply observe and draw inferences from your observations. It is a capital mistake to theorize before one has data. Insensibly one begins to twist facts to suit theories, instead of theories to suit facts."

"It is of the highest importance in the art of detection to be able to recognize out of a number of facts which are incidental and which are vital."

It also uses two others.

"How dangerous it is to reason from insufficient data. Data, Data, Data! I can't make bricks without clay."

Component Search™

"Detection is, or ought to be, an exact science, and should be treated in the same cold unemotional manner. When you attempt to tinge it with romanticism, you produce the same effect as if you worked a love-story into the fifth proposition of Euclid."

Dorian Shainin developed Component Search based on these principles. It is applicable whenever you can disassemble and reassemble a finished manufactured product, and it will still perform its intended function. When this is the case, Component Search™ requires just one good sample of product and one bad sample to determine which components are responsible for bad performance.

The basic concept is to switch components between the good and bad units, one-at-a-time, and to observe which switches affect the performance of the two units. If switching a component does not change the performance, then the component is non-critical. If the performance changes, the switched component is a critical factor.

Once the team knows the critical components, it can determine how to change the specifications of each component to eliminate the defects.

In many cases investigators will have completed a Multi-Vari experiment first and discovered that the category containing the most critical factor is Unit-to-unit, which suggests trying Component Search™ next, whenever the device can be disassembled and reassembled successfully. In some situations, Component Search™ may be the first experiment due to its simplicity and small sample size.

General Description:

Component Search™ has four stages. Dorian Shainin called Stage 1 the Ballpark Stage. It begins by selecting the good and bad samples to test. The larger the difference in performance between these two samples, the better this technique will work.

In Stage 1, first measure the performance of each unit, using the parameter that determines whether the units are good or bad. Then, disassemble and reassemble both units with no changes and measure their performance again. Finally, repeat disassembly and reassembly one more time, and measure performance for a third time. The two units pass Stage 1 when all three good readings are all better than all three bad readings, and the separation is wide enough that significant changes will be apparent.

If the performance of the two units changes in these Stage 1 rebuilds, then the most critical factor is a process condition, not a problem with one of the components. In that situation, study variation in process conditions.

If the separation of good and bad is not wide enough, then look for good and bad units with wider separation.

When the good and bad units pass Stage 1, proceed to Stage 2.

Stage 2 is Elimination. Begin by deciding the order of switching, beginning with the component with the highest probability of being the most critical factor. Proceed in descending order of expected importance. Label the components A, B, C, D, etc. (Choosing correctly means there will be fewer experiments to run.)

First, switch component A, putting A from the good unit into the bad unit, and vice versa. Then, measure the performance of each unit. There are three possible outcomes.

(1) If the good unit is still good, and the bad unit is still bad, then A is non-critical. Next, return the A components to their original units and recheck that nothing has changed. Then, move on to B.

(2) If switching A causes the good unit to become bad, and the bad unit to become good, a complete reversal, then A is the most critical factor, and the experiment is over.

(3) If there is some shift of the good unit, or the bad unit, or both units, but not a complete reversal, then A is critical, and so is something else. Put the A components back into their original units and move on to B. Continue until all the components have been switched, one at a time, or you find a most critical factor that acts alone.

Component Search™

Stage 3 is a Capping Run. In this last run, switch all the critical components and none of the others. The Capping Run is successful if there is complete reversal of good and bad performance. If so, proceed to Stage 4.

Stage 4 is Factorial Analysis of the data gathered in Stages 1, 2, and 3. It confirms most critical factor, and indicates if other critical factors are present as well, including any interactions among these factors.

Examples of the Tool in Action:

Example 1 – The Non-Firing Burner

This problem is from a company that manufactures oil-fired burners. About 3% of the burners failed to fire when tested at the end of the assembly line. They chose Component Search™ to look for the most critical factor because they could disassemble and reassemble the burners. The measurement was simply whether or not the burner fired.

In Stage 1, they selected one good (Firing) Burner and one bad (Non-Firing) Burner. They disassembled, reassembled, and measured each unit twice, and both burners remained good and bad respectively, so the units passed Stage 1.

In Stage 2, they prioritized the components as follows:
- Oil pump
- Nozzle
- Filters
- Oil hoses
- Electrodes
- Inner needle valve assembly

They tested the components in the indicated order, and the results are in the following table and graph.

Reasoning Backward

Non-Firing Burner Components Search

[Chart: Y-axis showing Firing vs. Non-Firing; X-axis "Components Swapped" with points: Initial, First rebuild, Second rebuild, Oil Pump, Nozzle, Filters, Oil Hoses, Electrodes, Needle Valve, Return Needle Valve. Lines for Good and Bad cross at Needle Valve.]

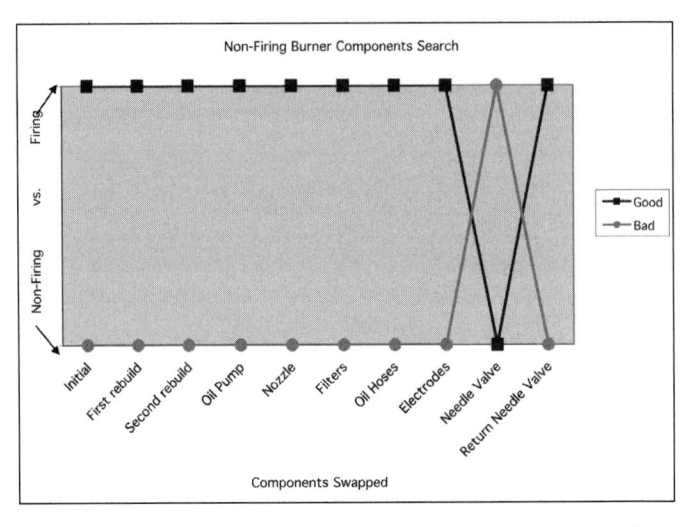

	Good	Bad	Importance
Initial	1	0	
First rebuild	1	0	
Second rebuild	1	0	
Oil Pump	1	0	
Nozzle	1	0	
Filters	1	0	
Oil Hoses	1	0	
Electrodes	1	0	
Needle Valve	0	1	**Important**
Return Needle Valve	1	0	

1 = Burner Fires
0 = Burner is Non-Firing

This result led to a second Component Search™ of the parts in the needle valves from the good and the bad units. The parts included a spring, a needle valve, a nozzle holder, and a seat. They tried the spring first and achieved the complete reversal they wanted, so they went to the spring supplier and developed a spring tension specification that eliminated the problem.

Component Search™

Example 2 – The Hourmeter

An hourmeter is a device designed to reliably record time, even at service temperatures as low as –40°C. Defective units would lock up at higher temperatures and stop recording, sometimes at temperatures as high as 0°C. The measurement they used for this experiment was the temperature at which the unit locked up, testing down to –40°C.

For Stage 1, they selected a good unit that worked down to –40°C and a bad unit that failed at 0°C. The two rebuilds of Stage 1 were successful, so they proceeded to Stage 2.

A	Solenoid, pin and shaft
B	Idler gear shaft
C	Numeral shaft
D	Mainframe
E	Bell crank
F	Idler gears
G	Numeral wheels
H	Electronic circuit board
R	Rest of the components

	D	d bar	D/d bar>1.25?
	-32	-6	5.33
Decision Limits = Medians +/- (1.53 x d bar)			
Good Dec. Lim.	-37.00		-37.00
Bad Dec. Lim.	-5.00		-5.00

	Good	Bad	High Lower Decision Limit	High Upper Decision Limit	Low Lower Decision Limit	Low Upper Decision Limit
Initial	-40	0	-27.82	-46.18	4.18	-14.18
1st Rebuild	-35	-5	-27.82	-46.18	4.18	-14.18
2nd Rebuild	-37	-7	-27.82	-46.18	4.18	-14.18

In Stage 2, they selected eight components to study and switched them all, one at a time. Six components had no effect, while two caused a partial reversal and were critical.

In Stage 3, they switched both D (the Mainframe) and G (the Numerical Wheels), the two critical components, and achieved complete reversal. The graphical representation of the data follows, along with Stage 4 Factorial Analysis.

Reasoning Backward

	Good	Bad	High Lower Decision Limit	High Upper Decision Limit	Low Lower Decision Limit	Low Upper Decision Limit
A swapped	-40	-5	-27.82	-46.18	4.18	-14.18
B swapped	-35	0	-27.82	-46.18	4.18	-14.18
C swapped	-35	-5	-27.82	-46.18	4.18	-14.18
D swapped	-18	-5	-27.82	-46.18	4.18	-14.18
E swapped	-40	0	-27.82	-46.18	4.18	-14.18
F swapped	-40	-5	-27.82	-46.18	4.18	-14.18
G swapped	-22	-5	-27.82	-46.18	4.18	-14.18
H swapped	-35	0	-27.82	-46.18	4.18	-14.18

As they studied the interaction, they discovered the Numerical Wheels were very close to the Mainframe. The combination of the mainframe shrinkage when the temperature dropped and variation in outside wheel thickness and centering caused the failures. When all three conditions were bad, the mainframe could contract enough to constrict the wheel's movement, and the unit would lock up. They solved the problem by making the outside wheel narrower and centering it more accurately. The number of defective units dropped to zero.

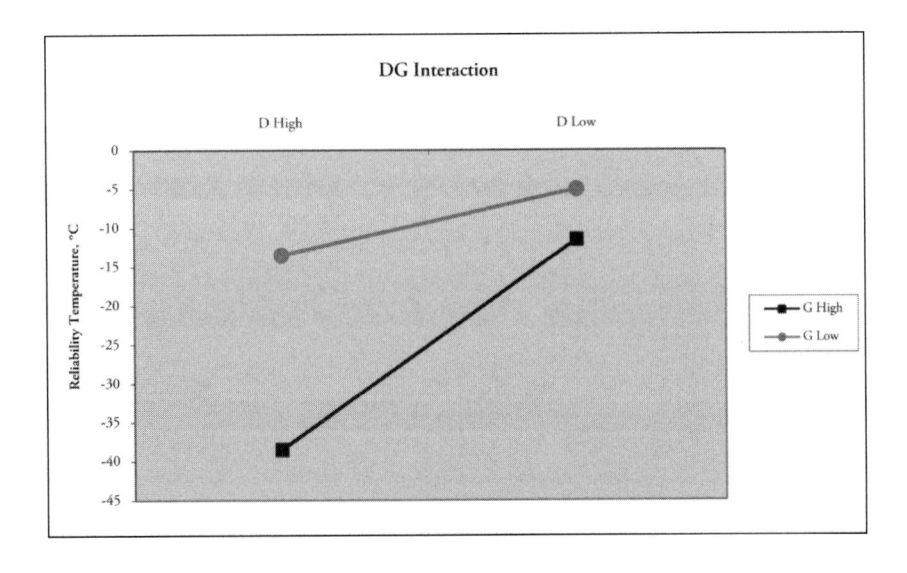

DG Interaction

Component Search™

	D High		D Low		
G High	-40	-35	-18		
	-35	-40	-5		
	-37	-40			
	-40	-35			-50
	-35	-40			
	Median =	-38.5	Median =	-11.5	
G Low	-22		0	-5	
	-5		-5	0	
			-7	-5	
			-5	0	-18.5
			0	0	
	Median =	-13.5	Median =	-5	
-25	-52		-16.5		-43.5

Main Effect D ((-38.5-13.5)-(-11.5-5))/2 = **-17.75**

Main Effect G ((-38.5-11.5)-(-13.5-5))/2 = **-15.75**

DG Interactio ((-38.5-5)-(-11.5-13.5))/2 = **9.25**

	D High	D Low
G High	-38.5	-11.5
G Low	-13.5	-5

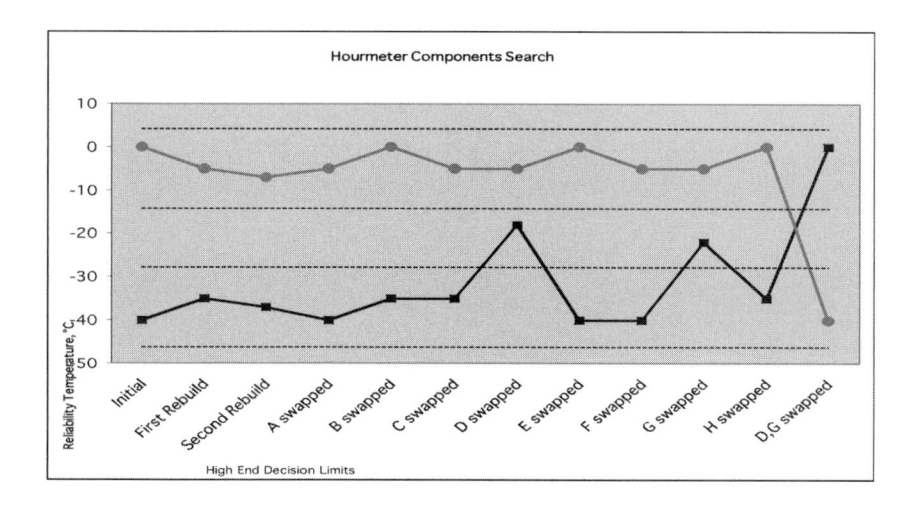

Hourmeter Components Search

[Chart showing Reliability Temperature, °C on y-axis (from 10 to -50) across stages: Initial, First Rebuild, Second Rebuild, A swapped, B swapped, C swapped, D swapped, E swapped, F swapped, G swapped, H swapped, D,G swapped. High End Decision Limits shown.]

129

Reasoning Backward

Problem Statement: Hourmeter is supposed to work down to -40°C, but some stop working at temperatures as high as 0°C.

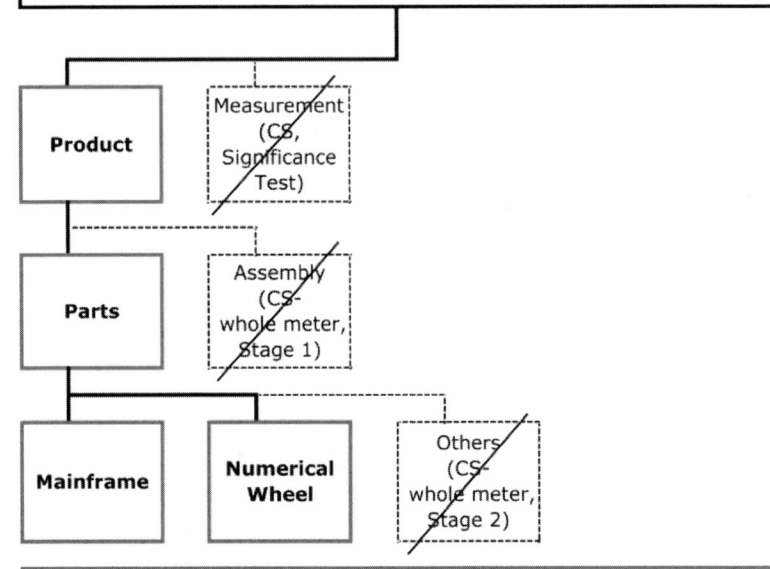

```
Product ─── Measurement (CS, Significance Test)
   │
Parts ───── Assembly (CS-whole meter, Stage 1)
   │
   ├── Mainframe
   ├── Numerical Wheel
   └── Others (CS-whole meter, Stage 2)
```

Action Taken: Most critical factor is interaction between off-center outside wheel and mainframe as thermal contraction occurs. Made outside wheel narrower and centered it further away from the mainframe.

Result: All hourmeters now work down to -40°C. Zero defects.

Example 3 – The Oscillator

This second electronics example is a Time-Delay Oscillator. The design called for a 16-millisecond delay, and good units performed as designed. The problem was that bad units had a delay longer than 32 milliseconds. The development team suspected five components in the circuit might be the most critical factor, as shown.

The good and bad units they selected passed Stage 1, so they conducted the Elimination switches in Stage 2.

Component Search™

A	Crystal
B	Microprocessor
C	Transistor
D	Capacitor C2
E	Capacitor C1

D	d bar	D/d bar>1.25?
20	3.5	5.71
Decision Limits	= Medians ±	(1.53 x d bar)
Good Dec. Lim.	15.00	15.00
Bad Dec. Lim.	35.00	35.00

Important

	Good	Bad	Good UDL	Good LDL	Bad UDL	Bad LDL
Initial	13	34	20.36	9.65	40.36	29.65
1st Rebuild	16	38	20.36	9.65	40.36	29.65
2nd Rebuild	15	35	20.36	9.65	40.36	29.65
A swapped	16	19	20.36	9.65	40.36	29.65
B swapped	16	35	20.36	9.65	40.36	29.65
C swapped	14	33	20.36	9.65	40.36	29.65
D swapped	15	37	20.36	9.65	40.36	29.65
E swapped	15	16	20.36	9.65	40.36	29.65
A, E swapped	32	17	20.36	9.65	40.36	29.65

Oscillator Time Delay Component Search™

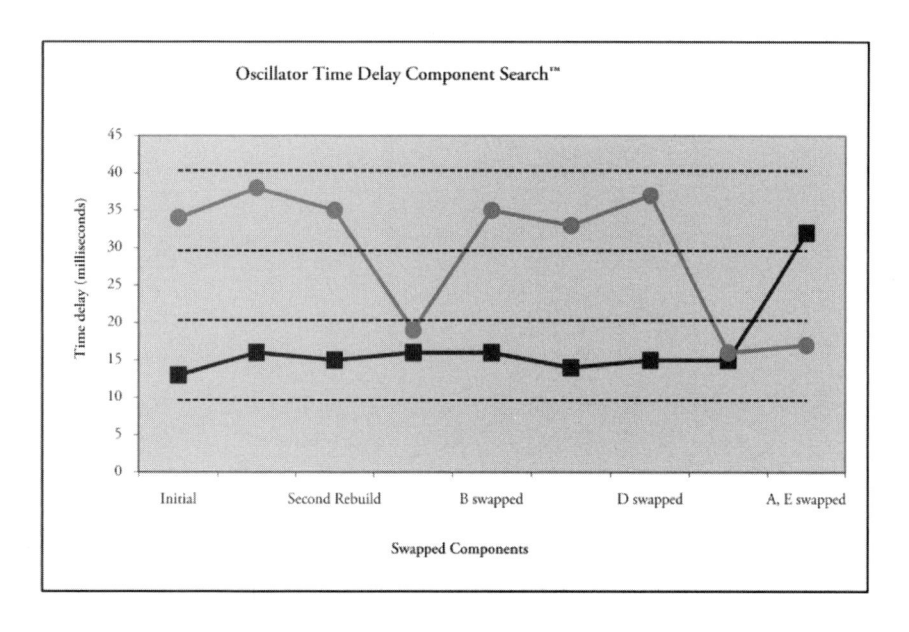

They discovered that switching components A and E each caused a partial reversal, so both were critical. The other three components were non-critical.

In the Stage 3 Capping Run, they switched A and E at the same time and achieved complete reversal. The most critical factor was the interaction between a bad crystal and a bad capacitor. It was much easier and less expensive to change the capacitor's leakage specification than to modify the crystal, so the team addressed the capacitor first. They tightened its leakage specification, and the problem disappeared, without having to modify the crystal at all. The Stage 4 Factorial Analysis for all three stages is shown.

	A High		A Low		
E High	13 15		16		
	16 17		16		
	15				
	16				31
	14				
	Median = 15.0		Median = 16.0		
E Low	19		34 37		
	15		38 32		
			35		
			35		52
			33		
	Median = 17.0		Median = 35.0		
33	32		51		50

Main Effect A = ((16+35)-(15+17)/2 = **-9.5**

Main Effect E = ((17+35)-(15+16))/2 = **-10.5**

AE Interaction ((15+35)-(16+17))/2 = **-8.5**

	A High	A Low
E High	15.0	16.0
E Low	17.0	35.0

Component Search™

AE Interaction

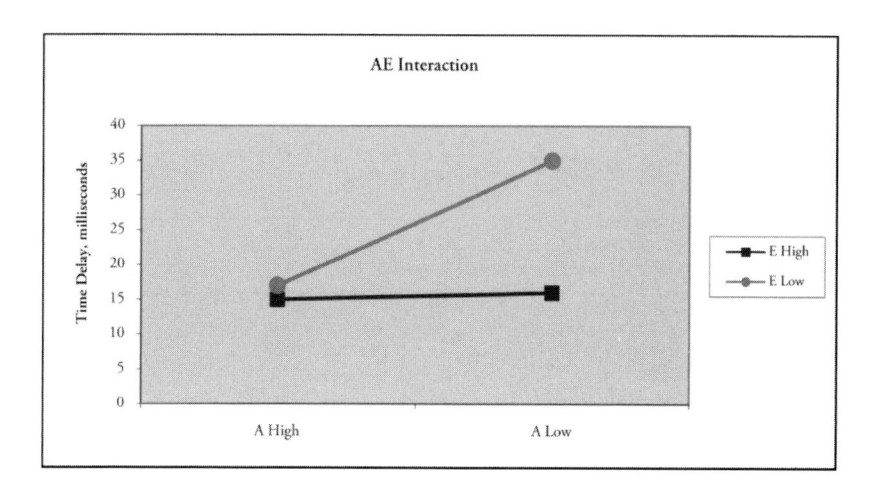

[Chart showing Time Delay (milliseconds) vs A High/A Low, with E High line roughly flat at ~15, and E Low line rising from ~17 at A High to ~35 at A Low]

Component Search™ Summary:

- Useful in any situation where disassembly and reassembly are possible because it doesn't interrupt the operation and only requires two samples
- Fast, easy, and effective, a workhorse tool because of its simplicity, small sample size, and power
- May have to conduct a series of Component Search™ experiments
- Also useful in other situations. In one case, two product inspectors made length measurements on a product coming off an assembly line, and one station reported a significantly higher percentage of defective parts. They applied the concept of Component Search™ and started switching factors. First, they checked the defective parts from one station on the other station, and the excessive defects from one line now passed inspection. Then, they switched operators, and both stations now reported similar very low defect rates. Operator competence was not an issue, but one person's readings were inaccurate. They looked closer and discovered that person making the mistakes was short, and seated on a shorter stool, which introduced parallax into her readings. When she used

the other station with its higher stool, her angle of vision improved, and her readings became accurate. The solution was to get her a taller stool. Switching needn't always be limited to components.

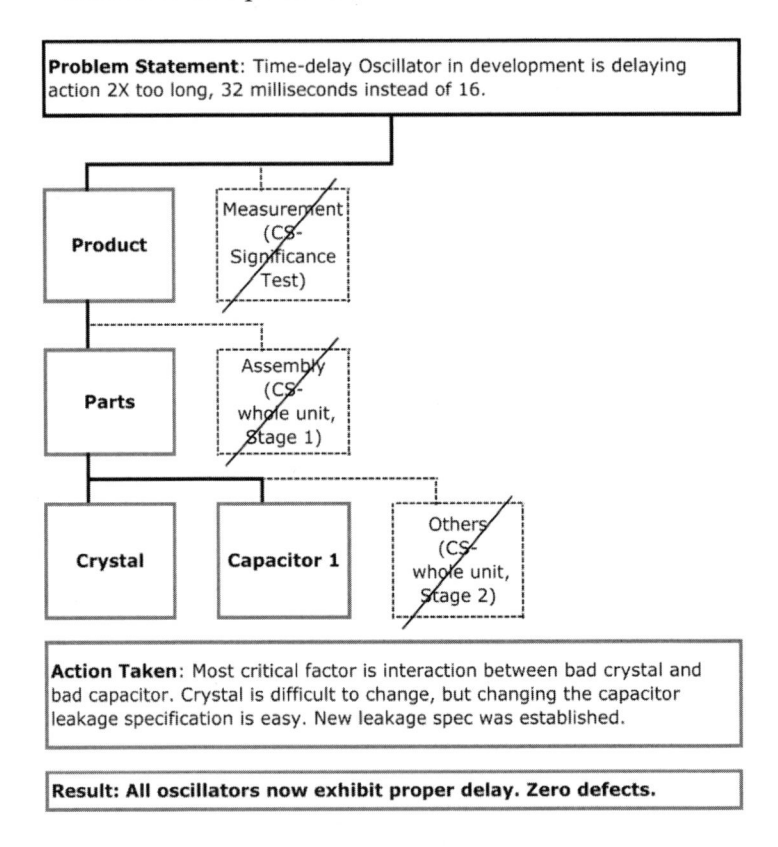

Problem Statement: Time-delay Oscillator in development is delaying action 2X too long, 32 milliseconds instead of 16.

- Product
  - Measurement (CS-Significance Test)
- Parts
  - Assembly (CS-whole unit, Stage 1)
- Crystal | Capacitor 1 | Others (CS-whole unit, Stage 2)

Action Taken: Most critical factor is interaction between bad crystal and bad capacitor. Crystal is difficult to change, but changing the capacitor leakage specification is easy. New leakage spec was established.

Result: All oscillators now exhibit proper delay. Zero defects.

The fundamental lesson is to **switch elements between good and bad performance** to discover which one or ones are affecting performance. This swapping strategy enables a problem solver to use the smallest possible sample size, just one good unit and one bad unit, and still make statistically valid conclusions. It offers the greatest advantage of any method, whenever it is applicable. Holmes would definitely approve.

Component Search™
(For Unit-to-unit comparisons of Good vs. Bad,
if disassembly and reassembly are possible)

Objective:
To identify the most critical component in an assembly when the Unit-to-unit category contains the most critical factor. This powerful method is so simple that line operators can do it with a minimal amount of coaching, and without interrupting production. It uses just two extreme samples, one very good and one very bad.

Procedure: This method has four stages.
 Stage 1: Ballpark Stage. This stage determines whether the right variables components are being tested. First, select the good and bad units. Then, disassemble, re-assemble and test each unit twice to determine that the results are reproducible. (If the results are not reproducible, then the most critical factor is in the assembly process, not the individual components.) If Stage 1 is successful, proceed to Stage 2.
 Stage 2: Elimination Stage. In this stage, swap components between units, one at a time, and retest the units. This eliminates all the unimportant causes and any interactions they may have. Only the important causes will show a significant effect.
 Stage 3: Capping Run Stage. This stage verifies that the important causes identified in Stage 2 continue to be important, and that all the unimportant variables continue to be unimportant. The team swaps all the important components at the same time and looks for a complete reversal of performance.
 Stage 4: Factorial Analysis. This stage is not another experiment, but simply an analysis of the data from Stages 1, 2, and 3. It is a full factorial matrix to quantify and separate the magnitude and direction of the important main effects and their interaction effects.

Reasoning Backward

<u>Prerequisites:</u>

Component Search™ is applicable in assembly operations, when identical processes or machines exhibit varying performance levels, and when parts are interchangeable between machines.

The performance must be measurable, with accuracy at least five times narrower than the specification tolerance or product spread.

The "good" and "bad" units must be capable of disassembly and reassembly without significant change in the outcome performance.

Stage 1: Ballpark Stage:
- Select a sample of just two units from a day's production as far apart as possible with respect to the property being investigated – one best sample and one worst. The further apart they are, the easier it will be to find the most critical factor. Measure their respective performance.
- Disassemble and reassemble the two samples twice each and re-measure their respective performance after each reassembly.
- Conduct the following Significance Tests.
  - All three best readings must rank better than all three worst readings with no overlap.
  - The difference (D) between the median of the best samples and median of the worst samples must be at least 1.25 times greater than the average range of the best and worst readings (d bar), and the higher the better. Consider the following example:
  - Assume that for a particular property, the best samples were 2, 4, and 1. The worst readings were 17, 21, and 19.
  - Median of best is 2. Median of worst is 19. $D = 19 - 2 = 17$.
  - Range of best is $4 - 1 = 3$, and range of worst is $21 - 17 = 4$. d bar $= (3 + 4)/2 = 7/2 = 3.5$.
  - D/d bar $= 17/3.5 = 4.86$, which is ≥ 1.25, so these samples pass the Significance Tests.

Component Search™

- If the ratio of D/d bar is less than 1.25, then Stage 1 failed. This means the performance measurements do not remain constant upon reassembly. In that case, the problem is in the assembly process, not in the components themselves. This calls for a progressive systematic disassembly and reassembly to determine which assembly step is the most critical factor.
- If the D/d bar ratio is ≥ 1.25, then the most critical factor is one of the components or subassemblies. Make a list, in descending order, of the subassemblies or components that are most likely to be causing the defects to occur. Label them A, B, C, etc. (By testing in order of descending likelihood, you can reduce the number of the experiments if your assumptions are correct.)

Stage 2: Elimination Stage.
- Switch the top ranked components (A) between best and worst, leaving everything else the same. Label these rebuilt assemblies $A_H R_L$ and $A_L R_H$. (R is for the Rest of the components.) Measure and record their performance.
- There are three possible outcomes:
  - $A_L R_H$ remains best and $A_H R_L$ remains worst within the decision limits. In this case, A is unimportant.
  - $A_L R_H$ becomes worst and $A_H R_L$ becomes best within the decision limits. A is important and is the most critical factor. Component Search™ is over.
  - $A_L R_H$ deteriorates partially, moving towards worst decision limit levels, but not reaching them, and/or $A_H R_L$ improves partially, moving towards best decision limit levels, but not reaching them. This indicates that A is Important, but so is at least one other component. There may also be interactions between A and another component or components.

Reasoning Backward

- Decision limits are the range of values around the best and worst medians that define the expected range of variation. Readings within the decision limits are not statistically different from the original readings. Values outside the decision limits are statistically different and indicate the swapped component is Important. The formula for decision limits simplifies to each median ± (1.5 x d bar). In the above example, best decision limits are 2 ± (1.5 x 3.5) = 2 ± 5.3 = –3.3 to 7.3. Worst decision limits are 19 ± 5.3 = 13.7 to 24.3.

  In this example, if swapping component A caused either reading to fall between 7.3 and 13.7, then component A would be Important, and so would at least one other component. (Caution: If the decision limits overlap, then the gap between best and worst is not wide enough. Look for more extreme differences between best and worst, or select another, earlier performance measurement that has a more extreme difference.)
- An alternative to decision limits is to use the point halfway between the median readings as a single decision limit. Any swap that crosses this point, or comes within about 10% of crossing this point would be important. In the example, 10.5 is halfway between 2 and 19, the median values of best and worst, respectively. Therefore, any best swaps with readings higher than about 8 or any worst swaps lower than about 13 would be important.
- After testing the units with component A swapped, return the components to their original units, and retest once again to assure that performance has not changed. If the values shift, then the disassembly/reassembly process is suspect, and progressive disassembly and reassembly is appropriate, as before.
- If A was not the most critical factor, proceed to swap component B, the next most likely component in the two units, and retest. Then return the B components to their

Component Search™

original units and retest. Use the same guidelines and decision limits as with component A. Continue to test all the components until you have identified all the Important components and eliminated all the Unimportant ones.

Stage 3: Capping Run Stage.
- The capping run validates that you have found all the important components. Swap all the important components from best and worst simultaneously, and none of the unimportant components. If successful, the unit with all best important components and all other components worst will test as best, and the other unit, with all worst important components and everything else best will test as worst.
- After completing the Capping Run, plot all the data on a graph that includes the decision limits to make the data easier to understand.

Stage 4: Factorial Analysis.
- This step uses all the data generated in Stages 1, 2, and 3. It determines quantitatively the magnitude and direction of the main effects and the interaction effects.
- Display the data in a 2^x matrix where x is the number of important components identified in Stages 1, 2, and 3. Calculate the medians in each cell of the matrix. Use the median values to calculate the main effects and the interaction effects using ANOVA. This analysis quantitatively identifies the most critical factor and any other critical factors.

Reasoning Backward

Component Search™ Template

Project: Date:
Investigator:
Performance Problem:
Defect Frequency and History:
Measurement (include target value and specification limits):
Accuracy of Measurement/Accuracy of Product Tolerance Ratio:
(If attribute, is a Likert scale possible?):

Stage 1: Ballpark Stage.

Select one truly best and one truly worst unit from a day's production. Measure the performance for each. Then disassemble and reassemble each unit twice, retesting after each reassembly.

Calculate D, d bar, and the D/d bar ratio. Do the data pass the Significance Rules? If so, proceed to Stage 2. If not, perform systematic disassembly and reassembly to find the process variation that is the most critical factor.

	Best	Worst
Initial output value		
Value after 1st rebuild		
Value after 2nd rebuild		

- Are all three best samples better than all three worst samples?
- D = difference in median values =
- Average of ranges = d bar = ((best high − best low) + (worst high − worst low))/2 =
- Is D/d bar ≥ 1.25? D/d bar =

Component Search™

- Calculate the decision limits. (Each median ± (1.5 x d bar)). Do they overlap? If so, find a best and a worst with greater separation.
- Calculate the alternate decision limit – the point midway between the median reading of best samples and median reading of worst samples. Alternate decision limit =

Stage 2: Elimination Stage.

List the components in descending order of likelihood of being the most critical factor and label them A, B, C, etc. Swap the A components, from best to worst and from worst to best, and measure performance. Label these $A_H R_L$ when A is from the best and the rest of the components are from the worst and $A_L R_H$ for A from the worst with the rest from the best. After testing, return A components to their original units and retest to assure that performance did not change.

- If $A_H R_L$ has a worst reading and $A_L R_H$ has a best reading, then A is unimportant.
- If $A_H R_L$ has a best reading and $A_L R_H$ has a worst reading, then A is the most critical factor, no other factor is important, and Component Search™ is over.
- If either $A_H R_L$ or $A_L R_H$ moves outside the decision limits of worst or best respectively, then A is important, and so is at least one other component.
- If A is not the most critical factor, then proceed to test component B in the same way. Continue until you have swapped all the components.

Build a table showing this data.

Label	Component	Factor Combination	Value	Decision Limits	Factor Importance
A		$A_H R_L$ $A_L R_H$			
B		$B_H R_L$ $B_L R_H$			
C		$C_H R_L$ $C_L R_H$			
D		$D_H R_L$ $D_L R_H$			
E		$E_H R_L$ $E_L R_H$			
...		...			

Stage 3: Capping Run.

Run one experiment with all the important components swapped and none of the unimportant components swapped. If this test is successful, $X_H Y_H Z_H R_L$ will have a best reading and $X_L Y_L Z_L R_H$ will be a worst.

Capping Run		$X_H Y_H Z_H R_L$ $X_L Y_L Z_L R_H$			

Plot all the data from Stages 1, 2, and 3 on one graph that includes the decision limits so the data will be easier to understand.

Stage 4: Factorial Analysis.

Build a factorial chart for the important factors using all the data from Stages 1, 2, and 3.

Component Search™

Calculate the medians in each cell.

Use the medians to quantify the main effects and interaction effects of the important variables in an ANOVA table.

Graph the interactions to see more clearly the interaction effects.

<u>Conclusion:</u>
Identify the critical components.

Use this result to find ways to reduce variation in the important components.

Work with suppliers of the components, including external suppliers, to find ways to reduce variation.

Section 2
"Identify the Truth" – (Causes)
Identification & Validation Tools

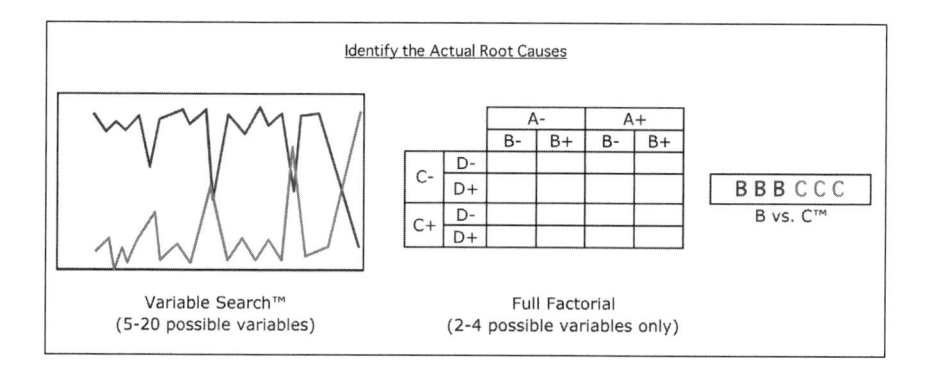

Identify the Actual Root Causes

		A-		A+	
		B-	B+	B-	B+
C-	D-				
	D+				
C+	D-				
	D+				

B B B C C C
B vs. C™

Variable Search™
(5-20 possible variables)

Full Factorial
(2-4 possible variables only)

Historically, the previous Clue Generation Tools completely solve 75% of all problems. The other 25% of problems require additional work. The investigator has narrowed the focus to just a few factors that include all the root causes. The tools in this section identify the most critical factor and any other critical factors that are active, and they go further to validate this solution by intentionally turning the problem on and off by varying these critical factors. At the end of this phase of problem solving, the investigator will know exactly which factors must be controlled more tightly to achieve Zero Defects.

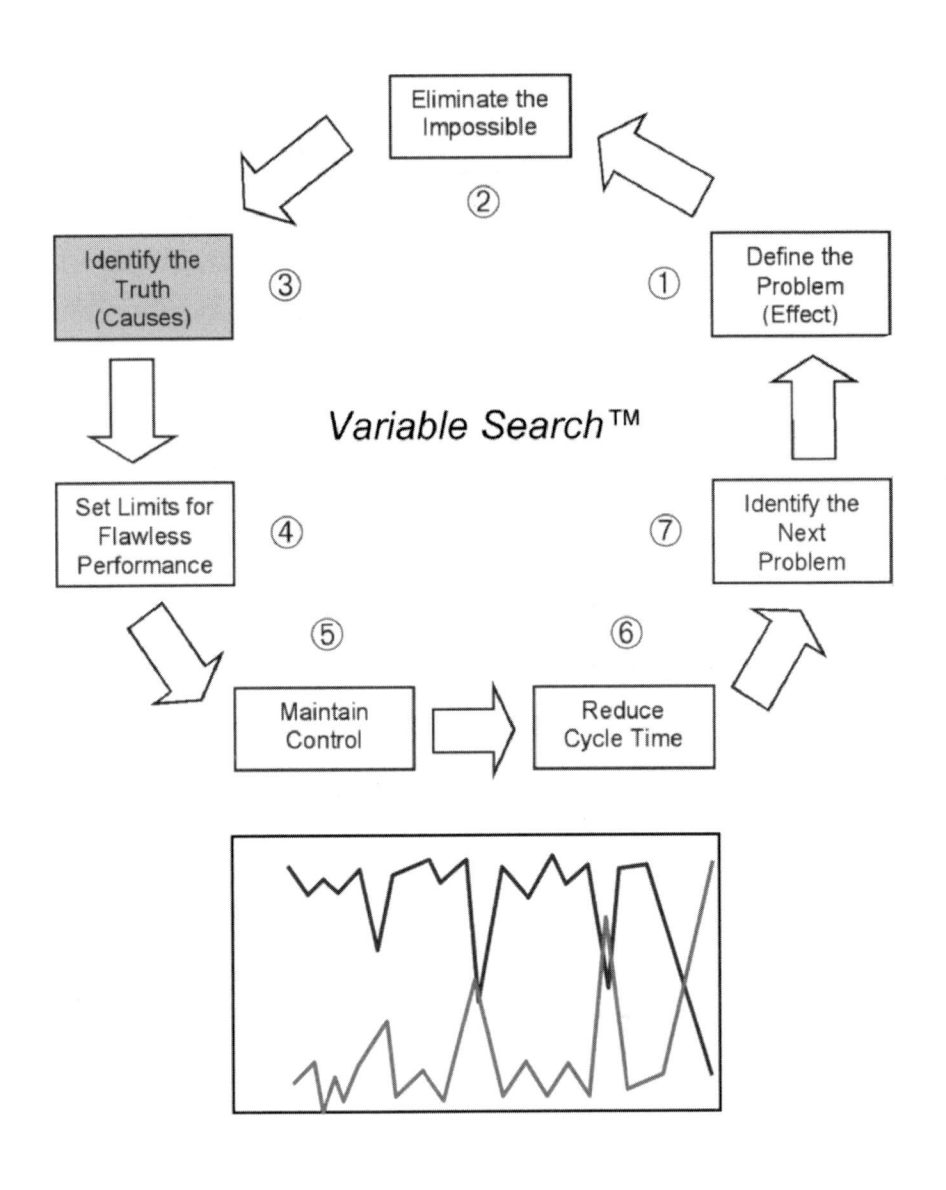

Variable Search™

1. Define the Problem (Effect)
2. Eliminate the Impossible
3. Identify the Truth (Causes)
4. Set Limits for Flawless Performance
5. Maintain Control
6. Reduce Cycle Time
7. Identify the Next Problem

Chapter 7

The Variable Search™ Tool

[**Note:** Variable Search™ and Full Factorials are primarily used in manufacturing operations. They are important parts of the complete set of best practice tools, but they may not be directly applicable for many people. These tools are included here to raise awareness and for future reference when the opportunity to use them may occur.]

Concept and Expected Results:

Variable Search™ uses the same Holmes' tips as Component Search™

"*Once you have eliminated the impossible, whatever remains, no matter how improbable, must be the truth.*"

"*Always approach a case with an absolutely blank mind. Form no theories, just simply observe and draw inferences from your observations. It is a capital mistake to theorize before one has data. Insensibly one begins to twist facts to suit theories, instead of theories to suit facts.*"

"*How dangerous it is to reason from insufficient data. Data, Data, Data! I can't make bricks without clay.*"

"*It is of the highest importance in the art of detection to be able to recognize out of a number of facts which are incidental and which are vital.*"

"*Detection is, or ought to be, an exact science, and should be treated in the same cold unemotional manner. When you attempt to tinge it with romanticism, you produce the same effect as if you worked a love story into the fifth proposition of Euclid.*"

147

The observation-based, non-invasive clue generation tools discussed in Section 1 have historically solved about 75% of all problems completely. Variable Search™ is usually the first experiment selected in the other 25% of cases when it becomes necessary to interrupt the activity to solve the problem. The clue generation tools will have eliminated dozens or even hundreds of non-critical factors. What remain are a few up to about a dozen factors that are involved in some way. If just 2, 3, or 4 factors remain, Full Factorial Design of Experiments is appropriate. If 5 or more factors remain, Variable Search™ is the next step.

Variable Search™ uses the same logic and methodology as Component Search™, but instead of switching components, Variable Search™ switches processing conditions. It normally follows one or more Clue Generation experiments. Variable Search™ will identify the most critical factor and any other critical factors in the operation.

B vs. C™ usually follows Variable Search™ to confirm the conclusions, followed by Scatter Plots or Simplex to establish the realistic target values and tolerances of the critical factors.

General Description:

Variable Search™ has the same four stages as Component Search™. Stage 1 is the Ballpark Stage to determine correct factors and the correct values for each factor. Stage 2 eliminates the non-critical factors. Stage 3 is a Capping Run to confirm the Stage 2 conclusions. Stage 4 is Factorial Analysis of the data from Stages 1, 2, and 3.

To begin, select two settings for each of the possibly critical factors. The first is at the best setting, the target value believed to give optimum performance. The second is at a marginal setting at the edge of the tolerance window that is believed to produce marginal outcomes. For Stage 1, make three runs with every setting in the best condition and three runs with every setting in the marginal condition. As before, every run with the all-best settings must be better than

Variable Search™

every run with the all-marginal settings, and the difference must be at least 80% of the range of variation observed in the operation.

In Stage 2, switch the best and marginal settings one at a time and look for partial shifts or complete reversals in performance. Any factor that causes a partial shift or reversal is critical. All the factors that don't shift performance when they are switched are non-critical.

Stage 3 is a Capping Run. Switch all the critical factors and none of the others. If successful, this will completely reverse performance. This will identify the most critical factor, as well as any other critical factors, if they exist.

As before, Stage 4 is Factorial Analysis of all the data from Stages 1, 2, and 3 to quantify the main effects and the interaction effects.

Examples of the Tool in Action:

Example 1 – The Press Brake

In this manufacturing example a metal fabrication process was unable to hold the acceptable tolerance of ±0.005" in a stamping and forming operation. The problem was deviation from the target value. The team identified six factors in the operation that could have been affecting forming accuracy. They selected a best setting and a marginal setting for each factor, as shown in the table.

They conducted Stage 1 using the all-best and the all-marginal settings, and they achieved excellent separation and consistency. The all-best results were within the specification limits, and the all-marginal results were an order of magnitude worse. These six factors definitely contained the most critical factor, so they ran Stage 2, switching the settings, one-at-a-time.

They discovered that two factors were critical, while four were not. Next, they ran Stage 3, the Capping Run with just the two critical factors switched. The data from Stages 1, 2, and 3 appear following, in table and graph form. The data are the variation from the target value, expressed as multiples of 0.001". Stage 4 Factorial Analysis follows.

Factors	Best	Marginal	D	d bar	D/d bar > 1.25?
A Punch, Die alignment	Aligned	Not Aligned	57	11	5.18
B Metal thickness	Thick	Thin	Dec. Lim = Medians ± 1.53 x d bar		
C Metal hardness	Hard	Soft			
D Metal bow	Flat	Bowed			
E Ram stroke	Coin form	Air form			Important
F Holding material	Level	At angle			

	All Best	All Marginal	Best LDL	Best UDL	Marginal LDL	Marginal UDL
1st Run	4	47	-12.83	20.83	44.17	77.83
2nd Run	4	61	-12.83	20.83	44.17	77.83
3rd Run	3	68	-12.83	20.83	44.17	77.83
A swapped	3	72	-12.83	20.83	44.17	77.83
B swapped	5	47	-12.83	20.83	44.17	77.83
C swapped	7	72	-12.83	20.83	44.17	77.83
D swapped	23	30	-12.83	20.83	44.17	77.83
E swapped	7	50	-12.83	20.83	44.17	77.83
F swapped	73	18	-12.83	20.83	44.17	77.83

The critical factors were that the metal sheet had to be flat, and the holding material had to be level. Nothing else mattered. To solve the problem, they modified the fixture to keep it level, and they make sure the metal sheet is flat. Now, they control dimensions to ±0.002", a C_{pk} of 2.5, or 7.5σ, and generate zero defects.

Variable Search™

Press Brake Case Study

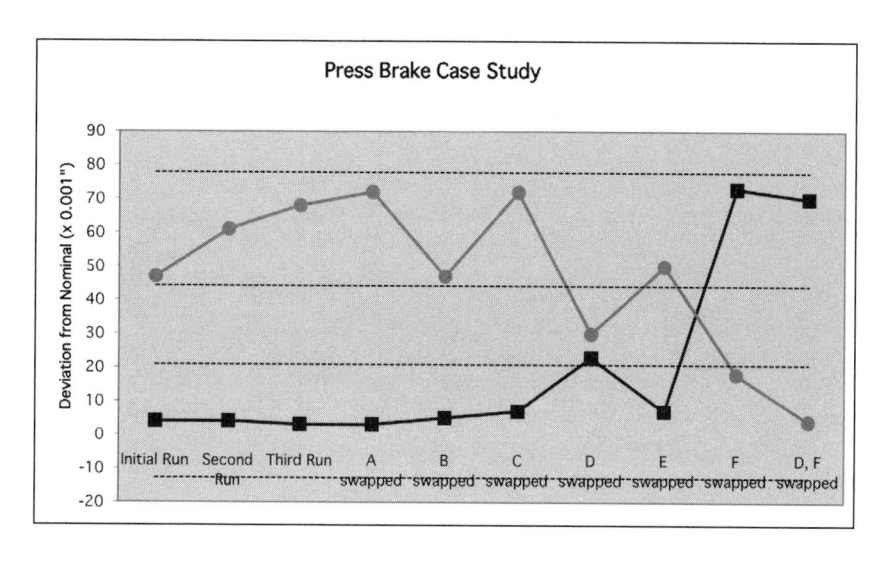

Chart: Deviation from Nominal (x 0.001") across Initial Run, Second Run, Third Run, A swapped, B swapped, C swapped, D swapped, E swapped, F swapped, D,F swapped

	D Best		D Marginal		
F Best	4	5	23		
	4	7	18		
	3	7			24.5
	3	4			
	Median = 4		Median = 20.5		
F Marginal	73		47	47	
	30		61	72	
			68	50	116
			72	70	
	Median = 51.5		Median = 64.5		
72	55.5		85		68.5

D Main Effect = ((20.5+64.5)-(4+51.5))/2 = **14.75**

F Main Effect = ((51.5+64.5)-(4+20.5))/2 = **45.75**

DF Interaction = ((20.5+51.5)-(4+68.5))/2 = 1.75

	D Best	D Marg
F Best	4	20.5
F Marg	51.5	64.5

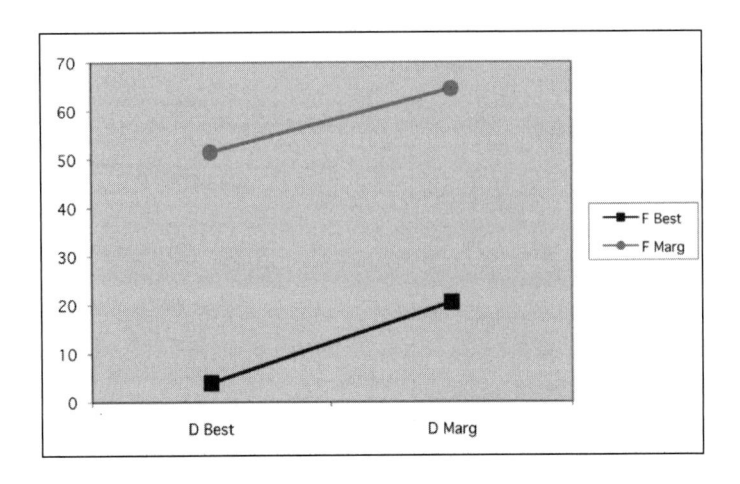

[Chart showing two lines: F Best (lower, from ~4 at D Best to ~21 at D Marg) and F Marg (upper, from ~52 at D Best to ~65 at D Marg), y-axis 0-70]

Problem Statement: Press Brake is unable to consistently form metal to acceptable tolerance of ±0.005".

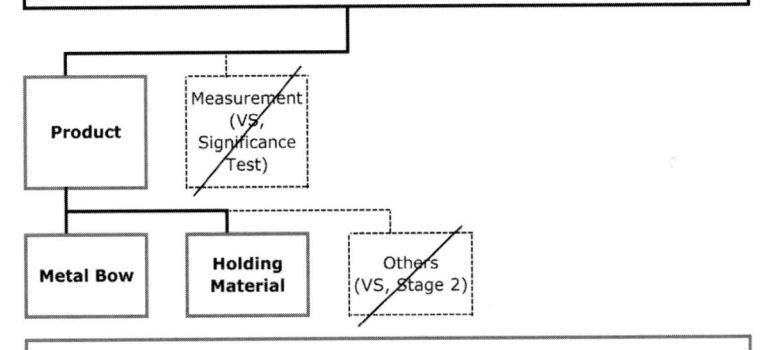

[Diagram: Product branches to Metal Bow, Holding Material, Measurement (VS, Significance Test) [crossed out], Others (VS, Stage 2) [crossed out]]

Action Taken: Most critical factor is Holding Material level. Metal Bow is next. There is no interaction. Make sure Holding Material is level and metal is flat.

Result: Press brake now holds to ±0.002", Cpk of 2.5, 7.5σ, Zero defects.

Example 2 – Prototype Engine Control Module

This problem is an R&D application, not a production problem. Researchers could not use the clue generation tools because there were too few samples, so they started with

Variable Search™

Variable Search™. The company was prototyping a complex engine control module that monitored up to 25 engine parameters and optimized the engine for maximum gas mileage and minimum pollution. One important parameter was idle speed current, which had to stay between 650 and 800 milliamps. If the current were too low, the engine would stall or stop; if it were too high, some components on the circuit board could burn up.

While in the prototype stage, some units had unacceptably high idle speed current. The development team chose seven components from the circuit design to test. They selected best settings (center of the design range) and marginal settings (at one end or the other of the proposed tolerance range, whichever end was thought to be worse) for each component. The components and their best and marginal settings appear in the table with the results of Stage 1. (Note that this is Variable Search™, not Component Search™, because the experiment did not involve swapping components from a good unit to a bad one. In this case, they built separate modules using components from the best and marginal settings.)

They knew at this point that the most critical factor was one of the seven components they had selected, so they proceeded to Stage 2. The table and graph show the Stage 2 results.

Stages 3 and 4 were unnecessary because G gave a complete reversal, and there were no interaction effects. In this case, the company tightened the specification on the Integrated Circuit chip, and then they loosened the ± 1% tolerance limits of the two resistors to lower costs. They reported total cost savings of $450,000 in Year 1 alone from the quality improvement and procurement cost reduction.

Reasoning Backward

Factor	Nominal value	Tolerance	Best value (B)	Marginal (M)
A R85 Resistor	0.68 Ohms	+/- 5%	0.68 Ohms	0.65 Ohms
B Vcc Pwr Sup	5.0 Volts	+/- 5%	5.0 Volts	4.75 Volts
C R77 Resistor	100 Ohms	+/- 1%	100 Ohms	99 Ohms
D R75 Resistor	787 Ohms	+/- 1%	787 Ohms	729 Ohms
E Xsister Q8	75 M.V.	150 M.V. max	75 M.V.	150 M.V.
F R79 Resistor	43 Ohms	+/- 5%	43 Ohms	40.2 Ohms
G IC 4 Int Cir	0 M.V.	+/-8 M.V.	0 M.V.	-8 M.V.

Stage 1 Initial	All Best	All Marginal
Initial Run	742	1053
Second Run	738	1050
Third Run	725	1024

	D	d bar	D/d bar >1.25?
	312	23	13.6
			Important

Stage 2 - Swapped components			Best LDL	Best UDL	Marg. LDL	Marg. LDL
A swapped	768	1020	703	773	1015	1085
B swapped	704	1051	703	773	1015	1085
C swapped	733	1028	703	773	1015	1085
D swapped	745	1018	703	773	1015	1085
E swapped	726	1022	703	773	1015	1085
F swapped	733	1020	703	773	1015	1085
G swapped	1031	718	703	773	1015	1085

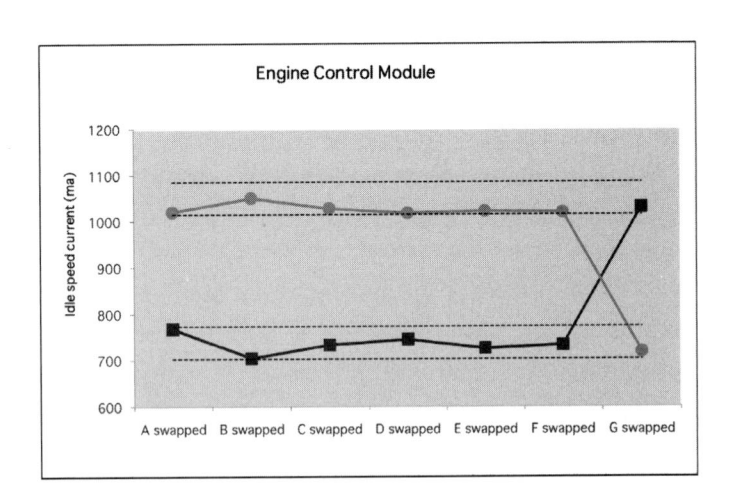

One technician ran all the Stage 1 and 2 experiments in just two days. If he had chosen component G first, the entire experiment would have taken less than one day because the answer would have been obvious after the first switch.

154

Variable Search™

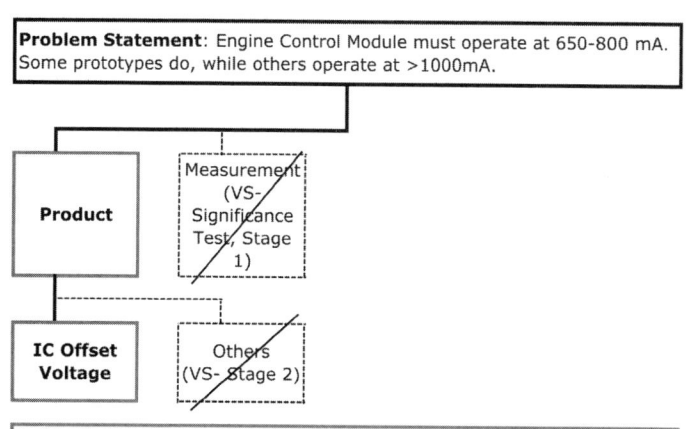

Problem Statement: Engine Control Module must operate at 650-800 mA. Some prototypes do, while others operate at >1000mA.

```
Product ─┬─ Measurement (VS-Significance Test, Stage 1)
         │
IC Offset├─ Others (VS-Stage 2)
Voltage  
```

Action Taken: Most critical factor is offset voltage of the integrated circuit. Nothing else matters. Tightened specification of IC chip, loosened resistor specifications to reduce costs.

Result: Module now operates flawlessly at <800 mA. Development cost savings were $450,000.

Example 3 – Cracked Epoxy Adhesive

This example involved an epoxy adhesive that developed cracks during its cure cycle. The problem had existed for three years, and the reject rate was 10%. The company used a Likert scale to measure the cracking, where 0 = No Crack and 10 = 100% crack across the bond line. The sample size was 20 units, so the range of possible scores was from 0 to 200. They chose six variables to evaluate as shown.

The table and graph show the results of Stages 1, 2, and 3. The most critical factor clearly was A, the cure temperature of the adhesive. They chose to use E in the marginal setting for other reasons, but as long as the cure temperature was high enough, the defect rate dropped to zero.

Variables D and F were opportunities to reduce cost. Reduced coverage meant lower material consumption,

Reasoning Backward

and lower viscosity resin cost less. With these changes in place, the 10% reject rate dropped to zero, and they saved an additional $40,000 per year in material costs.

Factor	Best Value	Marginal Value
A Cure Temperature (°C)	150	120
B Cure Time (min)	30	45
C Perpendicularity	0°	1.5°
D Lead coverage by epoxy	100%	75%
E Alignment of turning hole	No clipping	Clipping
F Epoxy viscosity (cps)	199,000	180,000

D	d bar	D/d bar
33	6	5.5

Sample size: 20 units   Important
Weighted Defects = (No. defective units) x (1-10 Likert scale)

Stage 1 & Stage 2	All Best	All Marginal	Best LDL	Best UDL	Marg. LDL	Marg. UDL
Run 1	0	41	-9.18	9.18	23.82	42.18
Run 2	0	29	-9.18	9.18	23.82	42.18
Run 3	0	33	-9.18	9.18	23.82	42.18
A swapped	37	0	-9.18	9.18	23.82	42.18
B swapped	0	25	-9.18	9.18	23.82	42.18
C swapped	0	19	-9.18	9.18	23.82	42.18
D swapped	0	22	-9.18	9.18	23.82	42.18
E swapped	12	0	-9.18	9.18	23.82	42.18
F swapped	0	27	-9.18	9.18	23.82	42.18
Cap run A, E swapped	30	0	-9.18	9.18	23.82	42.18
Cap run A swapped, E margin	24	0	-9.18	9.18	23.82	42.18

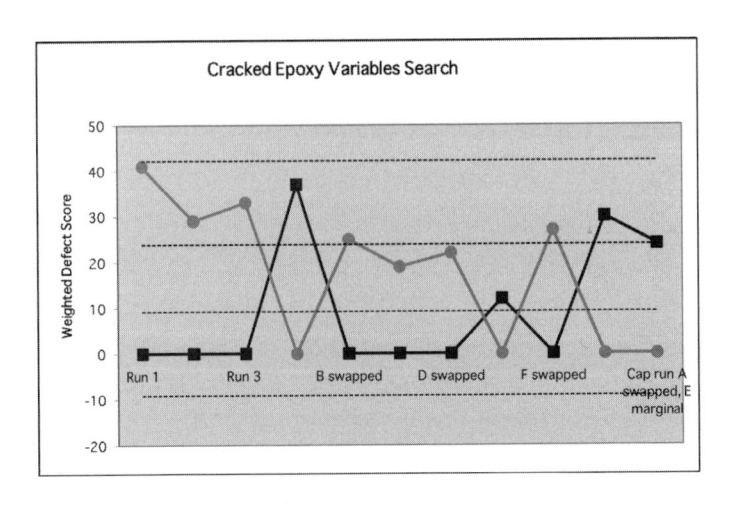

Cracked Epoxy Variables Search

	A Best		A Marginal		
E Best	0	0	37		
	0	0	0		
	0	0			
	0				18.5
	0				
	Median =	0.0	Median =	18.5	
E Marginal	12		41	22	
	0		29	27	
			33		
			25		34
			19		
	Median =	6.0	Median =	28.0	
24.5	6		46.5		28

Main Effect A= ((0+6)-(18.5+28))/2 = **-20.25**

Main Effect E= ((0+18.5)-(6+28))/2 = **-7.75**

AE Interaction= ((6+18.5)-(0+28))/2 = -1.75

	A Best	A Marginal
E Best	0.0	18.5
E Marginal	6.0	28.0

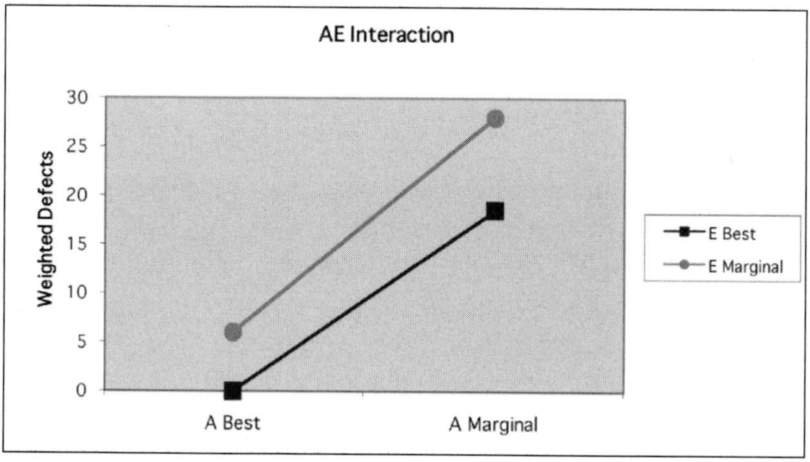

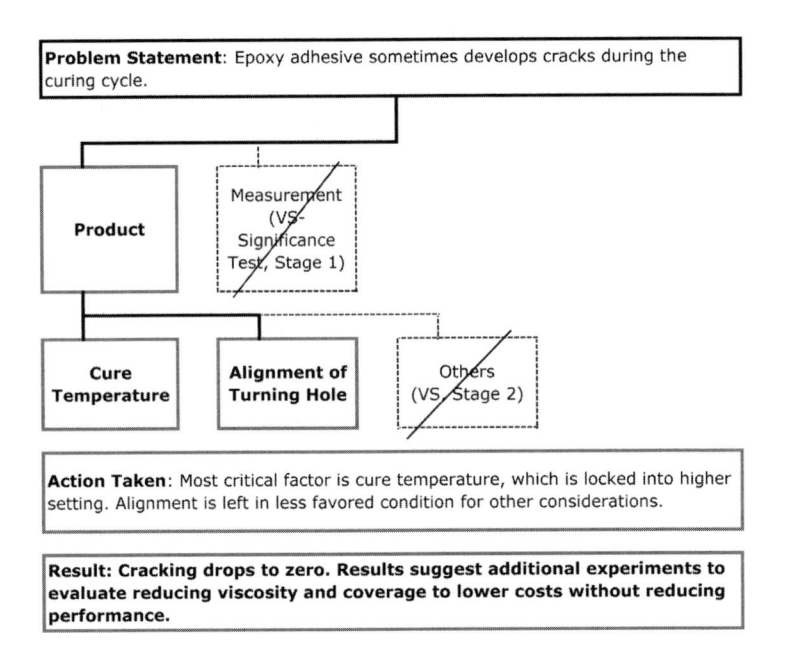

```
┌─────────────────────────────────────────────────────────────────┐
│ Problem Statement: Epoxy adhesive sometimes develops cracks      │
│ during the curing cycle.                                         │
└─────────────────────────────────────────────────────────────────┘
                                │
        ┌───────────────────────┼───────────────────────┐
        │                       │                       │
   ┌─────────┐        ┌──────────────────┐              
   │         │        │   Measurement    │              
   │ Product │        │  (VS-            │              
   │         │        │  Significance    │              
   └─────────┘        │  Test, Stage 1)  │              
        │             └──────────────────┘              
   ┌────┴──────┬──────────────┐                         
   │           │              │                         
┌─────────┐ ┌──────────┐ ┌──────────┐                   
│  Cure   │ │Alignment │ │  Others  │                   
│Tempera- │ │of Turning│ │(VS Stage │                   
│ ture    │ │  Hole    │ │    2)    │                   
└─────────┘ └──────────┘ └──────────┘                   

┌─────────────────────────────────────────────────────────────────┐
│ Action Taken: Most critical factor is cure temperature, which is │
│ locked into higher setting. Alignment is left in less favored    │
│ condition for other considerations.                              │
└─────────────────────────────────────────────────────────────────┘

┌─────────────────────────────────────────────────────────────────┐
│ Result: Cracking drops to zero. Results suggest additional       │
│ experiments to evaluate reducing viscosity and coverage to lower │
│ costs without reducing performance.                              │
└─────────────────────────────────────────────────────────────────┘
```

Variable Search™ Summary:

- Clue Generation Tools solve about 75% of problems without intervening in the activity. For the remaining 25% of cases, Variable Search™ is usually the first step.
- Easily handles up to about 20 variables, but rarely needs to.
- 5-10 variables is typical.
- Full Factorials are impractical for more than 4 variables, and Fractional Factorials lose too much information. Variable Search™ is the best answer for 5-20 variables because the number of experiments is manageable, and no data is lost.
- Variable Search™ is the workhorse tool whenever process intervention is necessary. As Holmes might say, "It quickly eliminates the impossible, and what remains is the truth."

Variable Search™
(Identifies the most critical factor and any other critical factors after Clue Generation has reduced the number of possibly critical factors to between 5 and 20)

Objective:

In about 75% of problems, the clue generation tools identify the most critical factor and any other critical factors without ever disrupting the operation. In the remaining 25% of cases, the clue generation tools will reduce the number of possible variables from hundreds to a few, usually less than a dozen. Variable Search™ reduces this number down to the critical factors with the fewest number of experiments and the least disruption of production.

While the most common use of Variable Search™ as a problem-solving tool is as the sequel to the various clue generation tools, its most important use is during the design stage of a product or process, to identify the critical variables early and prevent problems from reaching production in the first place.

Procedure:

Variable Search™ is the more general form of the switching technique used in Component Search™. Component Search™ swapped discrete components, parts, or subassemblies that were good or bad, and therefore, were the factors that made a final unit either good or bad. Variable Search™ extends that approach to include process or material parameters that are continuously variable, while still using the same four stages.

Stage 1: Ballpark Stage. (To determine that the right variables and the right levels for each variable have been selected for the experiment.)

Identify the performance parameter to investigate.

- Quantify and measure performance. Make sure the measurement accuracy is at least five times narrower than the specification tolerance(s).
- If the performance parameter is an attribute, convert it into a variable by using a Likert scale, if possible. This reduces the required sample size by changing a simple count of defects into an expanded scale of weighted defects.

Select the variables for the experiment.
- Make a list of the input variables or factors believed to be most important and label them A, B, C, D, E, F, G, H, and so on, in descending order of perceived importance. (Descending order is especially beneficial now because it can potentially mean having fewer experiments to run, and fewer production interruptions.)
- If a previous Paired Comparisons™ test has been run, the factors with higher Total End Count will have a higher probability of being important.

After selecting the factors for the experiment, assign two levels to each factor – a best level (B), which is most likely to contribute to the best performance (and hopefully, better than current performance), and a marginal level (M), indicative of a likely deviation from the best level in current day-to-day production with normal maintenance.
- The best level will often be the Target Value for the factor, and the marginal level is a judgment of how far the factor can deviate (on either side) from the best level to register a large, repeatable difference, within practical limits.
- If unsure about which level is better, assign them arbitrarily. The experiment will determine which level is better.

Determine the sample size.
- If the parameter is variable (continuously measurable), then the sample size is 1 best (all of the factors at their best levels) and 1 marginal (all of the factors at their marginal levels).

Variable Search™

- If the parameter is an attribute converted into a variable with a Likert scale, use 3 to 10 samples each of best and marginal.
- If the parameter is an attribute, such as number of defects, percent of defects, or percent yields, it requires a much larger sample size, from 16 to 500. The higher the defect percentage, the smaller the sample size, and vice versa.
- If the defect rate is ≤100 ppm, and a Likert scale is not possible, do not use Variable Search™. Use Paired Comparisons™ instead.

Run two experiments, one with all of the factors at their best levels, and one with all of the factors at their marginal settings.
- If there is a large difference between the readings at the all-best and all-marginal levels, then you have captured all the right factors in the list of factors. Continue on to the next step, Replication.
- If the all-best reading is only slightly better than the all-marginal reading, then chances are good that either:
  - You have not captured the right factors, or
  - You don't have the right levels for these factors, or
  - The most critical factor is being cancelled by another critical factor or
  - The most critical factor is an interaction among an even number of factors.
- If the all-best levels do show an improvement over the all-marginal levels, but the difference is not much greater than historic reading levels, then the experiment has not gone far enough in capturing the right factors or the right levels of the selected factors.
- If there is not a large enough difference to move on to Replication, then reevaluate the experiment. Run it again with different levels of some of the factors, or delete some of the factors and insert new ones.

Reasoning Backward

Replication. Repeat the previous step with two more samples at the all-best settings and two more samples at the all-marginal settings for a total of three all-best and three all-marginal samples. In random order, evaluate them. (Random order is important to prevent bias from affecting the experiment.)

Significance Test. As before in Component Search™, the samples must pass two significance tests.
- All three of the all-best readings must be better than all three of the all-marginal readings. (If all three of the all-marginal readings turn out to be better than all three of the all-best readings, then just reverse the headings and proceed. This does happen.)
- The ratio, D/d bar ≥ 1.25, where
  - D is the difference between the median values of the all-best and the all-marginal readings.
  - d bar is the average of the ranges of readings for the all-best and all-marginal samples. It is the lack of repeatability for each setting.

If the data pass the significance tests, Stage 1 was successful. You have captured the right factors. Proceed to Stage 2, which will pinpoint the critical factors.

If the data do not pass the Significance Test:
- Switch one pair of the most likely factors from its best value to its marginal one, and vice versa, to see if a cancellation of influence was taking place. If there is still no significant difference, switch a second pair of factors. This is rarely necessary, unless the engineering judgment of the best and marginal factor settings was reversed.
- If the repeatability, d bar, is poor, it indicates that an important factor, possibly the most critical factor, has been left off the list. Review the clue generation experiments to look for a

Variable Search™

better clue. Add one or two more factors to the list, and rerun Stage 1.

Stage 2: Separation of Critical and Non-critical Factors. (To eliminate the unimportant variables along with their interaction effects. As in Component Search™, switch the factors one at a time and measure the resulting performance.)

Run a pair of tests. The first test uses with marginal value of factor A (A_M) put with the best levels of the rest of the factors (R_B). The second test is the mirror image, ($A_B R_M$).

Calculate the decision limits as before.
- Median values ± (1.5 x d bar)
- The alternate decision limit is as before, movement to within 10% of the average of the two median values.

Compare readings of $A_B R_M$ and $A_M R_B$ with the decision limits for all-marginal and all-best respectively.
- If both tests are inside their respective decision limits, ($A_B R_M$ inside the marginal limits and $A_M R_B$ inside the best limits), then factor A, including all its interaction effects, is unimportant. Eliminate it from further study.
- If there is a complete reversal, ($A_B R_M$ inside the best limits and $A_M R_B$ inside the marginal limits), then factor A is the only critical factor. No other factor is important, and Variable Search™ is over.
- If either or both tests show results outside their respective decision limits, ($A_B R_M$ outside the marginal limits or $A_M R_B$ outside the best limits, or both), but not a complete reversal, then A is an important factor, but not the only one. Some other factor or factors, along with their interactions, are also important.

Reasoning Backward

Unless A is the only critical factor, move ahead to factor B and repeat the same process as was used for factor A. Continue on C, D, E, etc. until all the factors have been identified as either critical or non-critical.

Stage 3: Capping Run for Verification. (To validate that the critical factors actually are critical, and that the non-critical factors actually are not critical.)

After finding all the important factors, run a multiple-factor capping run that reverses all the critical factors and none of the non-critical factors. For example, assume factors A, B, and D to be critical, and all the rest, C, E, F, G, H, etc., are non-critical. The capping run experiment is $A_B B_B D_B R_M$ and $A_M B_M D_M R_B$. If this experiment is successful, $A_B B_B D_B R_M$ will show results within the all-best decision limits and $A_M B_M D_M R_B$ will show results within the all-marginal decision limits. (It is very rare to have to go further to a four-factor capping run.)

Graph the results of Stages 1, 2, and 3, including the decision limits, and to see more clearly the patterns in the data.

Stage 4: Factorial Analysis. (To quantify the magnitude and desired levels of the important variables and their associated interaction effects.)

As before, this is not a separate experiment, but only calculations to create a factorial analysis of the data from Stages 1, 2, and 3. It will quantify the main effects and interaction effects of all the important factors.

Variable Search™

Variable Search™ Template

Project: Date:
Investigator:
Performance parameter:
Defect Frequency and History:
Measurement (include target value and specification limits):
Accuracy of Measurement/Accuracy of Product Tolerance Ratio:
(If attribute, is a Likert scale possible?):

Stage 1: Ballpark Stage.

Create a list in descending order of all the factors to evaluate in Variable Search™. Label them A, B, C, and so on, and select a best level (B) and a marginal level (M) for each factor. Record this information in the following table.

Label	Process Parameter	Best Level (B)	Marginal Level (M)
A			
B			
C			
D			
...			

Run one sample with all the parameters in the best settings and one sample with all parameters in the marginal settings. Measure the performance. If there is a large difference in readings, replicate each sample twice, making six samples total. Evaluate all six in random order. Record the readings in the following table. (If there is not a large difference, adjust the parameter levels, or select new ones, and try again.)

	All-Best	All-Marginal
Initial output value		
Value of 2nd unit		
Value of 3rd unit		

Calculate D, d bar, and the D/d bar ratio. Do the data pass the Significance Tests? If so, proceed to Stage 2. If not, repeat Stage 1 with different settings or different factors.
- Are all three of the all-best values better than all three of the all-marginal values?
- D = difference in median values =
- Average of ranges = d bar =
- ((all-best high − all-best low) + (all-marginal high − all-marginal low))/2 =
- Is D/d bar ≥ 1.25? D/d bar =
- Calculate the decision limits. (Each median ± (1.5 x d bar)). Do they overlap? If so, find an all-best and an all-marginal with greater separation.
- Calculate the alternate decision limit, the point halfway between the median values of all-best and all-marginal readings.

Stage 2: Elimination Stage.
List the possible factors is descending order of likelihood of being critical and label them A, B, C, etc.

Run two experiments, one where the best level of A is run with all other factors in the marginal setting, and vice versa. Measure the performance. Label these $A_B R_M$ and $A_M R_B$ respectively. Record the readings in the following table.
- If $A_B R_M$ is within the marginal decision limits, and $A_M R_B$ is within the best decision limits, then A is unimportant.

Variable Search™

- If $A_B R_M$ is within the best decision limits, and $A_M R_B$ is within the marginal decision limits, then A is the only critical factor, and Variable Search™ is over.
- If either $A_B R_M$ or $A_M R_B$ moves outside the marginal or best decision limits respectively, but does not totally reverse, then A is important, and so is at least one other factor.
- If A is not the most critical factor, then proceed to test component B the same way. When two variables demonstrate a partial reversal, run a pair with just those two important variables reversed.

Build a table showing this data.

Plot all the data from Stages 1, 2, and 3 on one graph that includes the decision limits so the data will be easier to understand.

Label	Variable	Factor Settings	Value	Decision Limits	Factor Importance
A		$A_B R_M$ $A_M R_B$			
B		$B_B R_M$ $B_M R_B$			
C		$C_B R_M$ $C_M R_B$			
D		$D_B R_M$ $D_M R_B$			
E		$E_B R_M$ $E_M R_B$			
...		...			

Stage 3: Capping Run.

After identifying all the important factors, run one more experiment with all the critical factors reversed, and none of the non-critical factors reversed. If this test is successful, $X_B Y_B Z_B R_M$ will be inside the best decision limits and $X_M Y_M Z_M R_B$ will be inside the marginal decision limits.

Capping Run		$X_B Y_B Z_B R_M$ $X_M Y_M Z_M R_B$			

Stage 4: Factorial Analysis.

To validate the capping run, run the B vs. C™ test to turn the problem on and off. Graph the interactions to see more clearly the interaction effects.

Build a matrix of the data from Stages 1, 2, and 3.

Calculate the medians in each cell.

Use the medians to quantify the main effects and interaction effects of the important variables in an ANOVA table.

Use Scatter Plots or Simplex to further optimize the important factors.

Conclusion:

Identify the critical factors. Use the results to find ways to reduce variation of these factors. Work with materials suppliers, including external suppliers, to find ways to reduce variation.

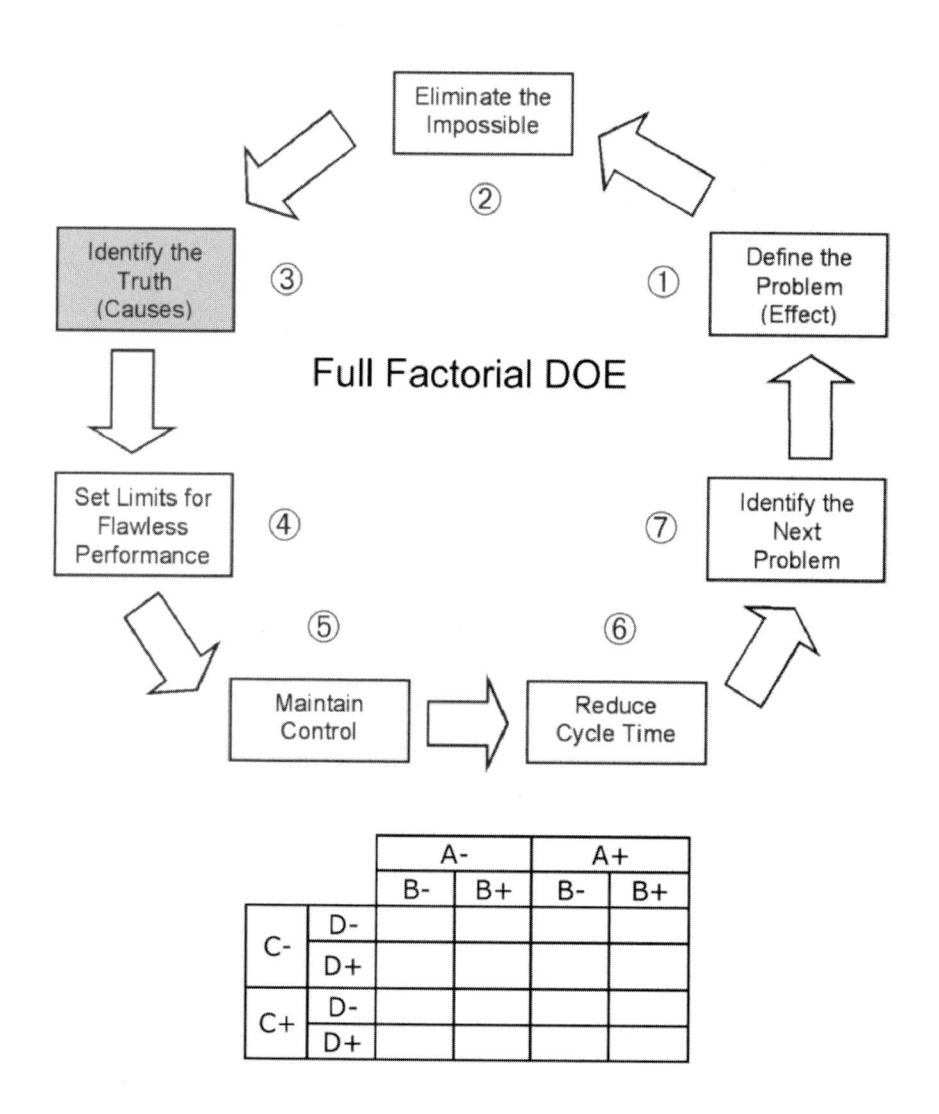

Full Factorial DOE

① Define the Problem (Effect)
② Eliminate the Impossible
③ Identify the Truth (Causes)
④ Set Limits for Flawless Performance
⑤ Maintain Control
⑥ Reduce Cycle Time
⑦ Identify the Next Problem

		A-	A-	A+	A+
		B-	B+	B-	B+
C-	D-				
C-	D+				
C+	D-				
C+	D+				

Chapter 8

The Full Factorial DOE Tool

Identifies all the critical factors from 2, 3, or 4 possibly critical factors

Concept and Expected Results:

Full Factorial DOE uses 7 of Holmes' Top 10 Tips.

"Once you have eliminated the impossible, whatever remains, no matter how improbable, must be the truth."

"Always approach a case with an absolutely blank mind. Form no theories, just simply observe and draw inferences from your observations. It is a capital mistake to theorize before one has data. Insensibly one begins to twist facts to suit theories, instead of theories to suit facts."

"How dangerous it is to reason from insufficient data. Data, Data, Data! I can't make bricks without clay."

"It is of the highest importance in the art of detection to be able to recognize out of a number of facts which are incidental and which are vital."

"Detection is, or ought to be, an exact science, and should be treated in the same cold unemotional manner. When you attempt to tinge it with romanticism, you produce the same effect as if you worked a love story into the fifth proposition of Euclid."

"I can see nothing," said Watson, handing it back to Holmes. *"On the contrary, Watson, you can see everything. You fail, however, to reason from what you see. You are too timid in drawing your inferences."*

"I never guess. It is a shocking habit -- destructive to the logical faculty."

The Full Factorial DOE Tool

Factorial Design of Experiments is the heart of most problem solving processes in use today. Most of these processes use Fractional Factorials or Taguchi Methodology when there are more than 4 variables to study, while the best practice approach uses Variable Search™ in these situations. All processes use Full Factorial DOE for 2, 3, or 4 factors.

This chapter presents examples of Full Factorial DOE, and it compares best practice Variable Search™ / Full Factorial DOE to Classical Full and Fractional Factorial DOE and Taguchi Methods. The basic concept and expected results are the same in all these techniques.

They all begin with a list of factors to evaluate. Establish two values of each factor being tested. The settings could be best and marginal settings for each factor, or they might be the current setting and a presumably better setting.

The concept in all three factorial methods is to test both settings of each factor with both settings of every other factor in order to determine all the critical factors by quantifying every direct effect and every interaction effect.

General Description:

In best practice problem solving, use Variable Search™ whenever testing 5 or more potentially important factors. It reduces the number of experiments to a manageable number, while still testing both settings of every factor against both settings of every other factor. Once Variable Search™ has identified the non-critical factors and eliminated them from further consideration in Stage 2, the Stage 3 Capping Run completes a Full Factorial matrix on just the 2, 3, or 4 critical factors.

Other processes address the issue of a large number of possible factors differently by introducing Fractional Factorials. Fractional Factorials lose data. They reduce the number of experiments, but some interactions are lost in the process. If the critical interaction happens to be one of the missing data points, the entire effort will be a waste of time and money.

Consider a humorous analogy. A (naïve?) farmer suspects that the newborn kid goat in his barn came from an interaction between its nanny goat mother and something else in the barnyard. As he looks for potential interactions with the dozens of things it could be, if he misses the one critical interaction with the billy goat, then his investigation will be a failure.

Some of today's other processes use the Taguchi Method as an alternative form of Fractional Factorials, but Taguchi also has a problem with lost data.

In the early 1980s, Motorola evaluated every system it could find in order to meet the first of three successive 10:1 improvement challenges issued by its CEO. It evaluated Classical Full and Fractional Factorials, Taguchi Methodology, and the Shainin® System. Keki Bhote, the Director of Quality for the Automotive and Industrial Electronics Division evaluated all three techniques and chose Shainin® as the only approach capable of meeting the company's improvement goals. Bhote's division achieved the five-year, 10:1 improvement goal in just three years, and the other divisions soon adopted its approach. Motorola's companywide use of the Shainin® methods achieved its 1000:1 improvement goal and resulted in Motorola winning the Malcolm Baldrige National Quality Award in 1988. Bhote created a table that compared the performance of the three alternative methodologies, which is reproduced here. He published it in his book, *World Class Quality,* 2nd edition, (2000) on pages 80-81.

Examples of the Tool in Action:

Example 1 – Summary of a Wave Soldering Project

This best practice example was a four-factor experiment on a Motorola wave soldering process for circuit boards from the early 1980s. The factors are listed in the table.

The Full Factorial DOE Tool

Factor	(−) Current	(+) Better?
A Flux type	A 19	880
B Belt speed	4 ft/min	6 ft/min
C Incline Angle	5°	7°
D Pre-heat Temp	160°F	220°F

The process was operating at a 10,000 ppm (1%) defect rate, which was typical of technology at that time. The company's goal was to reduce defects by 50:1, down to 200 ppm, lower than anyone in the world could achieve at that time. The team chose the current settings of the four factors as the (−) settings and selected four supposedly better settings for the (+) values.

A four-factor experiment needs 16 combinations to include a reading of both values for each factor with both values of the other three factors. The team made just two readings in each cell because the first two readings in each cell were within 10% of each other, as is shown in the table.

The results showed all four new settings were superior, so they completed a test run at the new settings. The defect rate dropped to 220 ppm, a 45:1 improvement, slightly short of their goal, but still the new state-of-the-art. (Subsequent experiments, described in other chapters, reduced the rate to 10 ppm, the performance standard at the time this study was published in 2000.)

The company implemented the same modifications on the other 12 wave solder machines inside that plant and eliminated 20 touch-up operators along with an equivalent number of inspectors. This project saved $750,000 per year.

Reasoning Backward

Green Y: Number of Solder Defects			A - Flux A 19	
			B - Speed 4 ft/min	B + Speed 6 ft/min
C - Angle 5°	D - Pre-Heat 160°F		1 - - - - Order of First Experiment: Order of Second Exp.: 21 Median: 19 17	3 - + - - Order of First Experiment: Order of Second Exp.: 14 Median: 15 16
	D + Pre-Heat 220°F		9 - - - + Order of First Experiment: Order of Second Exp.: 17 Median: 16 15	11 - + - + Order of First Experiment: Order of Second Exp.: 64 Median: 61 58
C + Angle 7°	D - Pre-Heat 160°F		5 - - + - Order of First Experiment: Order of Second Exp.: 4 Median: 4 4	7 - + + - Order of First Experiment: Order of Second Exp.: 43 Median: 45 47
	D + Pre-Heat 220°F		13 - - + + Order of First Experiment: Order of Second Exp.: 32 Median: 33 34	15 - + + + Order of First Experiment: Order of Second Exp.: 14 Median: 13 12

                               72   134

The ANOVA analysis of the Full Factorial experiment follows.

A- = 72 + 134 = 206   A- is worse than A+ by 35 defects.
A+ = 160 + 11 = 171

B- = 72 + 160 = 232   B- is worse than B+ by 87 defects.
B+ = 134 + 11 = 145

C- = 150 + 78 = 228   C- is worse than C+ by 59 defects.
C+ = 93 + 56 = 149

D- = 150 + 93 = 243   D- is worse than D+ by 91 defects.
D+ = 78 + 56 = 134

Table of Median Values

		A-		A+	
		B-	B+	B-	B+
C-	D-	19	15	108	8
	D+	16	61	1	0
C+	D-	4	45	41	3
	D+	33	13	10	0

The Full Factorial DOE Tool

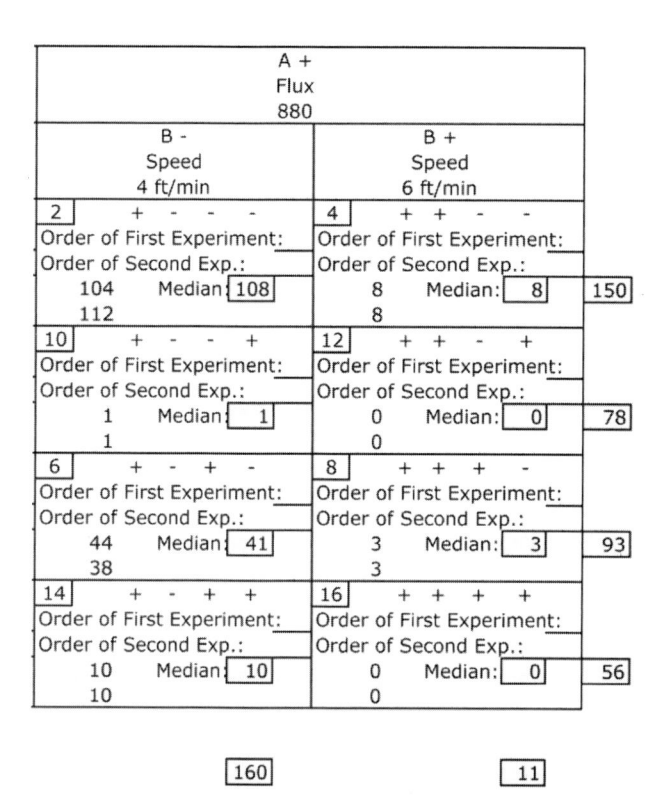

	A + Flux 880	
B - Speed 4 ft/min	B + Speed 6 ft/min	

2   + - - -
Order of First Experiment: ___
Order of Second Exp.: ___
   104   Median: 108
   112
	4 + + - -
	Order of First Experiment: ___
	Order of Second Exp.: ___
	   8 Median: 8
	   8
		150

10   + - - +
Order of First Experiment: ___
Order of Second Exp.: ___
   1   Median: 1
   1
	12 + + - +
	Order of First Experiment: ___
	Order of Second Exp.: ___
	   0 Median: 0
	   0
		78

6   + - + -
Order of First Experiment: ___
Order of Second Exp.: ___
   44   Median: 41
   38
	8 + + + -
	Order of First Experiment: ___
	Order of Second Exp.: ___
	   3 Median: 3
	   3
		93

14   + - + +
Order of First Experiment: ___
Order of Second Exp.: ___
   10   Median: 10
   10
	16 + + + +
	Order of First Experiment: ___
	Order of Second Exp.: ___
	   0 Median: 0
	   0
		56

160   11

Problem Statement: Previous work suggested presumably better settings for 4 critical factors in the Wave Soldering Process.

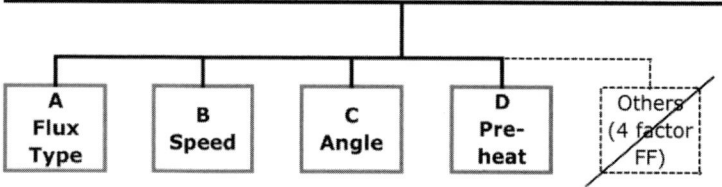

- **A** Flux Type
- **B** Speed
- **C** Angle
- **D** Pre-heat
- Others (4 factor FF) ~~crossed out~~

Action Taken: All the Better settings are better than all the Current settings, so all were introduced. Most critical factor is Flux-Speed interaction. Flux-Temp interaction and Speed-Angle-Temp interaction are also critical.

Result: Defect rated dropped from 10,000 ppm to 220 ppm, 45:1 improvement. Further experiments (described later) looked at other settings of Angle & Speed, establishing conditions that dropped defect rate to 10 ppm.

Reasoning Backward

Characteristic	Classical	Rating	Taguchi	Rating	Shainin	Rating
Techniques	Fractional Factorial, RSM	3	Orthogonal Array	2	Minimum of 10 approaches	10
Clue-generation ability	Poor: Guesswork	1	Poor: Guesswork	1	Powerful: Talk to the parts	10
Effectiveness	Moderate-Improvement range: 2:1 to 10:1; Retrogression possible	3	Low-Improvement range: 2:1 to 5:1; Retrogression likely	2	High-Improvement range: 5:1 to 100:1; No retrogression	10
Cost	High: 30 to 60 trials	4	High: 50 to 100 trials	2	Low: 2 to 30 trials	8
Complexity	Difficult concepts; Full ANOVA required	2	Difficult concepts; Inner and outer array multiplication; ANOVA; S/N	1	Easy, simple, logical concepts; Experiments done by line operators and engineers	8
(a) Time to understand; (b) Time to do	(a) Long: 3 days to 2 weeks; (b) Long: weak clues mean starting all over again	2	(a) Long: 1 to 2 weeks; (b) Long: weak clues, poor results require several trials	1	(a) Short: 1 day; (b) Short: Experiments finished in 1 day to 3 weeks	9
Statistical validity	Weak; Interaction effects confounded with main effects	2	Very weak; No randomization; Interaction effects confounded with main effects	1	Strong; Clear separation of main and interaction effects	8
Applicability	Requires hardware; Main use in production	2	Can be used in paper study with computer simulation, but danger of wrong results	4	Requires hardware; Has universal applicability in product/process design, production, field, suppliers, and administrative processes	8
Ease of implementation	Difficult; Wrong results if interactions are strong	2	Difficult; Wrong results likely because of high degree of fractionation	1	Easy; With clue-generation techniques, repeating experiment not needed	9
Disruption of production	Stoppage of production during experimentation	1	Stoppage of production during experimentation	1	No stoppage in clue-generation experiments, which can solve 70% of chronic quality problems	8
Total Score	Classical	22	Taguchi	16	Shainin	88

Source: Keki R. Bhote, *World Class Quality*, 2nd edition, (2000), pp. 80-81.

Example 2 – Paint Oven Defects

In this problem, a porcelain painting operation suffered from chronic poor yields on parts going through the paint oven, often just 70-80%. The workers thought temperature and humidity variations were responsible. Before doing a 2-variable Full Factorial study, the team carried out a Process Certification cleanup of the operation. The improved housekeeping resulted in the typical yield jumping to 92%, better than the operation had ever performed before. While this was a significant improvement, they still wanted to discover the causes of yield losses and the impact of temperature and humidity. They used the current settings as the (-) conditions and higher temperature and humidity as hypothesized better settings (+), as shown in the following table.

Factor	(-) Current	(+) Better?
A Temp.	Low	High
B Humidity	Low	High

The results were a surprise because the better settings were so much better than their current results.

Both temperature and humidity were important. Temperature was the most critical factor. Humidity was also critical. There were no interaction effects. The yield at the current settings was 92% as they expected after they completed the housekeeping, but the higher temperature and humidity increased the yield to 99+%. Process cleanup and one DOE experiment dropped a 25% defect rate to <1%.

Reasoning Backward

Measurement: Percentage of defective pieces.

	A − Low Temperature			A + High Temperature			
B − Low Humidity	1 Order of 1st Experiment: Order of 2nd Experiment: Order of 3rd Experiment: Gr.Y 8.5 Median: Gr.Y 7 Gr.Y	−	−	7.75	2 Order of 1st Experiment: Order of 2nd Experiment: Order of 3rd Experiment: Gr.Y 3.5 Median: Gr.Y 2 Gr.Y	+	−	2.75	10.5
B + High Humidity	3 Order of 1st Experiment: Order of 2nd Experiment: Order of 3rd Experiment: Gr.Y 5 Median: Gr.Y 7 Gr.Y	−	+	6	4 Order of 1st Experiment: Order of 2nd Experiment: Order of 3rd Experiment: Gr.Y 1 Median: Gr.Y 0.5 Gr.Y	+	+	0.75	6.75
			13.8				3.5

Run Number	Cell Group	A	B	AB	Output
1	(1)	−1	−1	1	7.75
2	a	1	−1	−1	2.75
3	b	−1	1	−1	6
4	ab	1	1	1	0.75
Main & Interaction Totals		−10.25	−3.75	−0.25	

Problem Statement: Porcelain painting operation is only achieving 70-80% yields from the paint oven.

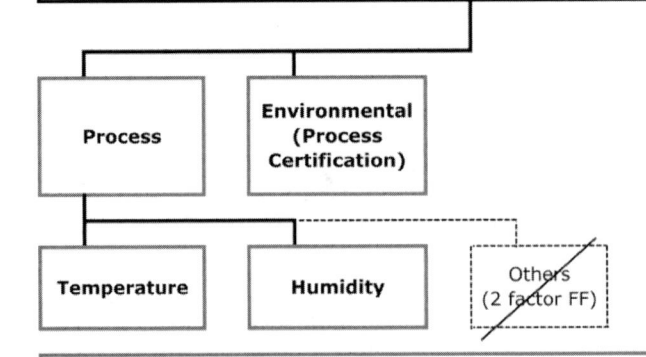

- Process
  - Temperature
  - Humidity
  - Others (2 factor FF) *(crossed out)*
- Environmental (Process Certification)

Action Taken: Fixing housekeeping increased yield to 92%, so it was most critical. Subsequent FF showed High Temp and High Humidity further increased yields.

Result: Paint oven now operates at 99+% yield.

Full Factorial Summary:

- Reserved for the situations where Clue Generation Tools have reduced the number of possible factors to just 2, 3, or 4
- Identifies all the critical factors in the shortest possible time, with the fewest interventions

Other processes suffer by comparison. They start by hypothesizing the factors to pursue. History has shown this is not effective. Most people pursue many wrong factors before finding one or more of the critical factors. Often teams never find the most critical factor, specifically in all cases where they fail to eliminate at least 50% of the defects.

Processes that don't use Clue Generation Tools first have no way to quickly eliminate non-critical factors, so teams usually have a large number of factors to test when they get to the Factorial Stage. Full Factorials are not efficient for 5 or more factors, so these teams that don't use Variable Search™ must choose Fractional Factorials or the Taguchi Methodology to move ahead. Both of these techniques lose data, which further diminishes the results they can expect to achieve. To reach best practice status, use Variable Search™ for situations when 5 or more factors remain for factorial DOE.

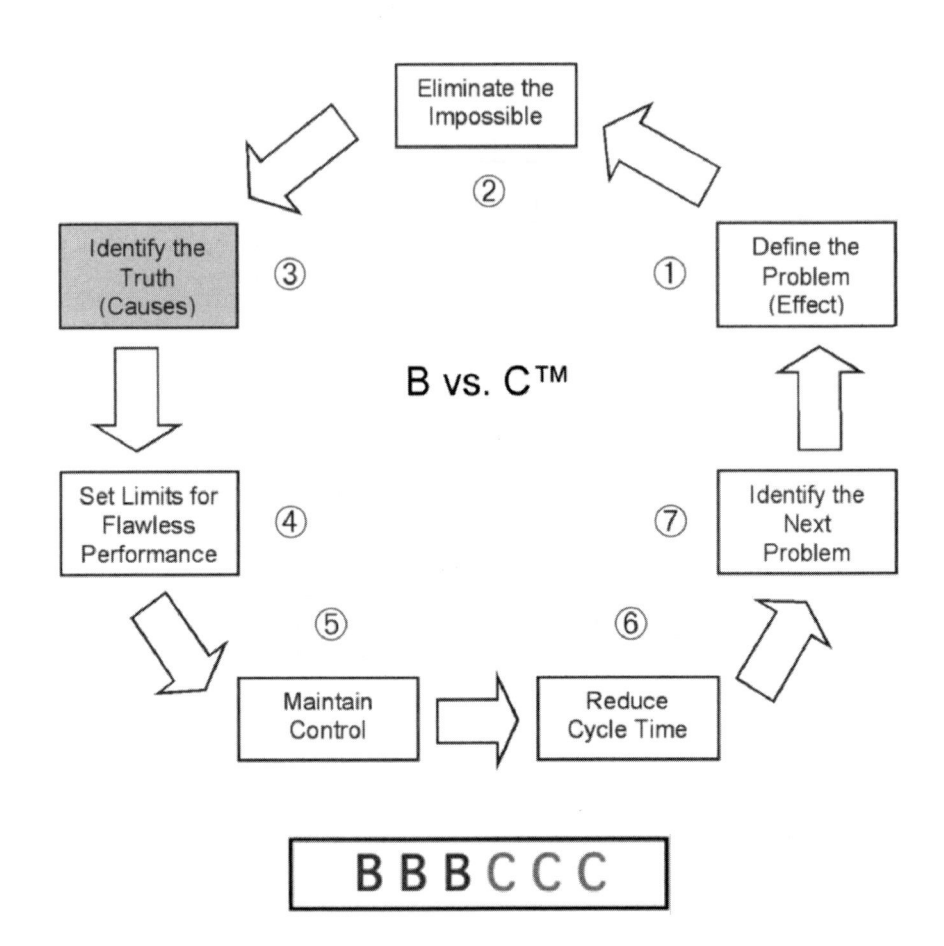

```
              Eliminate the
              Impossible
                  ②

Identify the              Define the
  Truth      ③        ①   Problem
(Causes)                   (Effect)

                B vs. C™

Set Limits for            Identify the
  Flawless   ④        ⑦     Next
Performance               Problem

          ⑤           ⑥
   Maintain          Reduce
   Control          Cycle Time
```

B B B C C C

Chapter 9

The B vs. C™ Tool

Turn problem on and off by varying the critical factors and applying Paired Comparisons™

Concept and Expected Results:

Recall that Paired Comparisons™ evolved directly from the original writings of Sir Francis Bacon nearly 400 years ago. List all things that include a phenomenon and all things that do not include the phenomenon. Next, rank the items relative to possible factors and looks for patterns and consistent differences to determine which are critical. The Tukey Guidelines make it easy to separate critical and non-critical factors. In B vs. C™, vary all the critical factors simultaneously to turn the problem on and off intentionally.

Paired Comparisons™ and B vs. C™ both use most of Holmes Top 10 Tips.

"In solving a problem of this sort, the grand thing is to be able to reason backward. That is a very useful accomplishment, and a very easy one, but people do not practice it much. In the everyday affairs of life, it is more useful to reason forward, and so the other comes to be neglected. There are fifty who can reason synthetically for one who can reason analytically."

"Once you eliminate the impossible, whatever remains, no matter how improbable, must be the truth."

"Always approach a case with an absolutely blank mind. Form no theories, just simply observe and draw inferences from your

observations. It is a capital mistake to theorize before one has data. Insensibly one begins to twist facts to suit theories, instead of theories to suit facts."

"How dangerous it is to reason from insufficient data. Data, Data, Data! I can't make bricks without clay."

"It is of the highest importance in the art of detection to be able to recognize out of a number of facts which are incidental and which are vital."

"I can see nothing," said Watson, handing it back to Holmes. "On the contrary, Watson, you can see everything. You fail, however, to reason from what you see. You are too timid in drawing your inferences."

"Detection is, or ought to be, an exact science, and should be treated in the same cold unemotional manner. When you attempt to tinge it with romanticism, you produce the same effect as if you worked a love story into the fifth proposition of Euclid."

"I never guess. It is a shocking habit -- destructive to the logical faculty."

Many times teams think they have solved a problem, only to find it comes back days, weeks or months later. They have found one of the critical factors and created a partial solution, but one or two other critical factors are still active. B vs. C™ tests the current settings (C) against the presumably better settings (B) directly. If the team can intentionally make the problem appear and disappear, then they have solved the problem. If not, they find out immediately that some other critical factor or factors are still active, so they continue to search for the complete solution.

General Description:

In B vs. C™, first run the operation at the original settings to create the problem, and then at the new settings to eliminate it. Next, repeat this switch two more times. Finally, evaluate the outcome from these six runs in random order using the Tukey Test (introduced in Chapter 5 as part of Paired Comparisons™) to determine if you have truly solved the problem.

B vs. C™ can use a very small sample size if no overlap of results is allowed. In its simplest form, B vs. C™ can use a "six pack" of samples, just 3 Bs and 3 Cs. If all three Bs are better than all three Cs, then the B settings are indeed better than the C settings with 95% confidence. Alternatively, you can test a larger number of samples and apply the Tukey guidelines for Total End Count.

Examples of the Tool in Action:

Example 1 – Warped Grills Revisited

In Example 6 from Chapter 5, the line workers had determined that straightness of the component pieces was the only critical factor affecting the acceptability of the finished grills. They tested this finding by applying the simple "six pack" variation of the B vs. C™ technique.

In random order, they made three grills using all straight pieces of wire and three grills using pieces with some residual curve remaining in the wire. Testing consisted of observing whether the final welded part was flat and square or warped and out-of-square. As expected, all three grills made from straight wire were flat and square, while all three grills made from curved pieces were warped and out-of-square. This confirmed that the problem was solved with 95% confidence. They implemented the correction and by making sure that all cut pieces are straight, they have never made another warped grill, which provides 100% confirmation of their solution.

Reasoning Backward

Example 2 – The Press Brake Revisited

As a follow up to the Press Brake example in Chapter 6, the team ran a B vs. C™ test for the two critical factors, Metal Bow and Alignment of the Holding Material. The specification called for ±0.005" accuracy. The data presented below are in multiples of 0.001". They ran 12 Bs and 13 Cs to allow for some overlap of the results, which follow.

Cs: 2, 5, 5, 4, 6, 9, 7, 1, 6, 4, 8, 2, 1
Bs: 2, 0, 1, 2, 2, 2, 1, 1, 0, 1, 2, 0

In rank order these are:
B 0 0 0 *1 1 1 1 1* 2 2 2 2 2 2 2 *4 4* 5 5 6 6 7 8 9 C

The overlap zone is 1 and 2 one-thousandths of an inch. The Total End Count is 3 + 9 = 12. The B conditions are better, with greater than 99% confidence.

Example 3 – Cracked Epoxy Adhesive Revisited

One of the best practice examples for Variable Search™ in Chapter 7 involved cracking in an epoxy adhesive. This team also used B vs. C™ on this problem to validate the conclusion they had reached.

Recall that most critical factor was Cure Temperature. At 150°C, there were zero defects, but at 120°C, the defect rate was 10%. They also concluded that viscosity and amount of adhesive were non-critical, so they could reduce both to lower cost. Therefore, they ran a B vs. C™ experiment with three samples at higher temperature with lower amounts of the lower viscosity resin as the B condition, and three samples at the low temperature with the higher amount of high viscosity material as the Current setting. The results follow.

Since there was no overlap in the six samples, they concluded that B was indeed better than C with 95% confidence.

Parameter	B Process	C Process
Cure Temperature	150°C	120°C
Epoxy lead coverage	60%	75%
Epoxy viscosity (cps)	150,000	180,000

Likert Scale
0 = no cracks
10 = 100% cracked

Process Condition	Number of Defects	Defect Type Likert Scale	Weighted Defect Score
B	0	0	0
B	0	0	0
B	0	0	0
C	1	2	2
C	1	4	4
C	1	5	5

Example 4 – Wire Bond Strength

Another best practice example involved the wire bond strength of a solder joint to an integrated circuit chip. In this case, the strength of the three B samples measured 225, 223, and 219 grams. The strength of the three C samples measured 217, 212, and 210 grams. Since all three Bs were better than all three Cs, B was better with 95% confidence.

Non-manufacturing applications

B vs. C™ has very broad utility in almost any area of human endeavor to compare two or more "things" directly. The key concept is to evaluate each choice and give it a numeric rating. Then, rank order the items, and the Total End Count provides a powerful result, often with a very high level of confidence. The following examples demonstrate the tool's versatility.

Focus groups (and other market research applications): A car company had two new styling options it wanted to test. It convened a focus group of 20 people and asked each person to provide a style rating of 1 to 10 on each vehicle, where 10 was best and 1 was worst. This created a rank ordered list of 40 entries, 20 for Style 1 and 20 for Style 2. The Total End Count was 11 in favor of Style 1 with greater than 99% confidence. The car company also ran traditional market research, at a cost of $45,000, at the same time and reached the same conclusion. B vs. C™ is a fast, accurate, inexpensive way to gather insight into trends and preferences using very small samples.

This same concept applies in surveys of all types – each respondent rates each choice on a 1 to 10 scale. The investigator calculates the Total End Count from all the data and reports the preferred choice with the Confidence Level.

In advertising, companies have run different ads and polled for preferences.

Companies have polled employees on various policy issues, like working conditions, benefits, flextime, etc. Small focus groups of employees provided initial guidance, so the company could evaluate possible options before introducing new plans.

Hospitals have used B vs. C™ to evaluate patient satisfaction with different departments, etc.

Schools have evaluated their recruiting efforts, methods of learning, methods of instruction, etc.

The possibilities are endless. Whenever someone needs to compare two or more alternatives, B vs. C™ provides a statistically powerful, fast, easy, inexpensive technique with a proven record of performance.

B vs. C™ Summary:

- Simple extension of the principles used in Paired Comparisons™
- Guarantees the validity and permanence of the solution

The effective problem solver achieves 90-100% defect reduction every time by using Sherlock Holmes' observation-based approach and the convergent Clue Generation Tools first to successfully find all the critical factors and address them. The convergence tools eliminate the non-critical factors, while retaining all the 1-3 critical factors. By using both Multi-Vari and Paired Comparisons™ first, the effective problem solver finds the most critical factor first, and then identifies what other factors are critical as well. B vs. C™ brings closure to this process by intentionally varying all the critical factors to turn the problem on and off, while holding everything else constant.

Contrast this approach with traditional Brainstorming-based methods. A team lists dozens to hundreds of possible root causes and selects which one or ones to pursue first. The odds are against them, with no more than a few percent chance of choosing any one of the critical factors, and more like a one-in-a-million chance of selecting all the critical factors. This investigation team eliminates non-critical factors one at a time. It eventually (in most cases) discovers one of the critical factors. Assuming there are three critical factors, the other two are still active. This team achieves partial success, usually 20-50% improvement. Most people who use Brainstorming are unaware of B vs. C™, but even if they were aware of this tool, it would merely show them they have more work left to do. They could turn part of the problem on and off and show some improvement, but it would prove they have only solved part of the problem.

Reasoning Backward

The first lesson is **always to test the validity and completeness of the solution.** Vary the critical factors to turn the problem on and off intentionally. Apply B vs. C™ to determine the Confidence Level that the problem is completely solved.

The second lesson is to **take advantage of the power of this tool whenever you need to compare two or more options in almost any situation.**

B vs. C™
(to validate the problem has been solved by turning it on and off and to create confidence the improvement is permanent)

[**Note:** The following directions go into more detail about other uses of B vs. C™. They are included as a to raise awareness and as a future reference.]

Objective:

To determine which of two products or processes is better in quality and reliability, with confidence of 90% or higher, using very small sample sizes. The test compares potentially better materials or processes (B) with current materials or processes (C). Other objectives include:
- Predicting how much better one product or process is than another, with confidence of 90% or higher.
- Assuring the permanency of an improved product or process over a previous one.
- Enabling the selection of one product or process over another, even if there is no quality improvement, because of some other tangible benefit, such as cost or cycle time reduction.
- Evaluating more than two products, processes, or materials simultaneously (B vs. C vs. D vs. E, etc.)
- Extending B vs. C™ into almost any field of human endeavor.

Procedure:

This technique answers the question, "Is one process or product different from or better than another, and at what level of confidence?"

The B vs. C™ technique can use just three Bs and three Cs to answer these questions with at least 95% confidence.
- Establish the sample size depending on the Confidence Level required. In most situations 95% confidence (5% risk) is adequate. If so, select 3 B and 3 C samples.

Reasoning Backward

- Measure the outcome parameter for the six samples, in random order. Random order is critical to eliminate bias from the data, and to assure the accuracy and validity of the readings.
- Rank order the six samples according to the outcome parameter.
- There are 20 possible different orders when ranking any three Bs and three Cs from best to worst. If the B product and the C product were identical, there is just a 5% chance for them to line up BBBCCC, from best to worst. If the rank order of 3 Bs and 3 Cs is BBBCCC, the probability is 19 out of 20, or 95%, that B is different from C. To put it another way, getting a BBBCCC result supports the conclusion that B is better, with only a 5% chance of being wrong.
- If the sample size totals six, three Bs and three Cs, there cannot be any overlap of results in order to conclude B is different from C. (If the results were BBCBCC from best to worst, there is not enough confidence to conclude that B is better than C.)
- By testing larger sample sizes, then some overlap of results is acceptable, by invoking the Tukey Test guidelines. For example, assume five Bs and five Cs produce a rank order of BBBCBBCCCC from best to worst. The End Count of Bs is 3, and the End Count of Cs is 4. The Total End Count is 7, which gives 95% confidence that B is better. The Tukey Test guidelines follow below.

Total End Count	Confidence Level
6	90%
7	95%
10	99%
13	99.9%

- Decide in advance, (a priori) what overlap guidelines and Confidence Level are necessary in order to conclude there has been a significant change.

The B vs. C™ Tool

Expanding the Number of Alternatives

The Tukey Test also enables simultaneous comparisons of several alternatives. For example, suppose several suppliers provide "equivalent" offerings. Test multiple samples from each supplier and rank them all from best to worst. The modified Tukey rules in the following table establish Total End Count criteria for determining which supplier is Best or Worst with 95% or 99% confidence, for different sample sizes, and for up to six alternative suppliers (labeled B, C, D, E, F, and G).

Modify B vs. C™ for single end-counts to prove C is worse than B

The previous cases described two-tailed Tukey tests because B could be better than C or C could be better than B, and the test uses the Total End Count (the sum of the Top End Count and the Bottom End Count). Sometimes the only requirement is that C be worse than B or, similarly, that B is no worse than C. In this situation, the only count that matters is the Bottom End Count. The table lists End Count guidelines for this situation.

B vs.	C		D		E		F		G	
	2 alternatives		3 alternatives		4 alternatives		5 alternatives		6 alternatives	
Confidence	n	Min. EC	n	Min. EC	n	Min. EC	n	Min. EC	n	Min. EC
99%	6-14	9	4-9	12	4	14	4	17	3	18
	15	10	10-12	13	5	15	5	18	4	20
			13	14	6	16	6	19	5	23
					7	16	7	21	6	24
					8	17	8	24	7	26
					9	18	9	24	8	28
					10	19	10	25		
95%	4	6	4	9	3	12	3	13	3	16
	5-13	7	5-7	10	4-5	13	4	15	4	18
			8-10	11	6-7	14	5	16	5	20
			11-13	12	8-9	15	6	18	6	23
					9	16	7	19	7	25
					10	17	8	21	8	27
							9	22		
							10	24		

When B is Better Than C	When B Is No Worse Than C
Design changes	Cost Reduction
Process changes	Cycle-time improvement
Manufacturing method changes	Variability reduction
Reliability life trials	Safety
New equipment	Easier manufacturability
New supplier/materials	Ergonomics (user friendly)
Yield improvement	Space reduction
	Environmental improvement
	Less expensive tooling
	Less capital equipment
	Increased uptime
	Machine efficiency
	Opening up tolerances
	Eliminating an operation or test

Confidence Level	Number of Cs	Min. Bottom EC for C
Critical, 99%	5 to 6	5
	7 to 19	6
	20 or more	7
Important, 95%	3	3
	4 to 15	4
	16 or more	5

Some such cases include an improved process, B, which will not make a better product, but will make the same product faster, at lower cost, or would include some other process improvements. In these cases the question becomes, "Is B no worse than C?" rather than "Is B better than C?" The table lists some industrial applications for both kinds of B vs. C™ tests.

B vs. C™ is also useful in transactional and administrative situations, almost anywhere that two (or more) alternatives must be evaluated. The following list is a small sampling of the situations where B vs. C™ has been useful.

- Focus groups, clinics, panels
- Surveys: marketing, political, economic, social, health
- Advertising
- Sales promotion, sales forecasting
- Job enrichment: vertical and horizontal
- Company policies: working conditions, fringe benefits, insurance, flextime, etc.
- Hospitals: admission, emergency rooms, nursing, billing, etc.
- Schools: recruitment, scholarships, methods of instruction, methods of learning, etc.

Reasoning Backward

B vs. C™ Template

Project: Date:
Investigator:
Performance Measurement:
Defect Frequency and History:
Measurement (include target value and specification limits):

Accuracy of Measurement/Accuracy of Product Tolerance Ratio:
(If attribute, is a Likert scale possible?):
Confidence level (Is B better than C?):
     90%   95%   99%   99.9%
Number of Bs:
Number of Cs:
Number of samples for each B and C:
Randomized order of testing:

Results, listed in rank order:

Conclusions:

Section 3
Set Limits for Flawless Performance
Optimization Tools

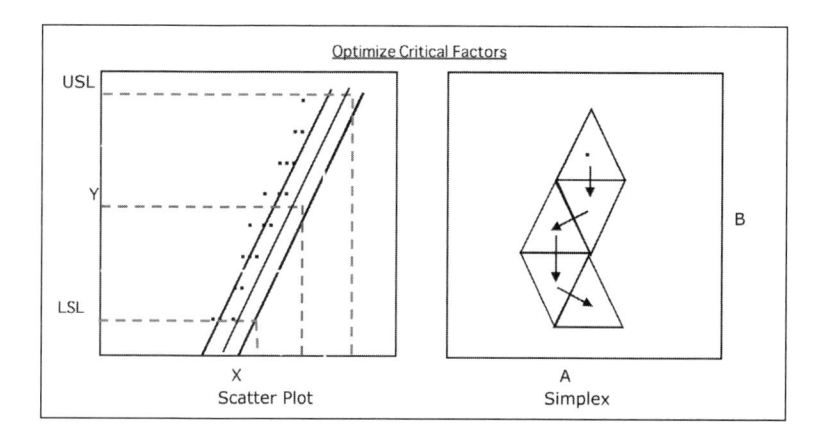

Optimize Critical Factors

Scatter Plot

Simplex

Once you have identified all of the root causes, it is time to optimize the process by establishing the Realistic Target Values and Realistic Tolerances for each Critical Factor. These settings enable the activity to operate flawlessly, to consistently generate Zero Defects. Choose a Scatter Plot for non-interacting factors and Simplex for interacting factors. This section introduces both techniques, but most people will find Scatter Plots to be immediately applicable. The Simplex technique is included to create awareness for the future.

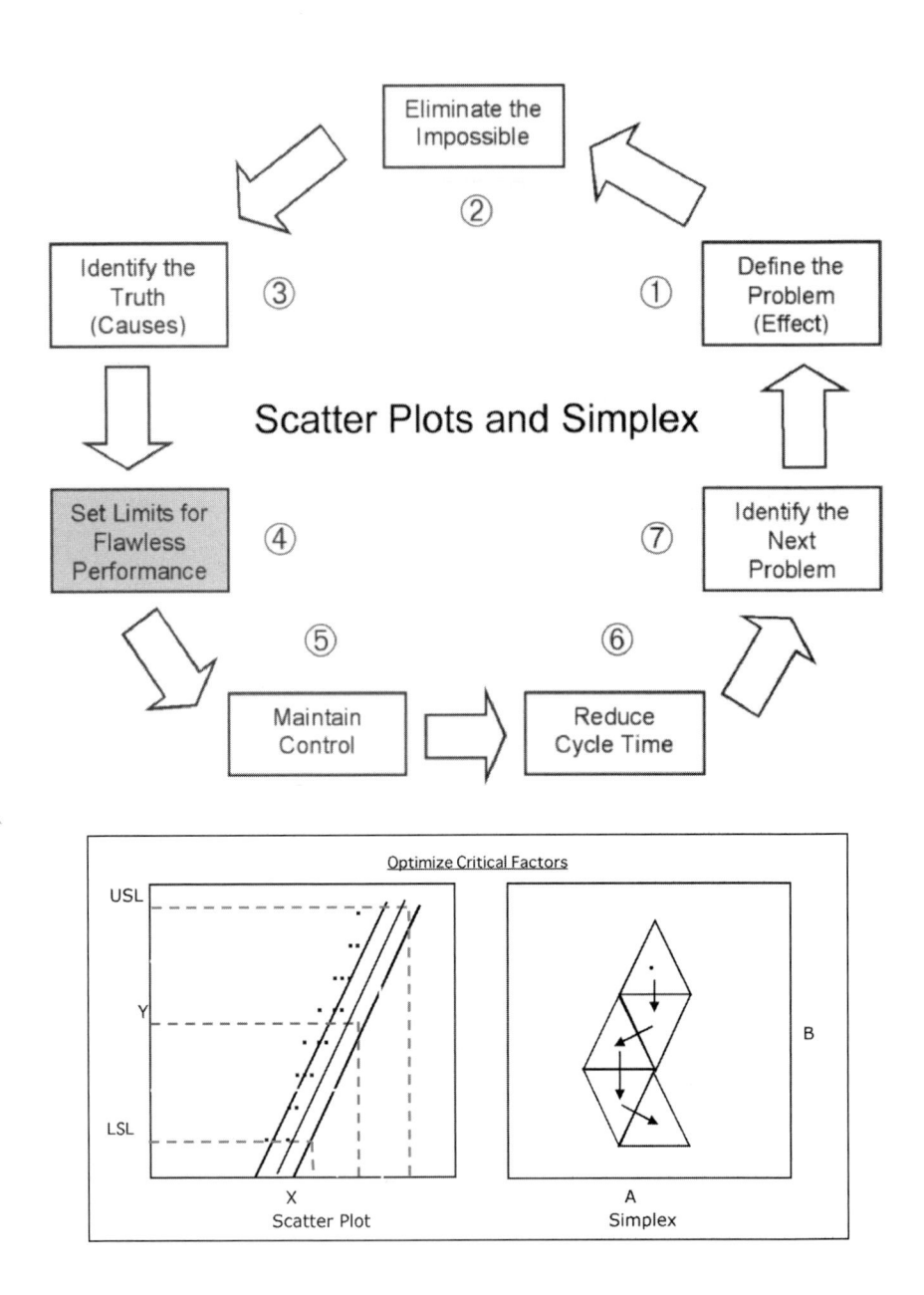

Scatter Plots and Simplex

1. Define the Problem (Effect)
2. Eliminate the Impossible
3. Identify the Truth (Causes)
4. Set Limits for Flawless Performance
5. Maintain Control
6. Reduce Cycle Time
7. Identify the Next Problem

Optimize Critical Factors

- X / Y axes with USL, LSL — Scatter Plot
- A / B — Simplex

Chapter 10

The Scatter Plot and Simplex Tools

To determine the limits of the critical factors that result in flawless performance

Concept and Expected Results:

Scatter Plots and Simplex use half Holmes' tips to establish realistic tolerances for the critical factors that guarantee flawless performance of the activity.

"In solving a problem of this sort, the grand thing is to be able to reason backward. That is a very useful accomplishment, and a very easy one, but people do not practice it much. In the everyday affairs of life, it is more useful to reason forward, and so the other comes to be neglected. There are fifty who can reason synthetically for one who can reason analytically."

"Always approach a case with an absolutely blank mind. Form no theories, just simply observe and draw inferences from your observations. It is a capital mistake to theorize before one has data. Insensibly one begins to twist facts to suit theories, instead of theories to suit facts."

"How dangerous it is to reason from insufficient data. Data, Data, Data! I can't make bricks without clay."

"It is of the highest importance in the art of detection to be able to recognize out of a number of facts which are incidental and which are vital."

"I can see nothing," said Watson, handing it back to Holmes. *"On the contrary, Watson, you can see everything. You fail, however, to reason from what you see. You are too timid in drawing your inferences."*

Most problem solving processes use both Scatter Plots and Simplex, but best practice operations use these tools differently. Others use statistical software to calculate correlation and regression data. Best practices use Scatter Plots and Simplex to establish realistic target values and tolerances for the critical factors. Because both these graphing techniques are familiar and straightforward, this chapter focuses on establishing realistic target values and tolerances.

The primary goal is to establish tighter specifications of the critical factors in order to eliminate defects and achieve flawless performance. The secondary goal is wider specifications of the non-critical factors, if doing so will reduce costs.

General Description: Scatter Plots of Non-Interacting Factors

After previous experiments have identified and validated the critical factors, it's time to establish the realistic target values and tolerances to achieve zero defects. Scatter Plots are the fastest and easiest way to do this when dealing with non-interacting factors, which is usually the case.

The graph plots the performance measurement on the Y-axis and the critical factor on the X-axis. The X-axis includes 30 data points from at least 10 different values of the critical factor that cover its entire range of variation. The Y-axis should show the entire range of variation of the performance measurement. Using Scatter Plots to establish target values and tolerances is a visual activity, so an example greatly helps the discussion.

Example 1 – Ignition Amplifier

This example is an engine ignition amplifier. The critical performance measurement was Off-Time with a specification range of 4.8-6.0 milliseconds. The defect rate had historically been over 10%. Previous experiments had identified the most critical factor as one particular resistor in the circuit, labeled R4, and there were no interaction effects. The team created a Scatter Plot of Off-Time vs. R4 resistance in ohms and added a series of lines to the chart as shown.

The existing specification for R4 was 110 ohms ± 10% – the team thought the acceptable range was about 100-120 ohms. It was clear from the graph that the low end of the specification was satisfactory, but the high end was a problem. In reality, any resistance over 115 ohms caused too long a delay, so the R4 specification had to change.

First, they drew the regression line that best fitted the data. The first critical guideline is that the data points and the regression line must tilt. The slope of the tilt doesn't matter, because it can be adjusted by changing the scale of the vertical axis.

If the regression line were vertical, it would mean that, for a given value of X, the value of Y could be anything, so X would be non-critical. Other factors would be controlling output value completely.

If the regression line had been horizontal, then all values of X would generate the same value of Y, so once again X would have no impact on Y, and X would be non-critical.

If the previous experiments had indicated that this X factor was critical, which they did, then the data and the regression line should have had a definite tilt, and they do.

Effect of R4 on Off Time

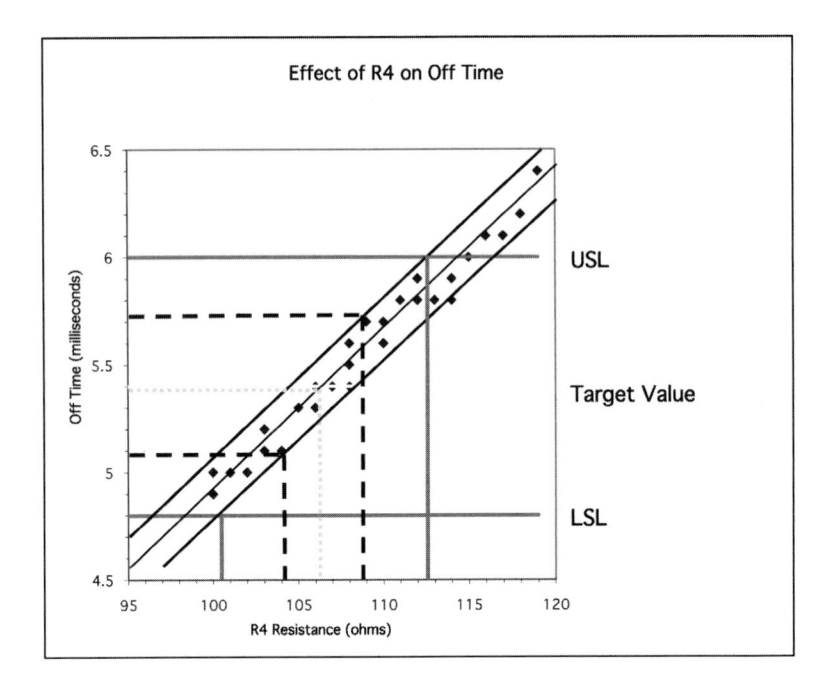

[Scatter plot showing Off Time (milliseconds) on the y-axis ranging from 4.5 to 6.5, versus R4 Resistance (ohms) on the x-axis ranging from 95 to 120. Data points follow a positive linear trend with two parallel diagonal lines bounding the data. Horizontal lines mark USL (near 6), Target Value (near 5.4), and LSL (near 4.8).]

Next, they drew two lines parallel to the regression line that just captured all the data (or all but one data point, if there had been an outlier). The critical feature about these two diagonal lines is their vertical separation relative to the specification range of the performance measurement. The closer together these two parallel diagonal lines are, the more critical this X-factor is.

In this example, the output specification range is 1.2 milliseconds, and the vertical separation of the diagonals is a little less than 0.3 milliseconds, or just under 25% of the specification window. This meant that all the variation of everything else in the system accounted for only 25% of the variation in Off-Time. R4 was definitely the most critical factor. If the separation had been greater, up to about 50% of the specification range, then the X would have been a critical factor, but not the most critical factor.

The third step is establishing the target value for the most critical factor. They began with the Off-Time target value at the center of its specification window, 5.4 milliseconds. They drew a horizontal dotted line from 5.4 on the Y-axis to intercept the regression line. Then, they dropped a vertical dotted line down to the X-axis. The X-intercept became the target value for R4, in this case, 106 ohms.

Then, they used the Off-Time Upper and Lower Specification Limits to establish the realistic tolerance for R4. They drew a horizontal solid line from the Y-axis at 6.0 milliseconds across to the top line parallel to the regression line, and dropped a solid vertical line from there to the X-axis, in this case at 112 ohms. At any R4 below 112 ohms, Off-Time will be under its Upper Specification Limit.

Then, they drew a similar solid horizontal line from the Off-Time Lower Specification Limit of 4.8 milliseconds to the lower parallel diagonal line and dropped a vertical line to the X-axis, intersecting it at 100 ohms. These two values were the realistic tolerance for R4, 100-112 ohms, or 106 ± 6 ohms. Any R4 resistor in this window would create an ignition with the correct Off-Time every time. If they wanted the process to operate at 3σ, they would have set 106 ± 6 ohms as the acceptable tolerance.

The company's goal for this project (and all its projects) was 6σ, so the team went one step further. They established tighter Pre-Control limits within this window to increase the capability of the process. They divided the Off-Time specification window into four equal quadrants by drawing two additional horizontal lines, which are the dashed lines on the graph. The top dashed line went from 5.7 milliseconds on the Y-axis (halfway between the 5.4 Target Value and the 6.0 Upper Specification Limit) to the upper parallel diagonal line, and then they dropped a vertical dashed line to the X-axis at 109 ohms.

The second dashed horizontal line went from 5.1 milliseconds on the Y-axis to the lower diagonal, and then they dropped a vertical dashed line to 103 on the X-axis. This established the specification for R4 at 106 ± 3 ohms, which would create a resulting Off-Time range of 5.1-5.7 milliseconds, and the circuit would achieve 6σ capability.

In this case, they could tighten the specification for the R4 factor to drop the defect rate to zero and loosen the specifications for the non-critical components to reduce costs. After they completed all these adjustments, the defect rate dropped to zero.

Other Examples

Scatter Plots are common to almost every situation where an investigator wants to examine the impact of a change in one independent X-variable on some dependent Y-variable (the outcome). For example, measuring the length of a metal bar at different temperatures produces a scatter plot. The slope of the regression line of the data is the Coefficient of Linear Expansion for the material. The vertical scatter of the data should be 0. Deviation from the regression line is a reflection of the accuracy of the experiment.

When studying trends in the population, Scatter Plots are also common. Just a few examples include studies of Income Level as a function of Level of Education, Cancer Deaths as a function of Level of Smoking, and Income Level as a function of the Reputation of a School. All of these have historically shown high levels of correlation, but understandably, there is more scatter in the data than in the Coefficient of Linear Expansion example. In any study of human systems such as Income and Cancer Death Levels, there will always be outliers, both high and low.

Most problem solvers focus on the slope and correlation coefficient in these applications, which provides some valuable information. However, the effective problem solver goes further and examines the vertical separation of the data to determine the criticality of the X-factor. This extra insight is significant. The effective problem solver knows by the narrowness of the vertical scatter whether this X is the most critical factor or simply one of one or two other critical factors, and there is more work to do. This insight is not readily available to problem solvers who do not examine the vertical separation of the data.

General Description: Simplex for Interacting Factors

A number of Response Surface Methods exist, all having the same desired outcome of discovering the optimal settings of two or more interacting variables. The most common are Evolutionary Operation (EVOP), Simplex, and Random Evolutionary Operation (REVOP). The most popular is Simplex because it requires fewer experiments in most situations. The following best practice example demonstrates the complete Simplex procedure.

Example 2 – Diode Baking Process

This example is from a diode baking process where the two interacting variables are Bake Time and Temperature. The performance measurement is the Percent Yield of the Batch. In the chart, Bake Time appears on the X-axis, Temperature is on the Y-axis, and Percent Yield appears as labels on the chart next to the data points.

In this variation of Simplex, the Stage 0 starting point was the current operating condition of 600°F for 60 minutes, which had a yield of 82%. They selected three points around Stage 0 for the Stage 1 runs. These points were 610°F for 60 minutes, 590°F for 55 minutes, and 590°F for 65 minutes. The yields of these three points were 76%, 84%, and 81% respectively. The next experiment, Stage 2, moves away from the lowest yield point to a distance equally far beyond the other two Stage 1 points, to 570°F for 60 minutes. This run yielded 87% good diodes, the best value yet. The Stage 2 triangle had values of 87%, 84%, and 81%, so Stage 3 moved directly away from the 81% reading, to 570°F for 50 minutes, which yielded 85%. Following this same logic again, Stage 4 was 550°F for 55 minutes, which yielded 89%. This led to their last experiment, Stage 5 at 550°F for 65 minutes with a 94% yield. They stopped the Simplex process at this point, but they had gone from an historic 82% yield to 94% in just eight experimental runs. Put another way, the defect rate dropped by 2/3, from 18% to 6% in just eight runs.

Experiment No.	Time (min)	Temperature (°C)	Yield (%)
Stage 0	60	600	82
Stage 1	60	610	76
Stage 1	55	590	84
Stage 1	65	590	81
Stage 2	60	570	87
Stage 3	50	570	85
Stage 4	55	550	89
Stage 5	65	550	94

The Scatter Plot and Simplex Tools

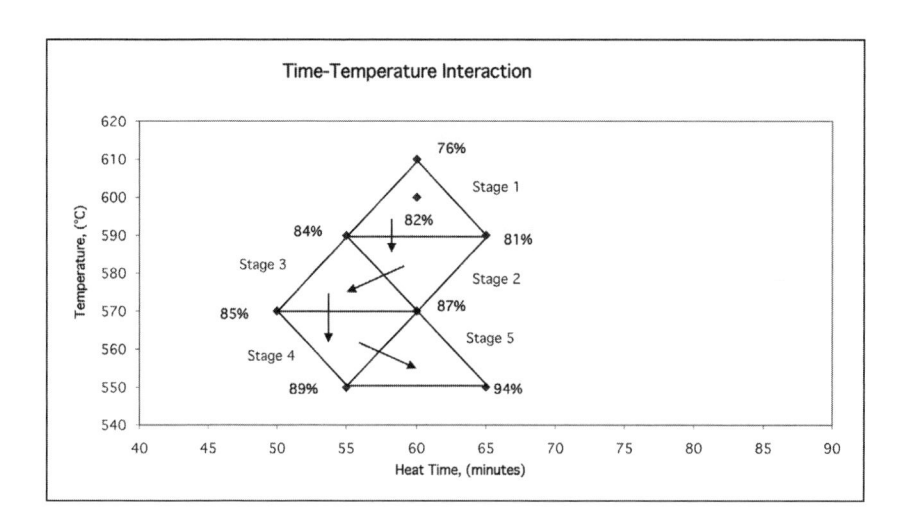

Scatter Plots and Simplex Summary:

- Used to determine realistic target values and tolerances visually in order to achieve defect-free production
- Significant contributor to the increased effectiveness of the best practice problem solving process.

The main lesson is to **use Scatter Plots to full advantage** – use them to **determine the realistic target values and tolerances for all the critical factors**. In any situation with an X input variable and a Y outcome parameter, a Scatter Plot can provide much more than correlation coefficients. It provides the necessary insights to achieve zero defects. **The vertical spread of the data also provides solid insight into how critical the variable is** and whether or not other critical variables remain undiscovered.

Scatter Plots
For optimizing the level of one variable
when there are no interactions with any other variables

Objectives: Experience has shown 90% of existing specifications and tolerances are wrong. They may come from old designs or drawings, may come from boilerplate settings, may be based on worst-case scenarios, may simply follow supplier recommendations, and worst of all, may not have included any customer input on what really is important.

When DOE testing is complete, the appropriate levels for the important variables will have been identified. Now is the time for Scatter Plots to optimize the target values and specification limits for important variables when there are no interaction effects. The objectives of Scatter Plots include:
- To establish realistic target values and tolerances of the critical factors.
- To tighten the tolerances of the critical factors to achieve high C_{pk}, flawless performance, and zero defects.
- To open up the tolerances of the non-critical factors to reduce costs.

Procedure: The Scatter Plot is a graphical technique. Take 30 readings that represent 10 or more levels from throughout the range of the critical factor. Plot them on the graph versus their corresponding output performance measurements. Then study the shape of the data points. If there is good correlation, a thin line will result, and you can determine appropriate target values and tolerances graphically. If the correlation is poor, the result will be a fat parallelogram. This indicates this X-factor is non-critical, so you can open up this factor's tolerances if it will reduce costs.

The Scatter Plot and Simplex Tools

- Select the performance measurement, its target value, and its upper and lower specification limits, always referencing such limits to customer requirements.
- Determine the critical factors to be optimized from previous DOE techniques. Be sure these critical factors have been verified as permanent improvements by using the B vs. C™ tool.
- Make sure there are no interaction effects between the critical factors, or that they are negligible. If interactions exist, use Simplex testing instead of Scatter Plots.
- Select a range of values for the X-variable. Run 30 samples from at least 10 different settings throughout this range and note the corresponding output performance measurements. Be sure to randomize the testing sequence.
- Plot the results. If there is a tilt in the graph and only a small vertical scatter, the most critical factor is further validated. If there is little or no tilt, or if the vertical scatter is large, then this X factor is non-critical.
- Draw a median line through the center of the 30 points. Draw lines on either side of the median line and parallel to it. The two lines should be equidistant from the median line and contain the 30 points between them. (If there is an outlier, then exclude it and use the other 29 points.) The vertical separation of this created parallelogram is the variation in the output performance due to all the other factors added together, except this one. If this input variable is the most critical factor, then the vertical intercept should be no more than about 20-25% of the performance specification. If the vertical intercept is about 25-50% of the specification, then this X factor is critical, but not the most critical factor.
- Next, draw a horizontal line from the Y Upper Specification Limit to intersect the top line of the parallelogram. Then, draw a vertical line from this intercept down to the X-axis. This X-axis intercept represents the maximum realistic

tolerance for this X factor. Any value of the X beyond this limit results in a defect above the Upper Specification Limit.
- Similarly, draw a horizontal line from the Lower Specification Limit across to the lower line of the parallelogram, and drop a vertical line from that intercept point down to the X-axis. This represents the minimum realistic tolerance for this X factor. Any value of X below this limit results in a performance defect below the Lower Specification Limit.
- The center of these maximum and minimum levels of the X factor is its target value. These maximum and minimum values will assure a C_{pk} of 1.0 relative to the customer's specification width.
- To achieve a C_{pk} of 2.0 relative to the customer's specifications, divide the specification range into four equal quadrants. Use the points that define the center half of the output specification range to draw horizontal lines to the parallelogram as before, and drop vertical lines to the X axis from these new intercepts. This narrower range of X values will determine the maximum and minimum values of the X to assure a C_{pk} of 2.0.
- Finally, compare these realistic maximum, minimum and target values of X to the current values and tolerances. Make whatever changes are necessary to ensure zero defects and 100% yields.
- Scatter Plots are useful in administrative and service applications as well, in industry, government, schools, hospitals, etc., in any situation to understand the correlation between any outcome performance measurement and an input X factor.

The Scatter Plot and Simplex Tools

Scatter Plot Template

Project: Date:

Investigator:

Performance Measurement:

Defect Frequency and History:

Measurement (include target value and specification limits):

Accuracy of Measurement/Accuracy of Product Tolerance Ratio:

(If attribute, is a Likert scale possible?):

Customer Specifications:

Target Value:

Range of Values for the X factor:

Randomize the testing sequence.

Data:

Point No.	X-value	Y-value
1		
2		
3		
4		
5		
6		
7		
8		
9		
10		
11		
12		
13		
14		
15		

Point No.	X-value	Y-value
16		
17		
18		
19		
20		
21		
22		
23		
24		
25		
26		
27		
28		
29		
30		

- Plot the data on a graph with the output specification limits shown.
- Draw a median line and two parallel lines that capture the data.
- If the vertical intercept $\leq \sim$ 20-25% of output specification width, then X is most critical factor.
- Draw a horizontal line from the upper specification limit to the top parallel line.
- Draw another horizontal line from the lower specification limit to the lower parallel line.
- Drop vertical lines from these two intercepts to the X-axis. These X-axis intercepts are the realistic specification limits for X to achieve C_{pk} of 1.0. (3σ)
- Divide the Y-axis performance specification into four equal quadrants. Draw horizontal lines from the center half of the output specification to the parallelogram as before.
- Drop verticals to the X-axis from these new intercepts. These intercepts are the X specification limits for achieving C_{pk} of 2.0. (6σ)
- The center of the X specification range is the realistic target value for the X variable.

Section 4
Maintain Control
Control Tools

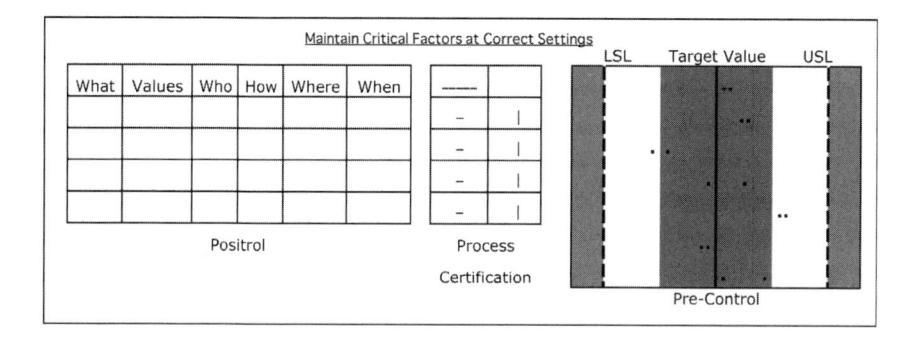

Maintain Critical Factors at Correct Settings

What	Values	Who	How	Where	When

Positrol

Process Certification

LSL   Target Value   USL

Pre-Control

Process Certification and Positrol

- ① Define the Problem (Effect)
- ② Eliminate the Impossible
- ③ Identify the Truth (Causes)
- ④ Set Limits for Flawless Performance
- ⑤ Maintain Control
- ⑥ Reduce Cycle Time
- ⑦ Identify the Next Problem

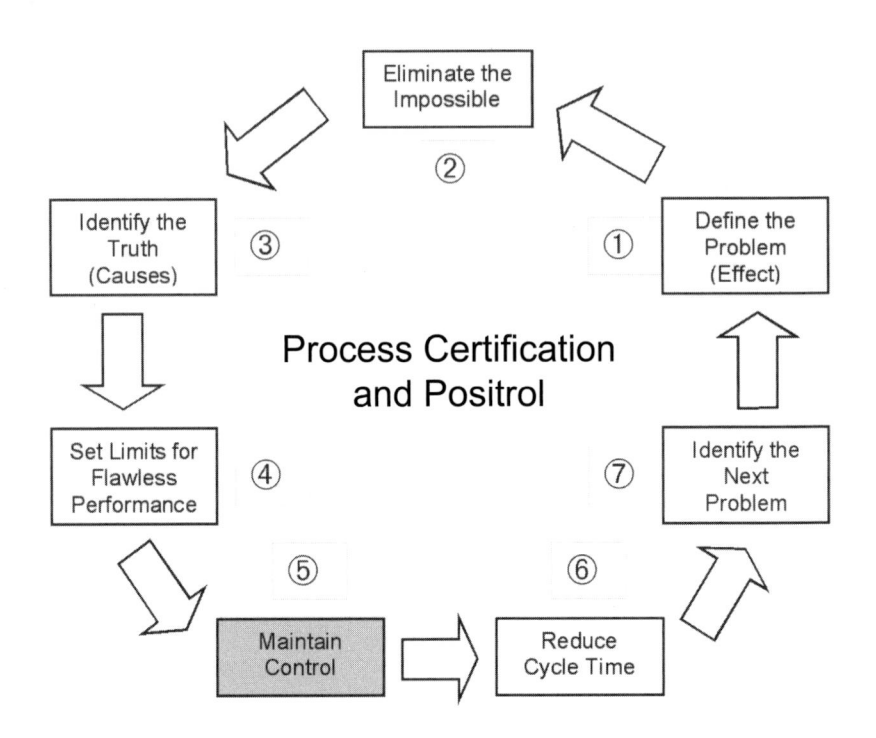

What	Values	Who	How	Where	When

Chapter 11

The Positrol and Process Certification Tools

To lock the critical factors into their ideal conditions and a checklist to eliminate background interference

Concept and Expected Results:

After problem solving is complete and a solution has been implemented, many activities revert to historic defect levels over time. This is especially true when one critical factor has been identified and is under control, but one or two other critical factors remain active. Positrol (short for Positive Control) and Process Certification eliminate this problem by locking in improved performance long-term.

Both these methods derive from Holmes' Tip #9. *"Nothing clears up a case so much as stating it to another person."* These tools document all the relevant issues and tell the people involved exactly what to do to maintain zero defect performance.

Positrol is a checklist for the critical factors (exclusively) that identifies what to control, to what levels, done by whom, where, how, and how often.

Process Certification is an exhaustive checklist of outside factors that can affect the continuous reproducibility of an operation.

When both are in place, history has shown that companies can control complex operations at zero defects for long periods.

General Description: Positrol

Positrol is the operational checklist that operators must follow scrupulously to keep an operation defect-free. It covers only the critical factors that previous experiments have shown to determine the quality of the outcome. Seeing an example is the easiest way to understand Positrol.

Example 1 – Positrol for Wave Solder

The following Positrol table comes from the wave solder example discussed initially in Chapter 4. Subsequent DOE testing established four critical factors that operators had to maintain in order to keep the defect levels below 10 parts per million. These were Temperature of the Preheat Zone, the Angle of Incline of the Circuit Board, the Speed of the Belt, and the Density of the Flux. The company created the following Positrol chart for line operators to track. With this chart in place, they maintained <10 ppm defects almost indefinitely.

Parameter	Spec and Tolerance	Who	How	Where
Preheat Temperature	220°F ± 5°	Automatic	Thermo-couple	Chamber entrance
Angle of Incline	7° ± 20%	Process technician	Angle scale	Tilt post
Belt Speed	6 ft./min. ± 10%	Process technician	Counter	Board feet
An 880 flux density	0.864 gm/cc ± 0.008	Lab technician	Specific gravity meter	Lab

General Description: Process Certification

Process Certification includes six categories, each with a detailed list of issues to consider. Any one issue can destroy the capability of the activity. The five generic categories include:

The Positrol and Process Certification Tools

- Management and Supervision Inadequacies
- Violation of Good Manufacturing Practices (GMP)
- Plant and Equipment Inattention
- Environmental Neglect
- Human Shortcomings

The sixth category is activity specific – any particular issues unique to the activity not covered in the generic lists.

A team should use Process Certification on an activity before conducting any experiments. More than one team has started experimenting only to discover later that the critical factor was an environmental issue, such as the housekeeping problem in the paint operation presented in Chapter 8. Once they properly maintained the area, the problem went away.

The second place to use Process Certification is at the end of experimentation, to lock-in performance at its best possible level.

Finally, Process Certification is appropriate as a periodic process review, once or twice a year for most operations, to assure that the performance does not drift out of control over time.

Example 2 – Process Certification Checklist

The following checklist of potential background issues is the result of decades of work with hundreds of companies around the world. Dorian Shainin developed this exhaustive list over many years. It first appeared in the book *World Class Quality, 2nd Edition* by Keki Bhote in 2000.

Some readers may not find this list to be immediately relevant, but it is an excellent reference for the future. When solving problems, use the list as a stimulus for thought, to consider if or how these conditions relate the specific situation.

Management/Supervision Inadequacies

- Pervasive fear among line workers
- Worker ideas stifled
- Error cause removal not encouraged
- Dictatorial line supervision
- No intra-department or cross-functional teams
- High people turnover
- High absenteeism
- No gain sharing
- Little or no training
- Little or no Poka-Yoke
- No operator certification
- Multi-skilled operators not encouraged
- No reach-out goals
- Measurements
  - Cost of poor quality not measured
  - Yields/cycle time not tracked
  - C_p, C_{pk} not measured
- Little feedback of results
- No audio/visual quality alarm
- Data pollution – little action on data
- No worker authority to shut down poor quality line
- No Positrol
- Supervisors chasing parts; excess paperwork
- Lack of recognition for job well done
- Poor working conditions

Violation of Good Manufacturing Practices (GMP)

- Standard Operating Procedures (SOP) not written or too difficult
- Poor safety for workers and products

The Positrol and Process Certification Tools

- Poor ergonomics
- Sloppy housekeeping
- Process flow vs. product flow
- Push vs. pull systems
- Set up and changeover time too long
- Excess inventory on floor; crowded aisles
- Tools difficult to access
- Frequent model changes
- Partial builds
- Unclear, confusing, contradictory instructions
- Excessive network

Plant/Equipment Inattention

- Total Productive Maintenance not used
- Poor ratio of preventive maintenance to "fix when broken"
- Inattention to:
  - Lubrication
  - Machine noise
  - Machine vibration
  - Overheating
  - Voltage surges
  - Conveyor speeds
  - Corrosion
  - Air hose pressures
- Instrumentation:
  - 5:1 accuracy not met
  - No traceability to national standards
  - Calibration infrequent, or not done
- Inadequate ventilation
- Poor fail/safe controls
- No airlocks for outside air

Environmental Neglect

- Lack of:
    - Temperature control
    - Humidity control
    - Water purity
    - Air purity
    - Dust control
    - Chemicals control
    - Lighting adequacy
    - Vent control
    - Electrostatic discharge protection
    - Electromagnetic compatibility protection
    - Smoking prohibition

Human Shortcomings

- SOPs not followed
- Lack of discipline
- "Diddle artists"
- Rugged individualism over team cooperation
- Personal problems brought to work
- Alcoholism/drugs
- Unreasonable union demands

Positrol and Process Certification Summary:

When Holmes solved a crime, the police arrested the criminals, and the story ended. Today's problem solvers are not so fortunate.

- Consistent procedures are key to long-term zero defect performance.
- Positrol locks in the critical factors to their optimum settings.

The Positrol and Process Certification Tools

- Process Certification keeps all the external factors under control.
- Together they guarantee that the zero defect performance created by the other DOE tools becomes permanent.
- Without them, activities tend to revert to the original conditions and defects reappear.
- Use the Positrol chart and the Process Certification checklist as guidelines to lock-in long-term zero defect performance.
- Each guideline is a stimulus for thought, not a substitute for it.

The lessons for readers are clear. First, **be aware these checklists exist**. Second, **use them when trying to lock-in long-term improvement in any activity**.

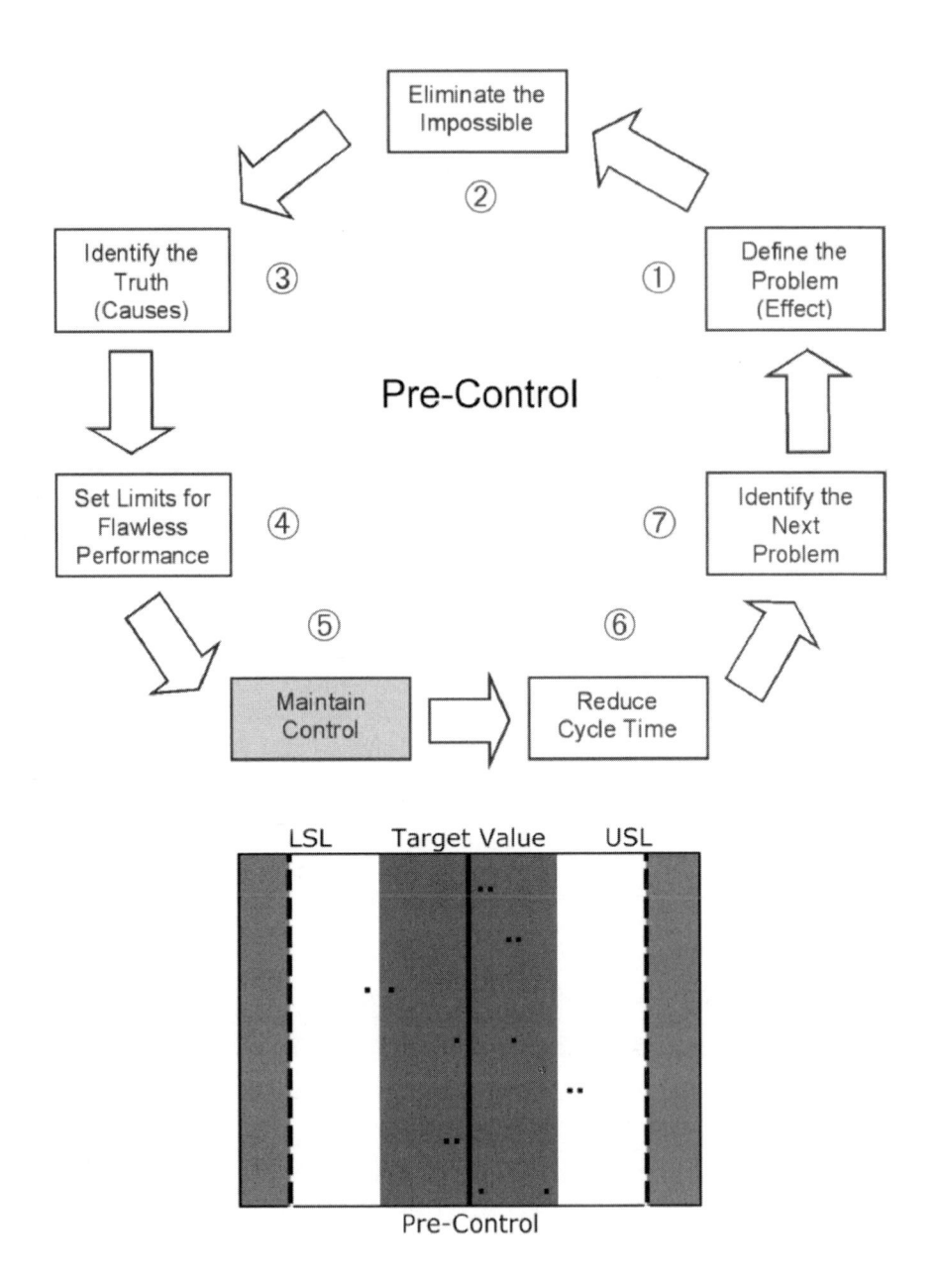

Pre-Control

① Define the Problem (Effect)
② Eliminate the Impossible
③ Identify the Truth (Causes)
④ Set Limits for Flawless Performance
⑤ Maintain Control
⑥ Reduce Cycle Time
⑦ Identify the Next Problem

LSL Target Value USL

Pre-Control

Chapter 12

The Pre-Control Tool

[**Note**: Pre-Control was designed for manufacturing operations, and it still finds the greatest use in production situations where operators must make decisions in real time. It is included here to increase awareness and as a reference for the future.]

Concept and Expected Results:

Pre-Control is the simplest, most powerful method of statistical process control yet devised. It is a key element of best practice problem solving because it gives the line operator the ability to control an operation much faster and more effectively than he could by using traditional control charts. Best practice companies use Pre-Control extensively, while many others include it only is as an afterthought, preferring the traditional control charts that Pre-Control was designed to replace. This chapter presents a comparison to traditional control charts in order to clarify the benefits of Pre-Control.

Pre-Control derives from Holmes' first tip: *"In solving a problem of this sort, the grand thing is to be able to reason backward. That is a very useful accomplishment, and a very easy one, but people do not practice it much. In the everyday affairs of life, it is more useful to reason forward, and so the other comes to be neglected. There are fifty who can reason synthetically for one who can reason analytically."* Pre-Control starts with the performance specifications established by the customer, and workers reason backward to determine production specifications and target values of the critical factors.

General Description:

Pre-Control begins with the Sales Specification for the performance parameter of a product. For a two-sided tolerance window, divide the range into the four equal quadrants as described in Chapter 10 on Scatter Plots. The center of the range is the Target Value. The two center quadrants are the Green Zone, and the outside edges of these two quadrants are the Pre-Control limits. The two outer quadrants are within the Sales Specification, but they are outside the Pre-Control limits. These are the Yellow Zones. Finally, the areas outside the Sales Specification are the Red Zones.

In Pre-Control, first establish that the operation is in control by testing five consecutive pairs of samples. They must all be in the Green Zone before proceeding with production. If they are not all in the Green Zone, adjust the process conditions until they are.

Once the conditions are right, production begins. Then, periodically, the operator collects two consecutive samples and tests them. If both are in the Green Zone, production continues.

If one is in the Green Zone, and one is in a Yellow Zone, production continues.

If both samples are in the same Yellow Zone, then the process has drifted, but it is still within the Sales Specification. The operator must determine what X-factor has drifted and adjust it. After the adjustment, the operator again tests five consecutive pairs of samples, and if they are all in the Green Zone, the operator restarts production.

If one sample is in one Yellow Zone, and the second is in the other Yellow Zone, then something major has changed in the operation. The operator must stop the process to determine what is wrong. As above, five consecutive Green pairs are required to restart the process.

Finally, if one sample is in either Red Zone, the process is out of control. (Note that this is the first time the process has actually created any out-of-specification product.) The operator stops the

The Pre-Control Tool

process to determine what has changed. Five consecutive Green pairs are necessary before the operator can restart the process.

Keki Bhote first introduced Pre-Control at Motorola during the 1950s. He prepared the following table that compares Control Charts and Pre-Control. It first appeared in *World Class Quality, 2nd Edition*, (2000) on pages 412-413.

Characteristic	Control Charts	Pre-Control
Simplicity	Complex – calculations of control limits.	Simple – Pre-Control limits are the middle half of the specification width.
Use by operators	Difficult – charting mandatory, interpretation unclear	Easy – green, yellow, red zones, a practical approach for all workers
Mathematical	Involved – X, R, control limits must be calculated	Elementary – must only know how to divide by 4
Process qualification	Twenty-five subgroups required, each with four or five units	Five green pairs in a row assures minimum C_{pk} of 1.33 (4σ)
Small production runs	Useless for runs below 500 units; must sample 80 to 150 units to establish trial limits.	Useful for runs above 20 units. Pre-Control lines derive from specs (which can narrow).
Decisions	Delayed–many points charted for plots.	Instantaneous – Green, yellow or red.
Recalibration of control limits	Frequent – no such thing in industry as a constant cause system.	None needed, unless specification "goal posts" move inward.
Machine adjustments	Time-consuming – any adjustment requires another 80 to 150 units.	Instant – based on two units.
Frequency of sampling	Vague, arbitrary	Simple rule – six samplings between two stoppages or adjustments.

Discriminating power	Weak – α risk of rejection when there are no rejects is high. β risk of acceptance where there are rejects is high. Little relationship to specifications.	Excellent – α risk of rejection is low, less than 2% under worst conditions, 0% with C_{pk} of 1.66 (5σ). β risk <1.36% under Worst conditions, 0% with C_{pk} of 1.66 (5σ).
Attribute chart	P and C charts do not distinguish between defect mode types or importance.	Attribute charts convert to Pre-Control charts by weighting defect modes and an arbitrary rating scale.
Economy	Expensive – complex calculations, paperwork, large samples, more frequent sampling, long trial runs.	Inexpensive – calculations simple, minimum paperwork, small samples, infrequent sampling if quality is good, process capability determined by just five pairs of units.

Example 1 – Wave Solder

This example comes from the wave solder example in Chapter 9 on Full Factorials. Recall that they had reduced the defect rate to 220 ppm. They created a Pre-Control system with two new measures to ensure they maintained the gains they had achieved. First, they increased the sample size from two units to two sets of ten boards each because of the low defect rate. Second, they created a Likert scale of over-solder and under-solder defects so they could create a two-sided tolerance situation. They established +100 point limit for over-solder and –100 point limit for under-solder. Then, they set the Pre-Control limits at +50 and –50, respectively. This led to the Pre-Control table and chart shown below.

The Pre-Control Tool

The operators embraced the Pre-Control chart's simplicity relative to the cumbersome control charts they had used previously. They could spot out-of-control situations almost immediately and make adjustments or take corrective actions on their own. Pre-Control became a way of life throughout the entire facility.

| Oversolder code | Demerits | Time Samples are Collected ||||||||||
		800	900	1000	1100	1200	1300	1400	1500	1600	1700
Solder short	20				X						XX
Nearshort	10										
Excess solder	5										
Capping	5										
TOTAL Oversolder					20						40

Undersolder code	Demerits										
Unsoldered connection	-100								X		
Insufficient solder	-20	XX									
De Wet	-20										
Blow hole	-5					XX					
TOTAL Undersolder		-40				-10			-100		

| TOTAL | | -40 | 0 | 0 | 20 | -10 | 0 | 0 | -100 | 0 | 40 |

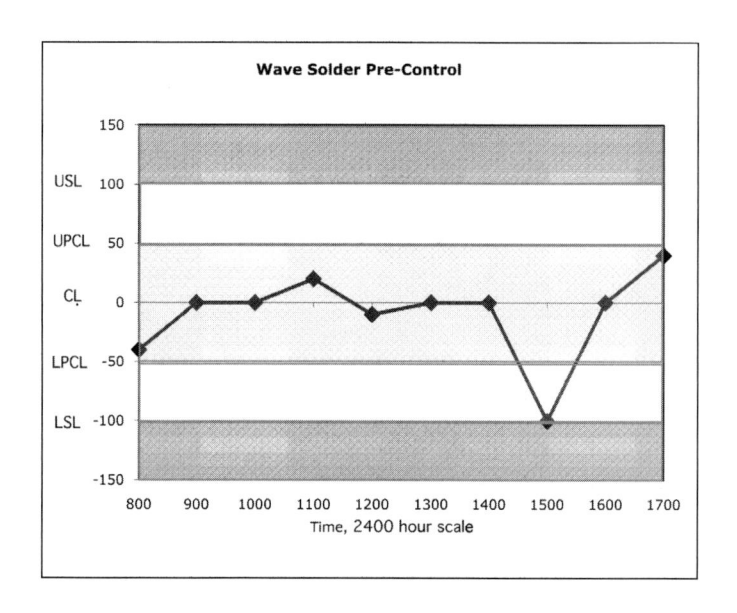

Wave Solder Pre-Control

- USL 100
- UPCL 50
- CL 0
- LPCL -50
- LSL -100

Time, 2400 hour scale

225

Reasoning Backward

Pre-Control Summary:

- The next generation of SPC chart
- Provides great value to the companies that use it
- Superior method for tracking on-going production to lock-in those performance gains

Its main lesson is that **customers define the quality of any product or service.** Their choice of supplier relates to the benefits they receive. Whether a business chooses to use Pre-Control or not, the concept of **targeting a center cut of the performance around the customers' performance window is sound business practice**. Apply that thinking in every pursuit and flawless performance with zero defects becomes an achievable goal.

Guidelines for Pre-Control

Condition	Action
5 consecutive units in the green zone to begin production	
2 units in the green zone	Continue
1 unit in the green zone and 1 unit in a yellow zone	Continue
2 units in the same yellow zone	Adjust*
1 unit in one yellow zone and 1 unit in the other yellow zone	Stop*
1 unit in a red zone	Stop*
* To resume production, 5 units in a row must be in the green zone.	

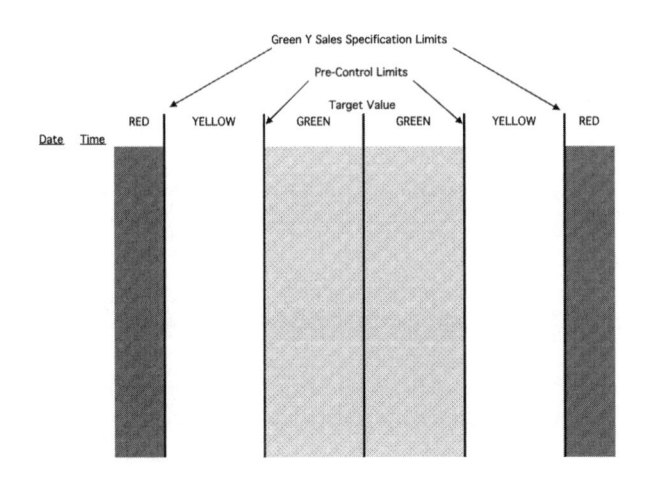

Chapter 13

Putting the Tools Together – A Best Practices Case Study

Concept and Expected Results:

Occasionally one tool alone will solve a problem, and the only required subsequent action is to lock-in the correct settings of the critical factors. Several of the examples in this book have been this type of problem, chosen because they demonstrate the tool so clearly.

However, it is normal to use a series of best practice tools. First, narrow down the number of critical factor candidates. Then, identify the most critical factor (and any other critical factors that might exist). Next, establish the realistic target values and tolerances of the critical factors. Finally, lock in the correct settings for all the critical factors.

This process is quite similar to Holmes' approach to solving a crime. He discovered clues by making observations of the crime scene and interviews, and then followed those clues wherever they led, discovering more clues along the way. Finally, he deduced the criminal's identity from all the clues he had collected.

Problem solving is hard work. The best practice tools are powerful because they make 90-100% defect elimination the expected outcome for any chronic closed-end problem. They work quickly, in days to weeks. This compares to the typical 20-50% defect elimination after several months effort that other problem solving approaches achieve. The best practice tools provide a

Reasoning Backward

structured framework that sets up the investigator for success, but only if he or she thinks analytically. This approach is a stimulus for thought, not a substitute for it. Success is the result of diligent application of the tools.

Golf provides another good analogy. Every new hole is a new problem. The tools are the golf clubs. To score well, different situations call for different clubs. Finally, while a hole-in-one is possible, it is not probable. However, a sequence of shots completes the hole every time.

The following practice example uses a series of observations to solve a mathematics problem.

Practice Problem: All the digits from 0 through 9 have been replaced with the letters a through j, but not in that order. The following six equations provide clues to which letter represents which number. Note that the "number" "gc" represents "g" in the 10s column and "c" in the 1s column, not the product of "g" times "c".

Equation 1 $e + d = e$
Equation 2 $h + i = gc$
Equation 3 $bc + i = cd$
Equation 4 $a - j = b$
Equation 5 $fa + j = fe$
Equation 6 $bb \times b = ff$

Identify which letter represents which number. The solution follows on the next page. Try to solve the problem before reading ahead.

Solution: This problem resembles many real life problems because a series of clues leads to the solution. It follows Holmes' basic process, "Eliminate the impossible, and whatever remains must be the truth."

Step 1: From Equation 1 ($e + d = e$), conclude that $d = 0$ because adding d to e does not change e.

Putting the Tools Together

Step 2: From Equation 2 (h + i = gc), conclude that g = 1 because adding two different 1-digit numbers can only yield another 1-digit number or a 2-digit number from 10 to 17.

Step 3: Equation 3 (bc + i = cd) reveals two additional facts. (A) using the same logic as in Step 2, b + 1 = c. (B) c + i = 10 because d = 0, and cd is a multiple of 10.

Step 4: Equation 6 (bb x b = ff) has two possible solutions. Either b = 2 and f = 4 (22 x 2 = 44), or b = 3 and f = 9 (33 x 3 = 99). Any larger value of b results in a 3-digit number. b ≠ 1 because 11 x 1 = 11, which would make b = f, which is not allowed.

Step 5: At this point, consider each of the two possible cases separately to eliminate the impossible. First, consider b = 2. Step 3A implies that c = 3, and Step 3B implies that i = 7. If i = 7, then Equation 2 (h + i = gc) implies that h = 6. The following table summarizes the situation at this point.

0	1	2	3	4	5	6	7	8	9
d	g	b	c	f		h	i		

Next, consider Equation 4 (a − j = b). The difference between a and j must be 2. The remaining three numbers are 5, 8, and 9. None of these differs from the others by 2. Therefore, this scenario of b = 2 is impossible, so b = 3.

Step 6: Check the values using b = 3. If b = 3, then f = 9 from Equation 6 (bb x b = ff). From Equation 3 (bc + i = cd), c = 4 and i = 6. Then, Equation 2 (h + i = gc) implies that h = 8. Now, the summary table looks like this.

0	1	2	3	4	5	6	7	8	9
d	g		b	c		i		h	f

The remaining numbers are 2, 5, and 7, and Equation 4 ($a - j = b$) says that $a - j = 3$. This implies that $a = 5$, $j = 2$, and by process of elimination, $e = 7$.

The final table becomes:

0	1	2	3	4	5	6	7	8	9
d	g	j	b	c	a	i	e	h	f

The six equations become:

Equation 1	$e + d = e$	$7 + 0 = 7$
Equation 2	$h + i = gc$	$8 + 6 = 14$
Equation 3	$bc + i = cd$	$34 + 6 = 40$
Equation 4	$a - j = b$	$5 - 2 = 3$
Equation 5	$fa + j = fe$	$95 + 2 = 97$
Equation 6	$bb \times b = ff$	$33 \times 3 = 99$

The following case study is a Motorola wave soldering operation from an improvement effort during the 1980s. It used seven tools to identify the most critical factor and two others and to establish realistic specifications for each. Finally, it used Positrol and Process Certification to lock in performance and drive the defect rate almost to 0. The source of this example is Keki R. Bhote's book, *World Class Quality: Using Design of Experiments to Make It Happen*, (1991), pages 142-158.

General Description:

The problem occurred in a wave soldering operation on a complex electronic circuit board. Five boards mounted on one panel go through the wave soldering station. Each board had about 1,000 solder joints. The performance measurement was defect level, and it varied from 2,400 to 3,500 ppm. The average was 2,970 ppm. The cost of the defects was about $8,900 per month, coming from inspection, scrap, rework, retest, and failures on the assembly line and in the field. The failure modes included solder shorts (80%), unsoldered connections (14%), and pinholes (6%). These problems had existed for 14 months. Investigators had tried various traditional problem-solving techniques, including process tweaking, maintenance at increased frequency, brainstorming, and Cause-and-Effect diagrams, but to no avail. Finally, they tried the tools that appear in this book to solve the problem.

Experiment 1: A Multi-Vari Study

They chose Multi-Vari first in order to spot non-random patterns of variation that would provide clues about the critical factors and to identify which category contained the most critical factor. They selected the categories of Time-to-time drift, Board-to-board variation within a panel, Panel-to-panel variation, and Within-board variation. They selected 3 consecutive panels of 5 boards each, sampled at 9:00 am, 11:00 am, and 2:00 pm, for a total of 45 circuit boards, each with about 1,000 solder joints.

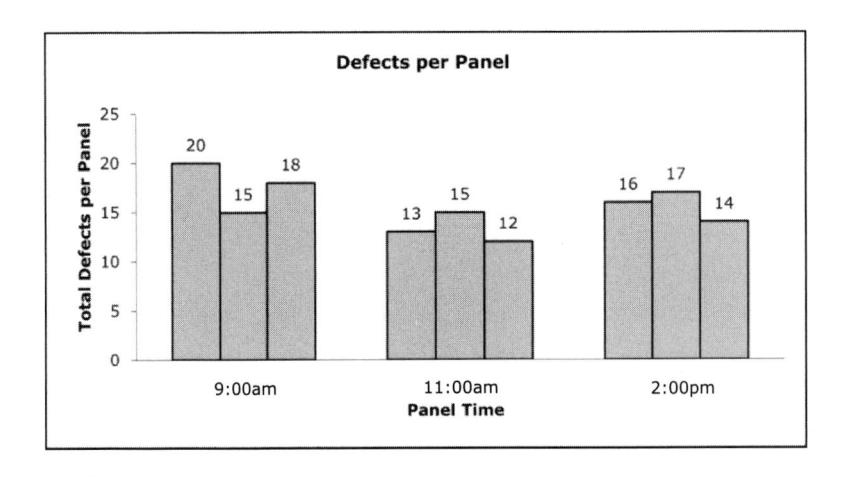

Defects per Panel

Panel Time	Values
9:00am	20, 15, 18
11:00am	13, 15, 12
2:00pm	16, 17, 14

When they analyzed the 45 boards, they found a total 140 defects (3,111 ppm), slightly higher than the historic average, so they had captured the problem. They observed the following patterns.

There was no significant Time-to-time variation, or from consecutive panels at each time, as shown. The range of Panel-to-panel variation was just 5 defects.

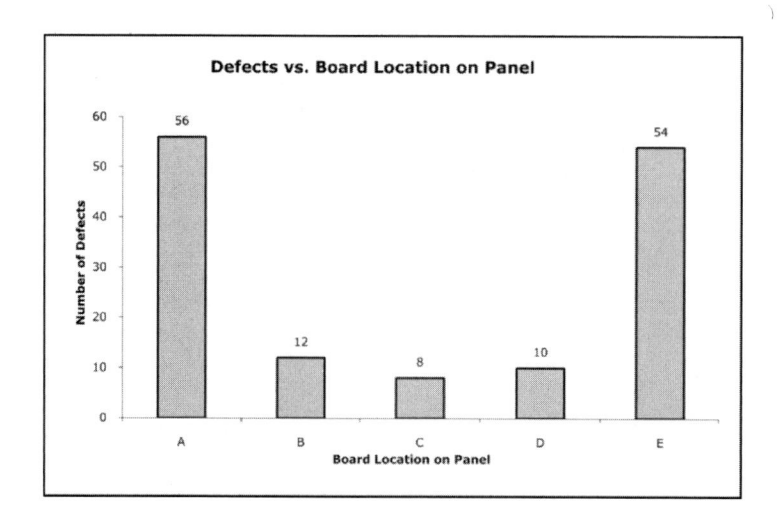

Defects vs. Board Location on Panel

Board Location	Number of Defects
A	56
B	12
C	8
D	10
E	54

They labeled the five boards on each panel A-E, from left to right. They observed that 79% of the defects occurred on the outer two boards, while the inner three boards had only 21%. The range of Board-to-board variation was 48 defects. This required further study.

The Within-board examination divided each board into four quadrants. The outer two quadrants accounted for 85%

Putting the Tools Together

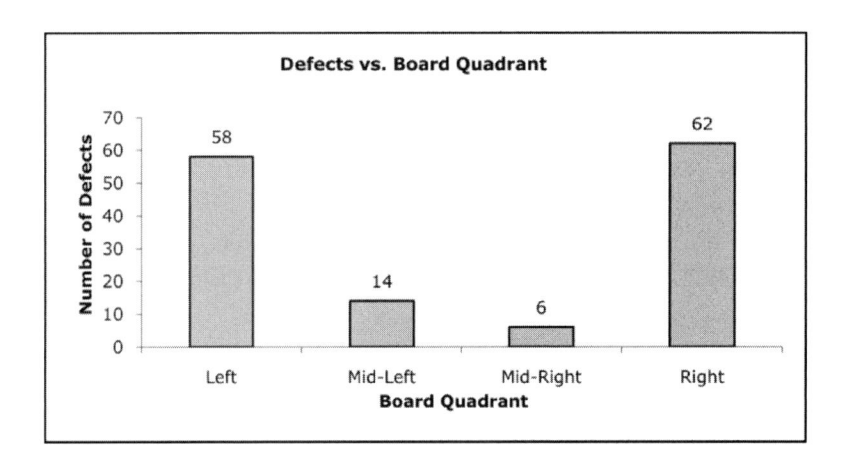

Defects vs. Board Quadrant

Board Quadrant	Number of Defects
Left	58
Mid-Left	14
Mid-Right	6
Right	62

of the defects, with just 15% coming from the inner two quadrants. The range of Within-board defects was 56 events.

Finally, they prepared a Concentration Chart to show the location and type of defect on the boards to look for non-random patterns. The distribution of 77% solder shorts, 16% unsoldered connections, and 7% other, mainly pinholes, was very close to the historical distribution.

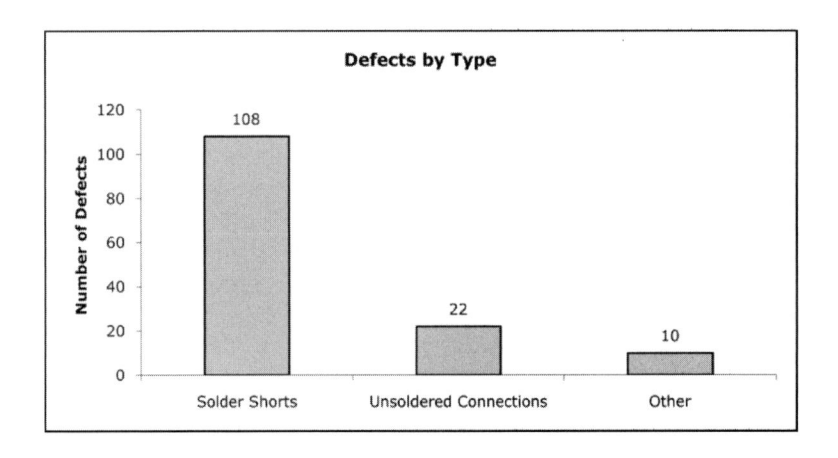

Defects by Type

Type	Number of Defects
Solder Shorts	108
Unsoldered Connections	22
Other	10

From this first experiment, they observed that the outer boards had defect rates four times higher than the inner boards. It provided a sample of "Good" and "Bad" boards for further examination using Paired Comparisons™. They also discovered there were two predominant types of solder shorts – one at an edge connection on the right side of the boards, and one at a particular integrated circuit connection on the left side of the boards. The unsoldered connections were all at just two holes, which again provided a sample of "Good" and "Bad" boards for another Paired Comparisons™ evaluation.

Experiments 2A and 2B – Paired Comparisons™

Experiment 2A compared inner and outer boards to discover consistent differences between them. The Multi-Vari data suggested a possible warp of the boards, which could indicate a process problem. They used four pairs of Good Inner and Bad Outer boards and measured the warp from the center of a panel to the center of each board, as shown in the table.

Panel No.	Pair	Warp in Inches (from Panel Center to Center of Each Board)	
		Left Board	Right Board
1	Inner Boards	0.008	0.010
	Outer Boards	0.150	0.170
2	Inner Boards	0.010	0.015
	Outer Boards	0.210	0.250
3	Inner Boards	0.015	0.012
	Outer Boards	0.300	0.260
4	Inner Boards	0.014	0.010
	Outer Boards	0.190	0.160

The larger warp of the outer boards suggested a fixturing problem and the pre-heat zone temperature might be too high, so they made the fixtures firmer and reduced the pre-heat zone temperature by 10°F.

In Paired Comparisons™ experiment 2B, they compared several boards with good and bad solder connections at the two unsoldered locations. They measured several properties, but found the only one with a significant difference was the ratio of hole diameter to wire diameter, as shown in Chapter 4. In the two spots where solder failed to make the connection, the hole-to-wire ratios were 1.4 and 1.7 times higher than the ratios at the good connections. They discovered that the same sized drill made all the holes, but that the components in question had finer wires than the other components on the board. The corrective action was to use a smaller drill bit on the holes with finer wires.

Experiment 3 – B vs. C™

Next, they wanted to measure the effectiveness of their initial corrective actions. The current settings were to use the existing fixtures, the traditional pre-heat temperatures, and original larger drill bit. The presumably better settings were to use new firmer fixtures, the lower pre-heat temperature, and the smaller drill bit for the two holes where the problems occurred. The total defects per panel follow.

Clearly, the new settings were better than the current process at the 95% Confidence Level. The defect rate for this small sample was 660 ppm (total of 10 defects out of 15,000

Reasoning Backward

Panels	Number of Defects
B2	5
B3	3
B1	2
C3	12
C1	16
C2	13

solder connections), but this was too small a sample to make that prediction without further testing.

The next step was Variable Search™ to determine what other factors were still at work, still generating defects after they had completed these three initial improvements.

Experiment 4 – Variable Search™

They decided on eight factors to consider in their first invasive experiment, as shown in the following table. High Level refers to the settings thought to produce the best results. Low Level settings are the levels to which the process drifts from day-to-day.

Code	Process Parameter	High Level	Low Level
A	Hot Air Knife Pressure, psi	14	10
B	Pre-Heat Zone Temperatures	Profile 1	Profile 2
C	Flux Density, g/cc	0.90	0.80
D	Conveyor Speed, ft/min	4	6
E	Conveyor Angle, °	7	5
F	Solder Temperature, °F	480	450
G	Solder Dwell Time, sec	3.5	3.0
H	Flux Foam Height	1.2	1.0

Putting the Tools Together

For Stage 1 they ran 10 panels with all settings at High Levels, and 10 panels at all Low Level settings. Then, they ran both sets of conditions two more times in random order and measured the defect levels to verify they were studying the right factors, that the settings were valid, and that the data had adequate separation and consistency. The data appear in the following table.

Stage 1 confirmed the experiment's validity, so they proceeded to Stage 2 to eliminate the non-critical factors.

Stage 1 - Ballpark	
High Level Defects	Low Level Defects
4	42
5	46
2	51

Stage 2 - Elimination of Non-Critical Factors			
Variable Combinations	Output	Range	Interpretation
$A_L R_H$	13	-5 to 13	A not important
$A_H R_L$	38	35 to 55	
$B_L R_H$	12	-5 to 13	B not important
$B_H R_L$	39	35 to 55	
$C_L R_H$	32	-5 to 13	C important, along with another factor
$C_H R_L$	15	35 to 55	
$D_L R_H$	20	-5 to 13	D important, along with another factor
$D_H R_L$	21	35 to 55	
$E_L R_H$	25	-5 to 13	E important, along with another factor
$E_H R_L$	22	35 to 55	
$F_L R_H$	10	-5 to 13	F not important
$F_H R_L$	40	35 to 55	
$G_L R_H$	9	-5 to 13	G not important
$G_H R_L$	42	35 to 55	
$H_L R_H$	8	-5 to 13	H not important
$H_H R_L$	38	35 to 55	

| Stage 3 - Capping Run ||||
Variable Combinations	Output	Range	Interpretation
$C_H D_H E_H R_L$	7	-5 to 13	R not important
$C_L D_L E_L R_H$	43	35 to 55	Search is finished

Three factors – Flux Density (C), Conveyor Speed (D), and Conveyor Angle (E) – were critical. This led to the Stage 3 Capping Run to look for complete reversal.

The last step was their ANOVA analysis of the data from the Variable Search™ experiment. It identified most critical factor as the interaction between the three critical factors, followed closely by Flux Density and Conveyor Angle as a weaker critical factor.

Experiment 5 – B vs. C™

They were confident from the Capping Run that they had found the critical factors, but they wanted to validate the corrective actions after several days in production. They elected to run another B vs. C™ experiment ten days later. This time the current process included the corrective actions from their previous work (firmer fixtures, lower pre-heat temperatures, and smaller drill bits) with the other settings left where they had been in the first experiment. The better settings were identical except the flux density was held at 0.9 g/cc, the conveyor speed at 4 ft/min, and the conveyor angle at 7°, with the results shown.

Putting the Tools Together

Panels	Number of Defects
B1	3
B3	3
B2	4
C2	25
C3	31
C1	29

		C High Flux Density = 0.9 g/cc	C Low Flux Density = 0.8 g/cc	
Metric: No. of Defects				
		1 + + +	2 - + +	
D High Conveyor Speed = 4 ft/min	E High Conveyor Angle = 7°	Gr.Y 4 Median: 8 Gr.Y 5 13 10 8 Gr.Y 2 12 9 7	Gr.Y 32 Median: 32 Gr.Y Gr.Y	40
		3 + + -	4 - + -	
	E Low Conveyor Angle = 5°	Gr.Y 25 Median: 25 Gr.Y Gr.Y	Gr.Y 21 Median: 21 Gr.Y Gr.Y	46
		5 + - +	6 - - +	
D Low Conveyor Speed = 6 ft/min	E High Conveyor Angle = 7°	Gr.Y 20 Median: 20 Gr.Y Gr.Y	Gr.Y 22 Median: 22 Gr.Y Gr.Y	42
		7 + - -	8 - - -	
	E Low Conveyor Angle = 5°	Gr.Y 15 Median: 15 Gr.Y Gr.Y	Gr.Y 42 Median: 42 Gr.Y 46 38 40 38 Gr.Y 51 39 42 43	57
		68	117	

	C	D	E	CD	CE	DE	CDE	Output
	1	1	1	1	1	1	1	8
	-1	1	1	-1	-1	1	-1	32
	1	1	-1	1	-1	-1	-1	25
	-1	1	-1	-1	1	-1	1	21
	1	-1	1	-1	1	-1	-1	20
	-1	-1	1	1	-1	-1	1	22
	1	-1	-1	-1	-1	1	1	15
	-1	-1	-1	1	1	1	-1	42
Main & Interaction Totals	-42	-13	-21	9	-3	9	-53	

The better process was indeed better at the 95% Confidence Level. The defect rate had dropped to an estimated 80 ppm.

Reasoning Backward

Experiment 6 – Optimization with Full Factorial

At this point, they had identified the two factors that absolutely had to be controlled – Flux Density and Conveyor Angle. They knew the two new settings they had chosen were better than the original settings, but they had no idea if these were the optimum settings. Since there were only two factors, it would be easy to test a value halfway between the original setting and the new setting to see if it performed even better. They designed an experiment to compare the

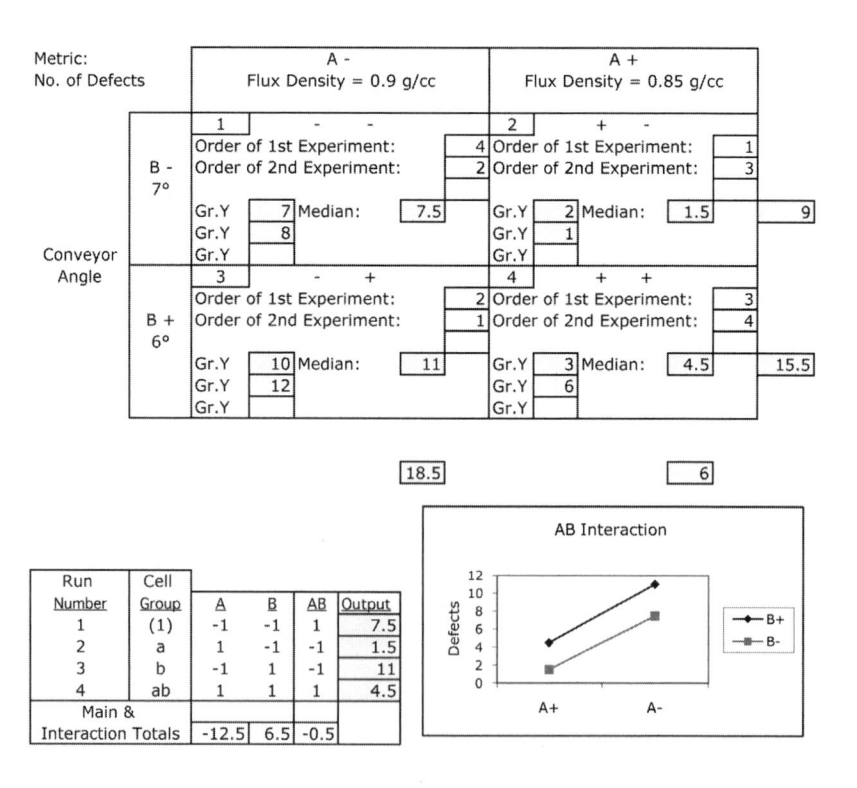

Metric: No. of Defects		A − Flux Density = 0.9 g/cc	A + Flux Density = 0.85 g/cc	
Conveyor Angle	B − 7°	1 − − Order of 1st Experiment: 4 Order of 2nd Experiment: 2 Gr.Y 7 Median: 7.5 Gr.Y 8 Gr.Y	2 + − Order of 1st Experiment: 1 Order of 2nd Experiment: 3 Gr.Y 2 Median: 1.5 Gr.Y 1 Gr.Y	9
	B + 6°	3 − + Order of 1st Experiment: 2 Order of 2nd Experiment: 1 Gr.Y 10 Median: 11 Gr.Y 12 Gr.Y	4 + + Order of 1st Experiment: 3 Order of 2nd Experiment: 4 Gr.Y 3 Median: 4.5 Gr.Y 6 Gr.Y	15.5
		18.5	6	

Run Number	Cell Group	A	B	AB	Output
1	(1)	−1	−1	1	7.5
2	a	1	−1	−1	1.5
3	b	−1	1	−1	11
4	ab	1	1	1	4.5
Main & Interaction Totals		−12.5	6.5	−0.5	

AB Interaction

(chart: Defects vs A+/A−, series B+ and B−)

240

new standard Flux Density of 0.9 g/cc with 0.85 g/cc, and the new Conveyor Angle of 7° with an intermediate value of 6°. The results of this 22 Full Factorial experiment follow. The results clearly indicated that the intermediate value 0.85 g/cc is better than 0.9 g/cc, but the previous angle of 7° was better than the intermediate setting of 6°. Notice that the two panel defect counts of the 0.85 g/cc and 7° setting were the best two readings from any of the experiments. With the angle now established, the last experiment was to characterize the effect of flux density more precisely. This suggested a Scatter Plot with all the other factors put at their optimum settings.

Experiment 7 – Scatter Plot of Flux Densities

The goal of this experiment was to establish the realistic tolerance for the most critical factor by collecting 30 data points from at least 10 different readings throughout the entire density range. They considered a range of densities from 0.74 to 0.90 g/cc. They selected 10 different densities and ran 3 samples at each setting. This time they reported the defect count as a defect rate in parts per million instead of defects per panel. The results, shown below, show a clearly defined optimum range that tails off quickly at higher and lower densities. Notice that the Scatter Plot need not be linear to provide very usable information. In this case, they were able to maintain a defect rate of less than 20 ppm by maintaining the flux density between 0.78 and 0.82 g/cc, which is what they did at that time. Also, notice the data suggest there could be a tighter tolerance window of 0.80 to 0.82 that might give performance in the range of about

Solder Defects vs. Flux Density

Realistic Tolerance

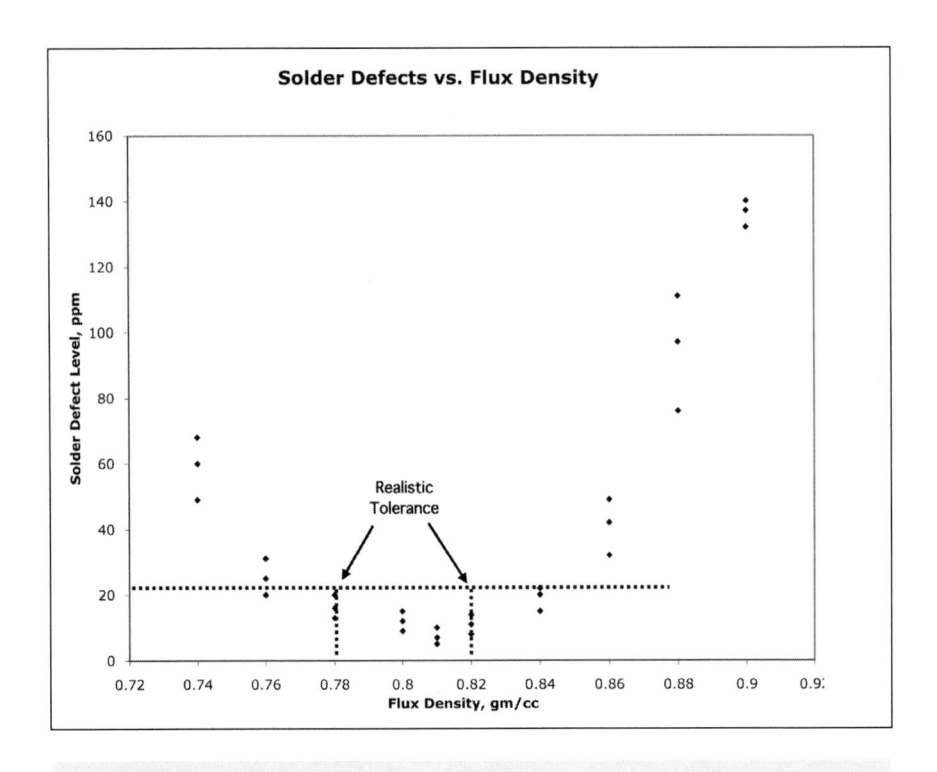

(x-axis: Flux Density, gm/cc; y-axis: Solder Defect Level, ppm)

10 ppm. (This was the subject of future experiments with this flux and other fluxes. After more experiments, Motorola was able to establish 10 ppm as the world class standard, one that remained the standard for at least the next 15 years.) This amazing accomplishment – going from about 3,000 ppm of defects to less than 10 ppm in a series of seven experiments over several weeks – took the company from average to best-in-the-world. It was an improvement of more than 300:1, 99.7% defect reduction.

Putting the Tools Together

Experiment 8 - Positrol

To lock in the improved performance, they had to control the three critical factors carefully, while simply providing normal maintenance for the rest of the operation. By keeping these three factors under control, the company established and maintained best-in-the-world performance of <10 ppm. The Positrol chart shows how they maintained this performance.

Once this schedule was in place, they used Pre-Control, the simplest and most powerful control tool known, for the solder technician to keep this operating steadily at <10 ppm defects.

Key Factor (What)	Who Controls	How Controlled	Where Controlled	When (How Frequently) Controlled
Flux Density	Solder Technician	Specific Gravity Meter	Flux Container	Once/Hour
Conveyor Angle	Solder Technician	Machine Setting	Conveyor	Once/Day
Conveyor Speed	Solder Technician	Counter	Conveyor	Each Model Change

Experiment 9 – Process Certification

This tool became the heart of the on-going maintenance program for the rest of the operation. The table shows the process specific parameters they had to maintain.

Quality Issue	Control Mechanism
Solder Technician	Certification; Periodic Recertification
Metrology	Assurance of 5:1 Accuracy on all instruments
Instrument Calibration	Per published schedule
Materials	Circuit boards, solder, flux certified with C_{pk} of 2.0 minimum
Environment	Temperature, humidity, electrostatic discharge, etc. controlled according to process sheets
Re-certification	Every six months

Summary and Conclusions:

This case study was both typical and unique. Typical in that a series of tools quickly identified the root causes of defects, tightened control of the three critical factors, dropped the defect rate to near zero, and locked in the performance gains.

This approach works in any repetitive activity – manufacturing or non-manufacturing, service activities, transactional, administrative, etc.

In this case, the company started with a defect rate over 3,000 ppm and dropped the rate to 600 ppm in a few days with the first three experiments.

The next two experiments took a few weeks more and dropped the rate to 100 ppm.

The sixth experiment took two more weeks and dropped the defect rate to 30 ppm.

The seventh experiment took another two weeks, and it dropped the rate to less than 10 ppm, which was better than anyone else in the world at that time.

The last steps were to lock-in the gains with Positrol and Process Certification and then to track performance with Pre-Control.

The use of a series of these tools in this fashion to deliver this level of improvement is typical of the results that best practice companies achieve in a variety of situations. In the same or less time than other processes would achieve perhaps 2:1 defect reduction (50%), this best practice process achieved over 300:1 improvement, (99.7%).

Putting the Tools Together

The uniqueness of this case study is the order of tool usage. Every problem is unique, so teams will use the various tools in a different order depending on the particular situation. Teams may solve many problems completely with just one, two, or three experiments. Complex problems, such as this one, may take more steps, but the fundamental concepts are the same.

1. **Quickly eliminate the non-critical factors from consideration, in order to focus on the 1-3 critical factors.**
2. **Identify and validate the critical factors and address them in descending order of importance.**
3. **Establish realistic target values and tolerances for the critical factors that will drive defects to zero.**
4. **Tighten control of the critical factors within their realistic tolerances and lock-in that performance for the long term.**

Most of today's problem-solving processes use this basic framework, but only the best practice organizations use the powerful tools described in this book.

The fundamental lesson is that **"zero defects" or "flawless performance" is always the reasonable goal. Never settle for partial improvement, because a series of experiments using the effect-to-cause, observation-based, convergent tools in this book will find the root causes every time**.

Solving closed-end problems is like playing golf. Every problem is a new hole to play. The tools are the golf clubs. Finding and eliminating the root causes creates zero defects, which is when the ball drops into the cup. Different situations call for different clubs, different tools. Settling for a partial solution is failing to finish playing the hole. This set of tools can completely solve any closed-end problem. Finally, just as golfers practice to improve their skills, problem solvers become more effective at spotting patterns and solving problems quickly as they gain experience with the tools. Have a great game!

Reasoning Backward

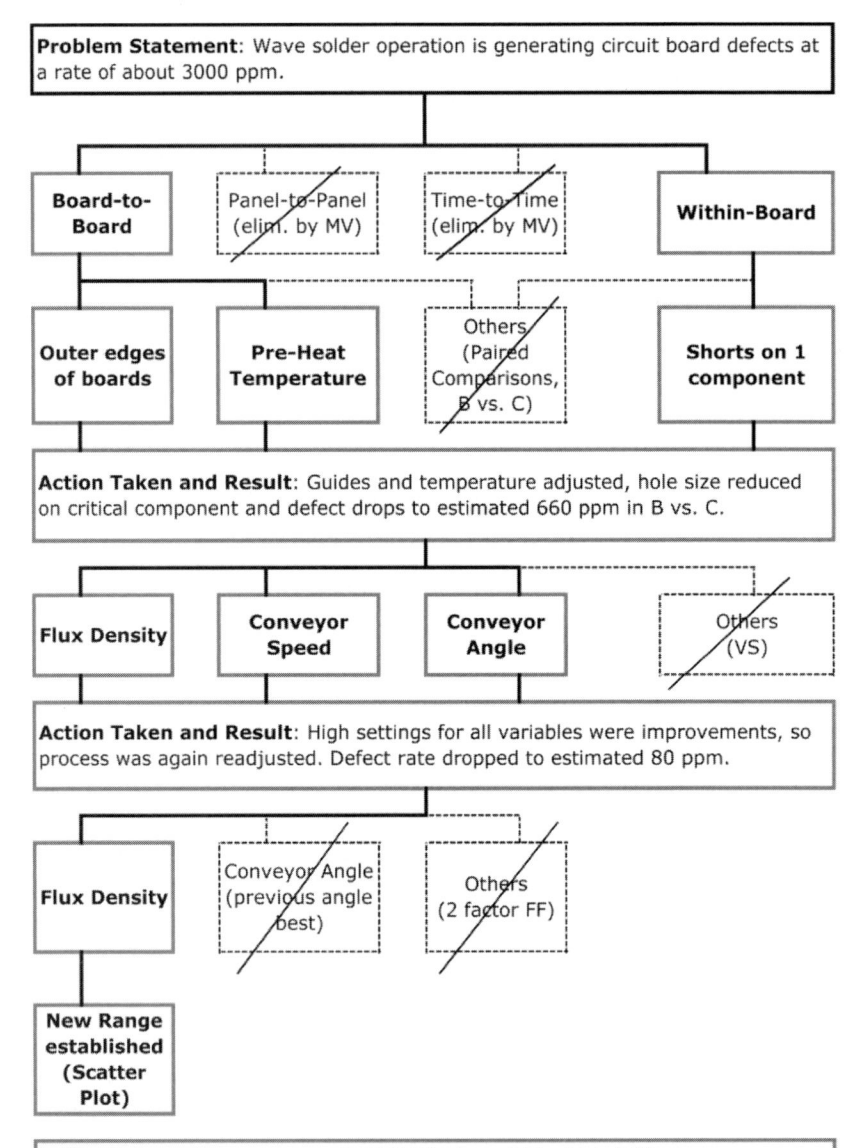

```
┌─────────────────────────────────────────────────────────────────────┐
│ Problem Statement: Wave solder operation is generating circuit      │
│ board defects at a rate of about 3000 ppm.                          │
└─────────────────────────────────────────────────────────────────────┘
         │
    ┌────┼─────────────┬──────────────┬─────────────┐
    │    │             │              │             │
┌────────┐ ┌──────────┐ ┌──────────┐ ┌──────────┐
│Board-to│ │Panel-to- │ │Time-to-  │ │Within-   │
│ Board  │ │Panel     │ │Time      │ │Board     │
│        │ │(elim. by │ │(elim. by │ │          │
│        │ │  MV)     │ │  MV)     │ │          │
└────────┘ └──────────┘ └──────────┘ └──────────┘
   │                                        │
   ├──────────────┬──────────┐              │
   │              │          │              │
┌────────┐ ┌──────────┐ ┌─────────┐  ┌──────────┐
│Outer   │ │Pre-Heat  │ │Others   │  │Shorts on │
│edges of│ │Temperat. │ │(Paired  │  │1 compo-  │
│boards  │ │          │ │Compari- │  │nent      │
│        │ │          │ │sons,    │  │          │
│        │ │          │ │B vs. C) │  │          │
└────────┘ └──────────┘ └─────────┘  └──────────┘

┌─────────────────────────────────────────────────────────────────────┐
│ Action Taken and Result: Guides and temperature adjusted, hole size │
│ reduced on critical component and defect drops to estimated 660 ppm │
│ in B vs. C.                                                         │
└─────────────────────────────────────────────────────────────────────┘

┌──────────┐ ┌──────────┐ ┌──────────┐ ┌──────────┐
│Flux      │ │Conveyor  │ │Conveyor  │ │Others    │
│Density   │ │Speed     │ │Angle     │ │(VS)      │
└──────────┘ └──────────┘ └──────────┘ └──────────┘

┌─────────────────────────────────────────────────────────────────────┐
│ Action Taken and Result: High settings for all variables were       │
│ improvements, so process was again readjusted. Defect rate dropped  │
│ to estimated 80 ppm.                                                │
└─────────────────────────────────────────────────────────────────────┘

┌──────────┐ ┌──────────┐ ┌──────────┐
│Flux      │ │Conveyor  │ │Others    │
│Density   │ │Angle     │ │(2 factor │
│          │ │(previous │ │ FF)      │
│          │ │angle     │ │          │
│          │ │best)     │ │          │
└──────────┘ └──────────┘ └──────────┘
    │
┌──────────┐
│New Range │
│established│
│(Scatter  │
│ Plot)    │
└──────────┘

┌─────────────────────────────────────────────────────────────────────┐
│ Action Taken: New range was 0.78-0.82 g/cc, which yielded 20 ppm    │
│ performance. Additional experiments further narrowed the range and  │
│ made other modifications.                                           │
└─────────────────────────────────────────────────────────────────────┘

┌─────────────────────────────────────────────────────────────────────┐
│ Result: Process reached 10 ppm defect level, best in the world      │
│ then, and for the next decade.                                      │
└─────────────────────────────────────────────────────────────────────┘
```

Section 5
Cycle Time Reduction Tools

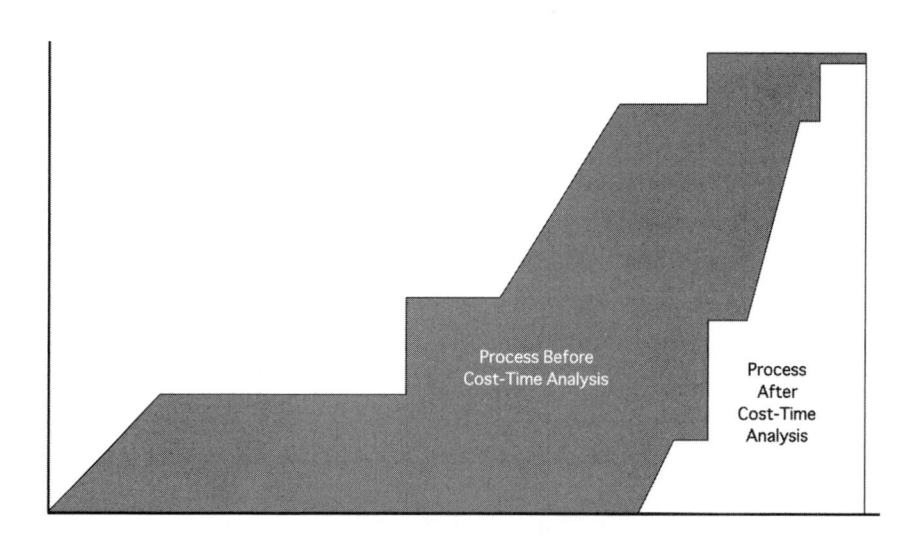

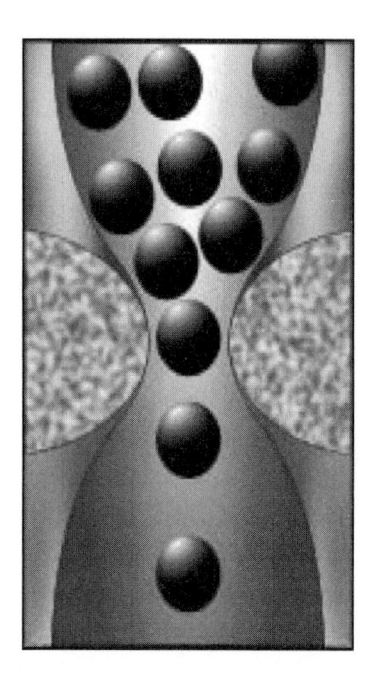

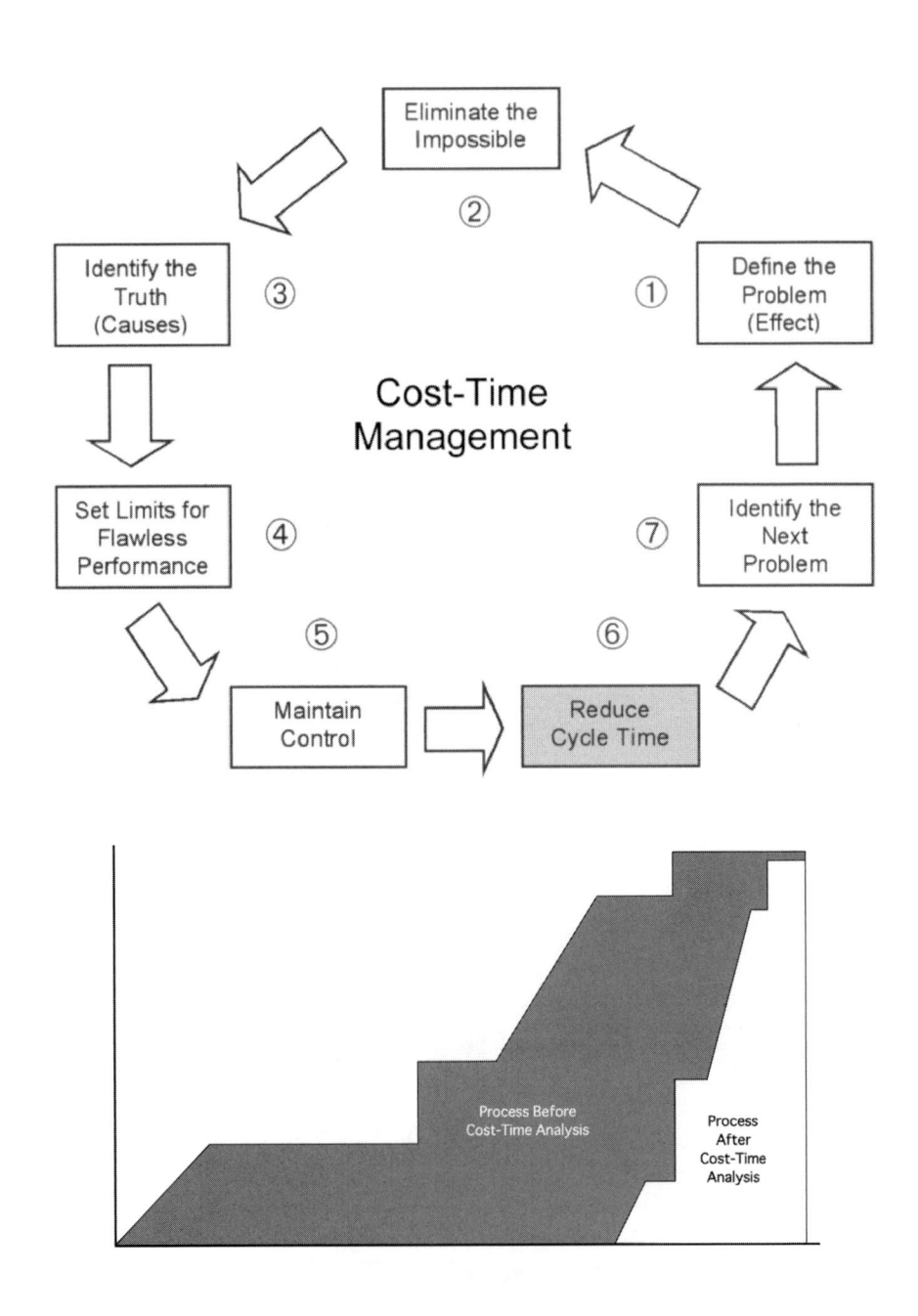

Cost-Time Management

① Define the Problem (Effect)
② Eliminate the Impossible
③ Identify the Truth (Causes)
④ Set Limits for Flawless Performance
⑤ Maintain Control
⑥ Reduce Cycle Time
⑦ Identify the Next Problem

Process Before Cost-Time Analysis

Process After Cost-Time Analysis

Chapter 14

Cost-Time Management

Concept and Expected Results:

At the same time Motorola used the Shainin® methods covered in this book to achieve 1000:1 quality improvement, and they were developing Six Sigma, Westinghouse was developing a cycle time reduction system. In 1988, both companies won the Malcolm Baldrige National Quality Award for their developments. Winning the award required them to teach other U.S. companies what they had done.

Westinghouse called its process for cycle time reduction Cost-Time Management. It taught this technique in workshops for several years after winning the Baldrige Award. In 1993, Westinghouse published a book by Jack H. Fooks about the technique, entitled *Profiles for Performance: Total Quality Methods for Reducing Cycle Time*. The Westinghouse workshops and that book are the original sources for the following overview of Cost-Time Management.

Cost-Time Management also uses half of Holmes' Top 10 Tips as the basis of its investigations. It starts by identifying what it is about the output that an organization's customers value, and it reasons backward through the activity to identify which parts of the activity generate that value. Everything that doesn't add value is waste. Holmes' relevant tips include

Reasoning Backward

"In solving a problem of this sort, the grand thing is to be able to reason backward. That is a very useful accomplishment, and a very easy one, but people do not practice it much. In the everyday affairs of life, it is more useful to reason forward, and so the other comes to be neglected. There are fifty who can reason synthetically for one who can reason analytically."

"Always approach a case with an absolutely blank mind. Form no theories, just simply observe and draw inferences from your observations." "It is a capital mistake to theorize before one has data. Insensibly one begins to twist facts to suit theories, instead of theories to suit facts."

"How dangerous it is to reason from insufficient data." "Data, Data, Data! I can't make bricks without clay."

"Detection is, or ought to be, an exact science, and should be treated in the same cold unemotional manner. When you attempt to tinge it with romanticism, you produce the same effect as if you worked a love story into the fifth proposition of Euclid."

"Nothing clears up a case so much as stating it to another person."

The heart of Cost-Time Management is the Cost-Time Profile. A Cost-Time Profile tracks the flow of cash over the cycle of a business process. Westinghouse used the concept at the Micro scale on individual products and processes, and at the Macro scale on plants, divisions, and the entire company.

At the Micro level, Westinghouse looked at the costs and cycle time for individual operations and discovered that virtually every process contains 50–99.9% dead time. There are huge opportunities to reduce cycle time and improve cash flow just by eliminating dead time. Westinghouse's initial objective was always to reduce cycle time by at least 50%. It found that doing so usually reduced costs by an additional 10-15% and reduced inventories as well.

At the Macro level, Westinghouse used Income Statement and Balance Sheet data to understand cash utilization. The Macro Cost-Time Profiles enabled Westinghouse to see the entire operation as inventory – both the obvious Visible Inventory in production operations and Invisible Inventory, the non-manufacturing office overhead. Best of all, the Macro Profiles gave Westinghouse a universal metric for comparing products, plants, and divisions to each other, so the company could make better resource allocation decisions.

This chapter provides a brief overview and some examples of Micro and Macro Cost-Time Profiles to show what is possible.

One final note is in order. The Shainin® methods Motorola used focused on defect reduction, but did not address cycle time reduction. The Westinghouse Cost-Time Management process focused on cycle time, but did not address defect reduction. The most successful companies do both. Companies can easily add any or all these tools to upgrade any existing improvement process. The most logical sequence is to add the defect reduction tools first for three reasons.

First, if a team shortens cycle time before eliminating defects, then the operation will just make defects faster.

Second, a series of defect reduction experiments usually delivers results in days to weeks, faster than a team can remove dead time from an operation. Eliminate defects first to make an impact quickly; then reduce cycle time.

Third, adding a few simple observation-based tools to the front end of any system is a fast and easy upgrade. Introduce the tools to an entire organization, and the workforce can quickly begin to deliver dramatic improvement. Both Motorola and Westinghouse were successful because they got everyone involved and taught them simple, powerful tools so they could solve problems effectively.

General Description:

Micro Cost-Time Profiles

The Micro Profile begins with a process flow chart. It can be a traditional linear flow chart that just links actions and decisions, or it can be a cross-functional flow chart that shows who does what. The

Reasoning Backward

cross-functional chart is more useful because it shows the handoffs and interactions that are often responsible for large amounts of dead time in an operation. The cross-functional flow chart begins to provide guidance about how to reduce cycle time.

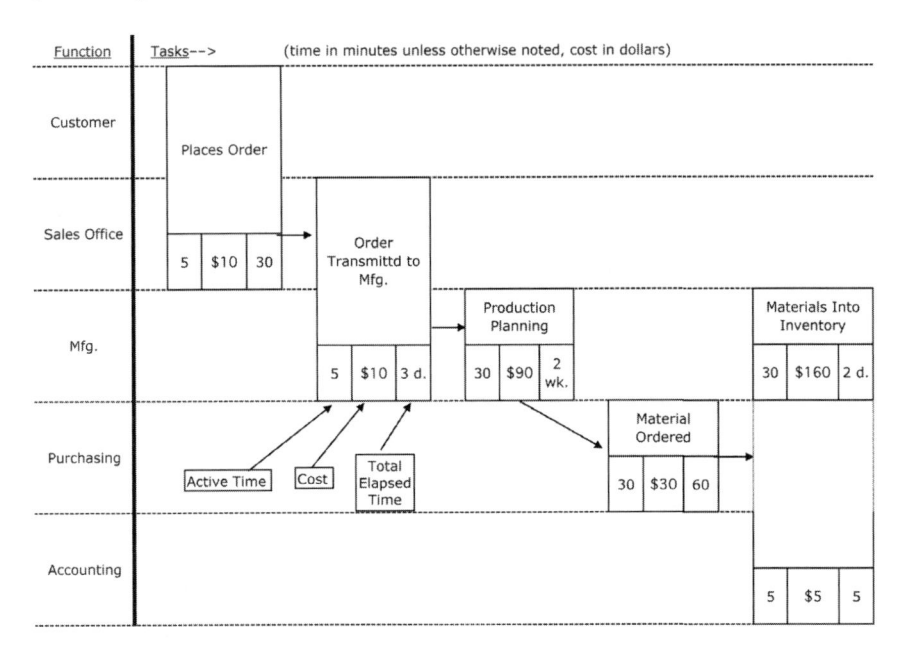

Function	Tasks-->	(time in minutes unless otherwise noted, cost in dollars)
Customer	Places Order	
Sales Office	5 | $10 | 30	Order Transmittd to Mfg.
Mfg.		5 | $10 | 3 d. 30 | $90 | 2 wk. Production Planning 30 | $160 | 2 d. Materials Into Inventory
Purchasing	Active Time | Cost | Total Elapsed Time	Material Ordered 30 | $30 | 60
Accounting		5 | $5 | 5

The second step involves answering three questions about each step in the operation.

1. How long is the active, hands-on time for this step?
2. How much does this step cost? (Include material consumption plus direct labor at the company's standard costing rate.)
3. How long is the total elapsed time for this step? (Start at the end of the active time of the previous step and count until the end of the active time on this step.)

Add these data to the process flow chart as shown in the example. Next, build a time line showing the total elapsed time and when the active time occurs within it.

Cost-Time Management

Micro Cost-Time Profile

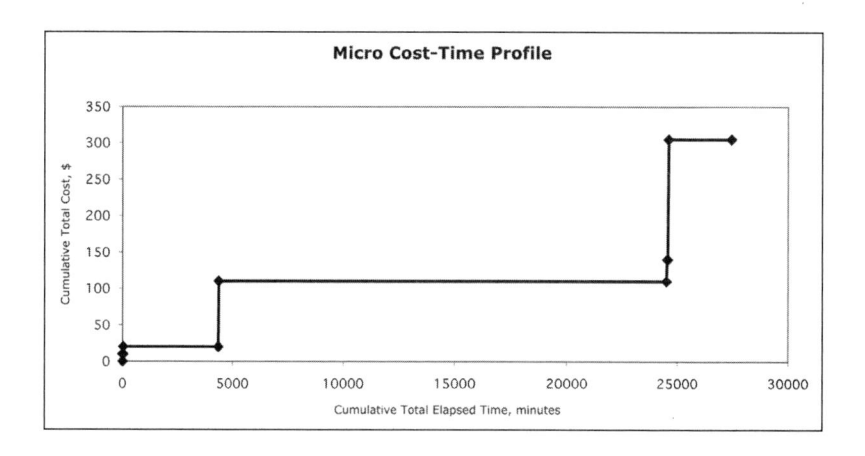

[Graph showing Cumulative Total Cost ($) on Y-axis (0–350) vs. Cumulative Total Elapsed Time, minutes on X-axis (0–30000). A step function starts near 0, rises to ~100 around 5000 minutes, remains flat until ~25000 minutes, then rises to ~300.]

Finally, construct a Micro Cost-Time Profile for the process by graphing Cumulative Cost on the Y-axis and Cumulative Total Elapsed Time on the X-axis, as shown below.

Micro Profiles contain three elements. Vertical lines (|) are material purchases, instantaneous expenditures of cash. Diagonal lines (/) are active, hands-on time. Horizontal lines (—) are dead time. The easiest way to address cycle time is to attack the horizontal lines.

In this example, there are 103 minutes of work spread over 19 days, 98.1% dead time on an 8-hour/day basis, or 99.6% dead time on a 24-hour/day basis.

There are three primary ways to attack a Micro Cost-Time Profile.

First, shorten cycle time, especially by eliminating dead time.

Second, to address costs, look at the steps with the greatest vertical displacement.

Third, the area under the curve is cash flow. Reduce the area to improve cash flow.

Many people believe this visual picture of cash flow is the most powerful aspect of the Micro Cost-Time Profile. It becomes the basis for comparing different activities and products for their impact on the business now, and how that could change in the future when improvements occur.

Reasoning Backward

Macro Cost-Time Profiles

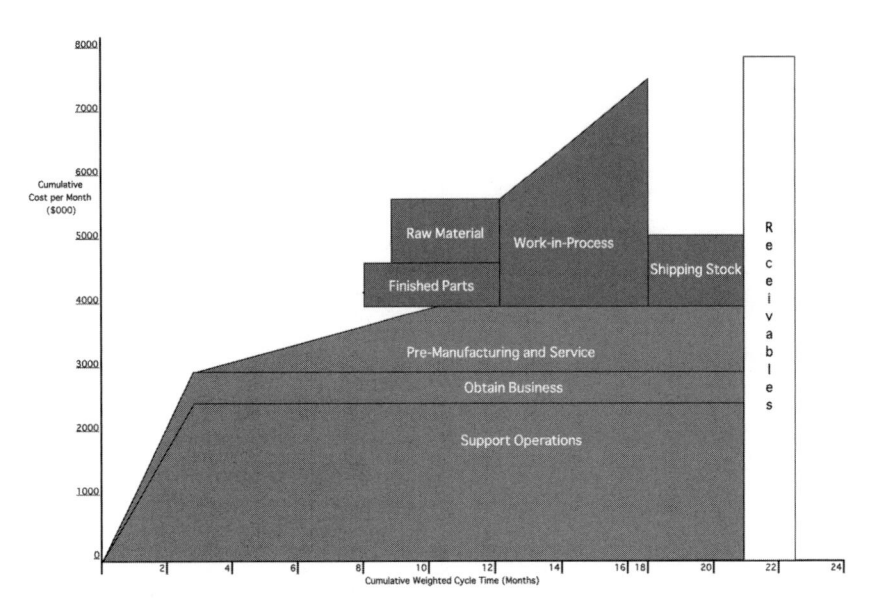

The Micro Profile looks at individual processes and measures costs per unit, costs per operation, and cycle time. The Macro Profile combines all these data for every operation in a business or division. It uses itemized Income Statement data to create a cash flow picture of the entire business unit, as shown in the generic Macro Profile.

The dark gray areas of the Profile are the on-going overhead operations that Westinghouse named Invisible Inventory. Note that in this generic example Invisible Inventory consumes 50% of sales revenue.

The medium gray areas are Visible Inventory from the manufacturing operations. The height of each box is the amount of cash per month tied up in each resource. The width of each box shows how many months supply is in inventory. The diagonal portion of Work-in-Process is direct factory labor. This model assumes direct labor is a variable cost, just like traditional accounting systems do.

Finally, the light gray region on the right is Accounts Receivable. The height of the box shows the monthly revenue. The width shows the average receivables days outstanding for business.

Cost-Time Management

There are four steps to creating a Macro Profile.

1. Gather the business data.
2. Develop a flow model of the business.
3. Create the Macro Profile from the flow model and the data.
4. Validate the data to assure the flow model and breakdown of resources are accurate. The following example shows the Income Statement data and flow model for the preceding generic Macro Profile.

	Total ($000)	A Support Operations	B Obtain Business	C Pre-Mfg. Or Svc.	D Mfg. Material	E Mfg. Labor	F Sales & Revenue	G Collect Receivables
Sales Revenues	7880						7880	7880
Transport Cost	94	94						
Sales Compensa	79	79						
Labor Direct Cos	783					783		
Material Direct C	1670				1670			
Factory Expense	660					660		
Cust. Order Dev	125			125				
Eng'g. Contracts	719			719				
Product Warrant	50		50					
Other	371		371					
Manufacturing	437					437		
Engineering	180			180				
Marketing	385		385					
Admin & Genera	474	474						
Other	223	223						
Strategic Mngd.	358	358						
R & D	44	44						
Depreciation & L	423	423						
Ins., Tax, Holida	190	190						
Inv.Chng Eff on	9	9						
HQ Selling Costs	106			106				
Corp Mngd Cost:	158	158						
Total Cost of Sal	7538							
Operating Profit	342							
a) Total Cost; Revenue		2473	491	1024	1670	1880	7880	7880
b) Weighted Cycle Time (Mo.)		0	3	8	10		-	1.5
c) Cumulative Cost; Revenue		2473	2964	3988	5658	7538	7880	7880
d) Cum. Wtd. Cycle Time (Mo.)		3	3	11	21		21	22.5

Customer Needs → Obtain Business → Pre-Mfg. Or Service → Mfg. → Collect Receivables

Support Operations

The last data needed to create the Macro Profile are the cycle times for each step in the business flow, which create the X-axis of the Profile. In the end, the Profile shows the cash outlay per month over the life of the business cycle. It provides an easy-to-understand picture of the business that can show management the largest opportunities to improve the business.

Reasoning Backward

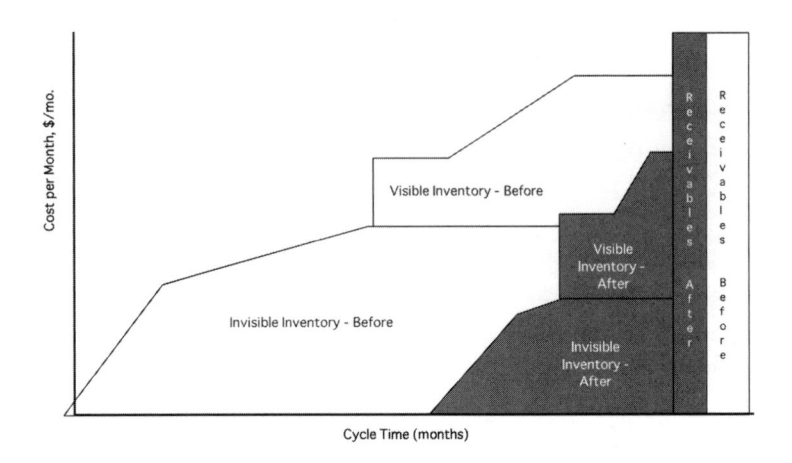

As with the Micro Cost-Time Profile, the goals of any business are to improve cash flow (reduce the area under the curve), and increase profits (increase the gap between the top of the cost boxes and the top of the receivables box.) The Macro Profile is a simple visual tool for seeing how different parts of the business are contributing to the overall success of the company.

In the final chart, a long cycle time, low profit, and long average receivables business (the light gray area) improved all aspects of the operation to become a short cycle time, high profit, and short average receivables operation (the dark gray area). This change reduced the cash demands of the business by about two-thirds.

Summary:

- Dorian Shainin gave everyone simple, powerful tools for defect elimination that build on Sir Francis Bacon and Sherlock Holmes' methods, but his tools ignore cycle time reduction.
- Westinghouse used Bacon and Holmes' reasoning backward strategy to reduce cycle time while ignoring defect reduction.
- Cost-Time Management provides an easy-to-understand visual tool for understanding cycle time and how resources

are committed in any process, plant, division, or to an entire business.
- Its strength is its ability to clearly show where dead time is hurting a business's cash flow.
- The Micro Profile clearly identifies the cycle time and cash flow improvement opportunities in individual processes, which creates a roadmap for process improvement.
- The Macro Profile provides the same insights at the business unit level, which leads to a roadmap for business improvement.
- Cost-Time Management complements defect elimination, which is why it is part of this book. Eliminate defects first, and then reduce cycle time to achieve maximum advantage.

The fundamental lesson is **most activities are at least 90% dead time. A good goal for any activity is to reduce the total cycle time of any activity to no more than twice the active time. (<50% total dead time)** The Cost-Time Profile shows where to focus to achieve this goal.

Cost-Time Management
to eliminate dead time and reduce cycle time
after defects have been eliminated from a process

Objective:

Dorian Shainin maximized the effectiveness of processes by tightening control to eliminate the root causes of defects. Cost-Time Management maximizes the efficiency of a process by eliminating dead time, reducing cycle time, and improving cash flow in order to increase profitability. One can apply Cost-Time to any process at any time, but for maximum impact, eliminate defective outcomes first because this is normally achieved in days to weeks. Then, examine the now-flawless process for opportunities to reduce cycle time. Reducing cycle time first, before eliminating defects, simply causes the process to generate more defects faster.

Cost-Time Management works at two different levels. Micro Cost-Time Management is applicable to individual processes. Macro Cost-Time Management focuses on entire plants, divisions, businesses, or corporations to examine the cash flow and cash conversion efficiency of the overall operation. This discussion focuses on the Micro level to maximize process efficiency after the defect reduction tools have maximized process effectiveness.

Procedure:
- Identify the process to be studied.
- Select a cross-functional investigation team of people who know how the process actually works, not just how it should work.
- Begin by identifying the expected outcome of the process and everything that customers value about this outcome.
- Next, create a Cross-functional Process Flowchart of the process. Begin by asking, "What happens first in the process, and who does that?" Show the Who in a box in a column on

Cost-Time Management

the left side of the paper. Show the What in a box to the right of the Who box.
- Then ask, "What happens next, and Who does that?" Show the Who in a box beneath the Who of the first task if it is a different person or function. Put the What on the appropriate line, connected to the first task with an arrow showing the flow of the operation.
- Continue by asking, "What happens next, and Who does that?" until the process is complete. Show tasks in boxes and decisions in diamonds as in other flowcharting methods.
- For each step in the process, ask,
  - "Does this step add value for customers?"
  - "Does it add value for our company?"
  - "Is it included in order to comply with some legal or regulatory requirement?"
- If the answers are all "No", then this step is a candidate for elimination to reduce cost. Highlight it on the flowchart.
- Gather cost and time data on every step in the process. Ask three questions:
  - **How much active (hands-on) time does this step require?**
  - **How much does this step cost? (Labor cost of the active time, materials, equipment time.)**
  - **How long is the total elapsed time for this step, including all the dead time until the next step begins.**

- Display these three data points for each step on the Cross-functional Process Flowchart.
- Create a data table for these data in order to construct a Cost-Time Profile of the process. An automated Excel spreadsheet is available that creates the Cost-Time Profile automatically from this data.
- Create the Cost-Time Profile. Plot Cumulative Cost on the Y-axis versus Cumulative Total Elapsed Time on the X-axis. The Profile will consist of three different kinds of lines.
  - Diagonal lines (/) are active, hands-on time.

- Vertical lines (|) are material purchases, instantaneous costs.
- Horizontal lines (–) are dead time.

Begin to search for cost and time reduction opportunities, including:
- Dead time (Usually 85-99% of a process is dead time. A reasonable goal is 50%, so that total process time is no longer than twice the active time.)
- Redundancies in the process
- Approvals – they do not add value to the outcome
- Any other steps that do not add value, such as inspections, scrap, rework, etc.

Analyze the Cost-Time Profile in three ways.
- Slice the Profile vertically to see time saving opportunities, especially dead time.
- Slice the Profile horizontally to see significant cost saving opportunities.
- The area under the profile is the cash flow demand of the process. Look for ways to shrink the area under the profile to improve cash flow.

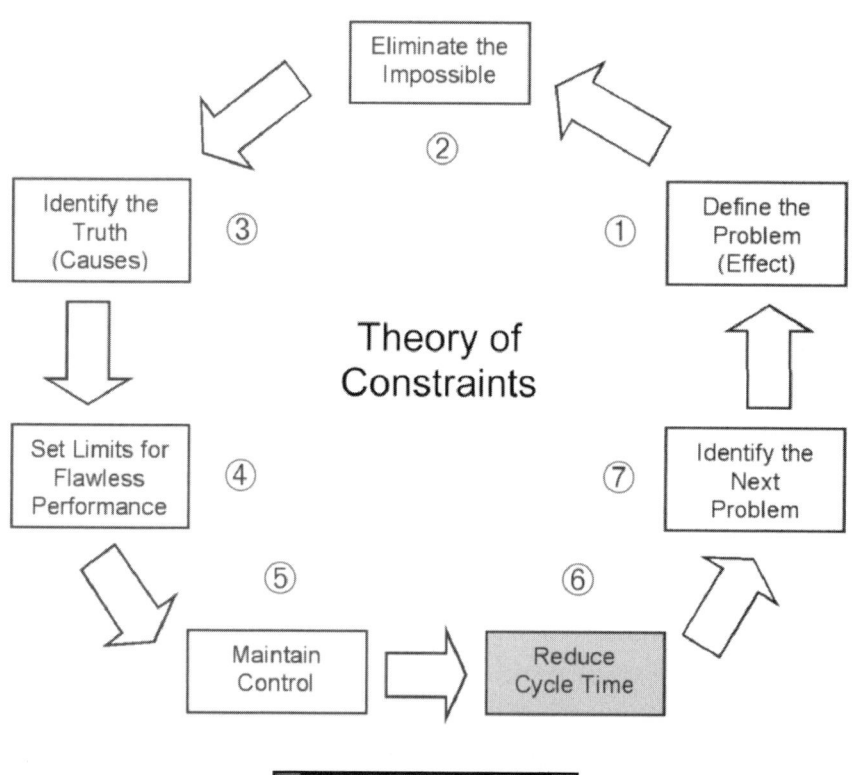

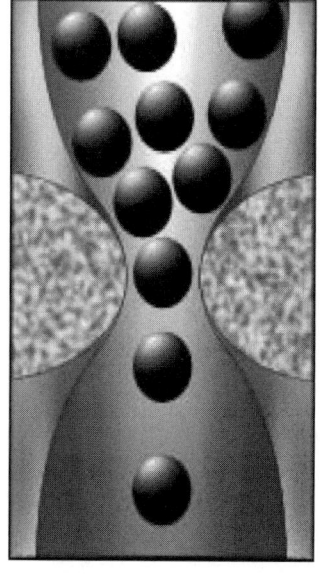

Theory of Constraints

① Define the Problem (Effect)

② Eliminate the Impossible

③ Identify the Truth (Causes)

④ Set Limits for Flawless Performance

⑤ Maintain Control

⑥ Reduce Cycle Time

⑦ Identify the Next Problem

Chapter 15

The Theory of Constraints

Concept and Expected Results:

During the 1980s, the late Dr. Eliyahu Goldratt developed the Theory of Constraints (TOC) and introduced it to the world in his 1984 landmark book, *The Goal*. He used the analogy of a scout troop on a hike to introduce the constraint concept.

The scouts start out together, but quickly get spread out as some of the boys in front get out ahead of one boy in the middle, the slowest hiker, Herbie. All the other boys are jammed up behind Herbie because they want to go faster. After a few stops and starts, when the spread reoccurs each time, the troop starts to make some changes to increase the speed of the troop, so they can reach their campsite before dark. First, they shift some of Herbie's load to other scouts, so he can go faster. This helps because the lead scouts do not get as far ahead, but the troop is still spreading out along the trail. The breakthrough in thinking comes when they decide to make Herbie's pace the pace for the entire troop. They use a long rope as the tool to regulate everyone's pace. Each scout grabs the rope, and the boys set out together. Herbie's pace determines how fast the rope advances, which is the overall progress of the troop. Faster boys in front of Herbie or and behind him can speed up and slow down only as much as the rope allows. This plan keeps Herbie moving all the time, and the troop reaches the campsite on time, determined by Herbie's pace.

Theory of Constraints

This scout troop is the model of manufacturing or paperwork processes in a business. Every process is a series of steps, each represented by a scout. The speed of each scout corresponds to the capacity of each step in the business process. The speed of the whole troop (and the rope once they started using it) corresponds to the overall capacity of the business process. Herbie is the constraint of the troop – it can go no faster than he can go. In the same way, the lowest capacity step in a business process determines the overall capacity of the operation. This model leads to a new way of managing processes.

In the business world, TOC starts with the fundamental goal of all businesses, to make more money, now and in the future. Businesses accomplish that goal by simultaneously Increasing Throughput (Margin), Decreasing Operating Expenses, and Decreasing Inventory.

The principle metric for any business is profit per year (assuming it has positive cash flow). TOC directly links profit per year to profit per hour for every product, every customer, every process, and every business unit. It leads managers to make decisions based on the one resource that is always limited, time.

For any activity, there is always one step that is the constraint, or bottleneck. The overall capacity of the activity cannot be any greater than the capacity of the constraint.

For example, if one step in the activity can turn out 100 units per hour, and every other step in the process can turn out between 150 and 200 units per hour, the total capacity of the activity is only 100 units per hour. Common sense dictates the constraint must be kept running at all times. Any down time on the constraint is capacity lost to that step and to the entire process forever.

While this concept is easy to understand and accept, most people have a much harder time with the conclusion that follows. Consider the foreman who is in charge of one of the stations that can operate at 200 units per hour, but the overall capacity of the whole activity is limited to 100 units per hour by another station. How should he run his equipment?

If management is measuring efficiency according to traditional "cost per unit" metrics for each individual station, then he is expected to run at full capacity of 200 units/hour to minimize cost/unit. However, what happens to the overall system? In one hour, this foreman's activity generates 100 pieces that end up moving ahead to become finished product, plus another 100 pieces that increase inventory costs and reduce profitability. Is there a better alternative?

To keep the flow balanced, this foreman should run his station just 30 minutes per hour and let the equipment sit idle for the other 30 minutes. While this is obviously the right answer for the business's bottom line, it is not what traditional accounting and management practices dictate.

Conventional theory teaches that optimizing each individual operation optimizes the total system. The Theory of Constraints teaches that optimizing ONLY the constraints optimizes the overall system. The system's constraints must control the utilization of the non-constraints. TOC guides a business to different, better solutions.

General Description:

The Theory of Constraints uses five steps to improve any activity.

- **Identify the system's constraint.**
- **Exploit the constraint.**
- **Subordinate all non-constraints to the constraint.**
- **Elevate the constraint.**
- **After the constraint has been removed, start over at Step 1 with no carry over assumptions.**

Identify the system's constraint. Every process has one constraint – the one operation with lower capacity than every other operation in the process. In the scout troop, this was Herbie. The first step is to identify this constraint. In many business situations, it will be the operation with the biggest amount of inventory stacked up in front of it. This could be parts inventory, or where paperwork stacks up, waiting for approvals or data entry. If the process uses expediters, they will have a good idea which operation is the constraint – the one that gets most of their attention. The capacity of the constraint limits the overall capacity of the process.

Exploit the constraint. Do anything that will enable the constraint to produce more good output. When the scouts lightened Herbie's load so he could walk faster, the entire troop could move faster. In business situations, add an extra shift on the constrained operation. Stagger coffee breaks so this equipment is never idle. When model changeover requires downtime on the constrained equipment, complete as much of the changeover activity offline to minimize the actual time the equipment is down. Determine if other equipment or resources can absorb some of the load to expand the capacity of the constraint. Explore ways to shorten the active time and eliminate dead time on the equipment as much as possible. Be creative. Every boost in the constraint's capacity increases the overall capacity of the entire system.

Subordinate all non-constraint operations to the constraint. This is the hardest step for most organizations. In the scout troop, the rope subordinated everyone else's pace to Herbie's pace. In business situations, every manager's scorecard has historically been efficiency, the "cost per unit" of his or her operation, which requires every manager to generate as much outcome per hour as possible. In Theory of Constraints, that metric is only appropriate for the constraint. All other operations must run inefficiently, producing at lower than capacity levels, to minimize inventories. Their metrics must change to focus on never starving the constraint and keeping inventories low. Everyone's goal shifts away from optimizing individual operations to optimizing the overall flow of the entire process.

Elevate the constraint. If all the activities to exploit the constraint are inadequate to eliminate the constraint, then as a last resort, and only if the market demand will support it, invest in new equipment or old equipment that can provide additional capacity at a lower cost. Make the constraint operation cease to be the constraint.

Reasoning Backward

When that occurs, some other operation in the process will become the new constraint in the system.

Once the old constraint is no longer a constraint, go back to Step 1 and take a completely fresh look at the system. Some assumptions that were valid before will have changed. Begin again with no pre-conceived notions. Find the new constraint, exploit the new constraint, subordinate all the non-constraints, and elevate the new constraint. Product mix decisions often change once a new constraint starts to dominate an operation.

Time Profiling

One visual tool for understanding constraints and cycle time is the Time Profile, a variation of the Cost-Time Profile. It starts with a flow chart of the complete process that includes four pieces of data:

- What happens in this step?
- Who does it?
- How long does it take? (Active, hands-on time)
- How long is the total elapsed time for this step? (Active hands-on time plus dead time)

Use the first two pieces of data to construct a Cross-functional Flow Chart as shown. Then, add the Active Time and Total Elapsed Time data for each step to the box on the flow chart. Finally, use the time data to construct a Time Profile by plotting Active Time on Y-axis and Total Elapsed Time on the X-axis as shown.

The power of the Time Profile is the insight it provides into the amount of Dead Time in the current operation and its impact on overall productivity. In this example, just 8% of the cycle time is Active Time. (Remember from Cost-Time Management that a reasonable target is 50% of the cycle to be Active Time.) The time spent when nothing is happening is excess Inventory in the system. The Time Profile shows where excess Inventory is stacking up in the process, increasing costs, lengthening cycle time, reducing

Theory of Constraints

productivity, and hurting cash flow. The easiest way to improve a process is to eliminate Dead Time, which reduces Inventory and shortens Cycle Time, which in turn increases Productivity.

Task	Active Time, minutes	Elapsed Time, minutes	Cumulative Elapsed Time, minutes	Cumulative Active Time, minutes
Release Material	0	0	0	0
In Queue for Step 1	0	0	0	0
Step 1	60	60	60	60
In Queue for Step 2	0	180	240	60
Step 2	240	240	480	300
In Queue for Step 3	0	2880	3360	300
Step 3	120	120	3480	420
In Queue for Step 4	0	4320	7800	420
Step 4	12	12	7812	432
In Queue for Step 5	0	240	8052	432
Step 5	600	600	8652	1032
In Queue for Step 6	0	4320	12972	1032
Step 6		0	12972	1032
In Queue for Step 7	0		12972	1032
Step 7		0	12972	1032
In Queue for Step 8	0		12972	1032
Step 8		0	12972	1032
In Queue for Step 9	0		12972	1032
Step 9		0	12972	1032
In Queue for Step 10	0		12972	1032
Step 10		0	12972	1032

Percent Dead Time   92.0%

Function	Tasks-->	(time in minutes unless otherwise noted, cost in dollars)

Customer: Log and Stamp Order

Sales Office: 60 | $50 | 240 — Check Order

Mfg.: 240 | $200 | 2 d. — Resolve Discrepancy 120 | $100 | 3 d. — Engineer Customer Order 600 | $500 | 3 d.

Purchasing: Active Time | Cost | Total Elapsed Time — Enter Order in Database 12 | $10 | 240

Accounting: 5 | $5 | 5

267

Reasoning Backward

Once an investigator has identified the constraint in the operation, the Time Profile helps guide optimization. The two keys to overall productivity are keeping the constraint fully utilized, which runs the whole operation at the pace dictated by the constraint. The third element of TOC is to keep a small buffer of inventory just ahead of the constraint, so it is never starved for input. All other steps in the process can operate with no buffer, no wasted inventory. The Time Profile guides this improvement activity.

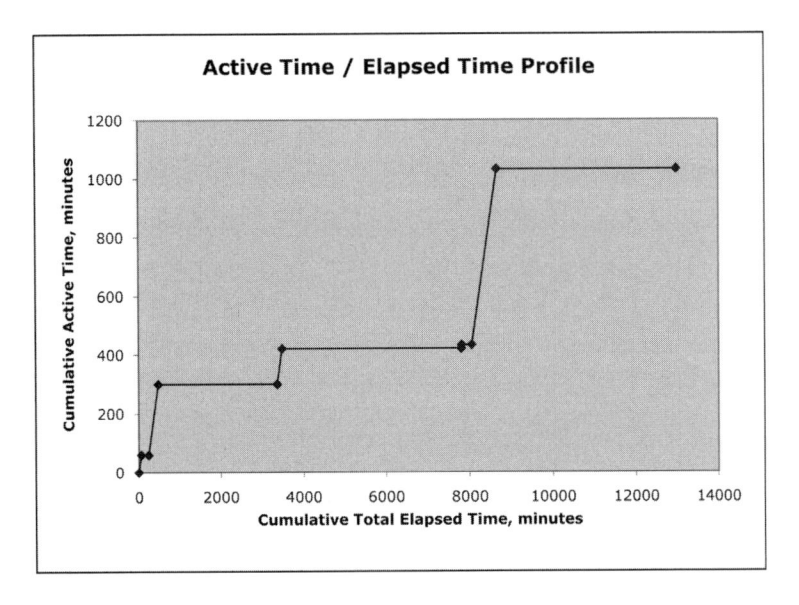

Summary:

The conflict between the traditional Cost per Unit approach and the Theory of Constraints is partially a result of when each system was developed.

The Cost per Unit, efficiency-based management approach comes from the early 20th century, when direct labor was a variable cost that contributed over 50% of the total cost to make a product. Laborers were hired or laid off depending on product demand. Today's accounting systems originated at that time, when management focused on the labor cost per piece. Overhead costs were less than 5% of a business's costs, and accounting systems treated them all as an add-on factor, a fraction of the direct labor cost.

Today, direct labor has become a fixed cost, not variable, and it usually accounts for only 5-10% of the total cost of a product. Overhead is now more than 50% of the cost of a product. Direct labor is only a variable cost when a company hires temporary workers for a specific job and lays them off when the job is finished. Now that labor is a fixed cost, it no longer matters whether people are busy or not, as long as the constraint is operating at full capacity. This is the hardest lesson for most people to accept, even after their logical brains know it is true. Emotionally, we are so conditioned to stay busy that we feel uncomfortable and at risk if we are idle, even when we know being idle is the right thing to do.

The fundamental lesson is to **treat cycle time as the second dimension of problem solving.** The previous tools addressed the elimination of defects to increase productivity, wasting less material and saving the time spent creating scrap. TOC addresses productivity by shortening cycle time, which increases capacity and reduces the cost of each item produced. A fully optimized system uses both approaches.

The second key learning from TOC is to **think globally**. Conventional thinking optimizes each individual step to optimize the whole system by optimizing its individual parts, but in reality, this will always sub-optimize the total operation. True optimization only occurs when people realize the flow rate of the entire operation is dictated by its constraint. First, they identify the constraint in the system. Then, they fully utilize it, share its workload if possible, and determine if its cycle time can be reduced. Finally, they subordinate the other operations to the constraint in order to maximize the capacity and productivity of the entire process. This logic applies everywhere. Learning to think this way will create both long-term and short-term benefits for anyone.

Reasoning Backward

One Final Note on the Merits of Cost-Time Management vs. Theory of Constraints

Cost-Time Management is a product of the conventional accounting system. It inaccurately treats direct labor as a variable cost in Micro Profiles, which only allows the analyst to see its small contribution to total cost. Nonetheless, Cost-Time Management is still useful, even in a company that uses Theory of Constraints.

For example, the Micro Cost-Time Profiles show where the dead time is in both constraint steps and non-constraint steps. It is shows where to focus to improve the constraint steps, and how to manage dead time to reduce inventories throughout the system. Its ability to visually present cash flow is valuable in either approach. The power of Cost-Time Management is not the absolute precision of the Cost-Time Profile. Profiles are always approximations. The power is the insight Cost-Time Management delivers about where and how to improve a system. These insights are valuable in both management systems.

Theory of Constraints requires new metrics that derive from the global performance of the system. In today's world, it is a more effective way to manage a business. It would be possible to modify the traditional Cost-Time Profile Tool to show direct labor as a fixed cost, the same way that it treats Invisible Inventory now, but valuable insights would be lost. It is much more useful to adapt the Cost-Time Profile to TOC by removing the cost element of labor and material, and simply considering active time and total elapsed time for each step. Then the Time Profile enables the analyst to see visually all the critical improvement opportunities:

- Dead time in front of non-constraints, which is excess inventory
- Dead time in front of constraints, which creates a desirable buffer that the analyst can now see and begin to manage
- Impact of eliminating dead time vs. impact of shortening active time when reducing overall cycle time

- Relative importance of different improvement alternatives on increasing capacity and improving productivity

Both approaches are valuable to a business, but the specifics will depend upon the situation. Just as different defect elimination tools are appropriate for different situations, using both these very different tools for cycle time reduction provide better guidance than just one. Recall that looking at a problem from a different perspective is one of the powerful strategies for effective problem solving. Seeing the operation from these two opposing perspectives leads to better insights into the operation and the possibilities. Both Cost-Time Management and Theory of Constraints have delivered very impressive results in the past. Both are valuable upgrades for any system that has never addressed cycle time issues before, or as a precursor to implementing Lean techniques.

Chapter 16

Solving Organizational Problems
Adapting the Tools to Solve Complex Problems Within and Between Organizations

Concept and Expected Results:

The previous chapters covered individual tools applied in different situations. The case study problem in Chapter 13 required a series of these tools to discover the fundamental root cause of a physical problem and eliminate it, like peeling back the layers of an onion. A similar systematic approach with these tools also works for complex problems inside large organizations and between companies in a supply chain. However, it requires two additional tools to deal with this extra complexity. This chapter introduces these two tools and the entire process.

Organizational problems occur within companies because each function involved in an activity tries to optimize its own operation independent of the other functions. This internal focus within each function is the problem. Recall that the traditional management and accounting systems in Chapter 14 use this paradigm. Optimizing each of the parts always sub-optimizes the whole. This is the essence of organizational problems.

The Theory of Constraints from Chapter 15 uses the opposite paradigm. TOC recognizes that optimizing the individual functions automatically sub-optimizes the performance of the entire system. TOC focuses on optimizing the overall flow of the entire operation.

Solving Organizational Problems

It identifies and optimizes the constraints to maximize the throughput of the entire system. Non-constraints operate at less than full capacity to minimize inventories while keeping the constraint satisfied at all times. Scorecards for each function change to reflect overall productivity.

Supply chain management adds another dimension because the different functions are inside different companies, not simply different departments inside the same company.

Organizational problems arise because companies are using the traditional functional optimization paradigm in a world where global optimization is critical, and no one is managing the flow between functions.

In 1991, Geary Rummler and Alan Brache introduced the concept of "White Space" in an organization. An organization chart or a supply chain drawing shows a number of different functions separated by white space. Managers in each area focus on their individual area, but no one manages the flow between areas, the white space on the chart. This chapter addresses the white space and provides the tools to fix the problems that arise because different functions or companies are involved.

The problem solving process for these complex organizational problems includes four phases.

1. Apply White Space Management principles to establish a common definition of the problem, the functions involved, and the relationships between the functions.
2. Apply Multi-Vari or Paired Comparisons to the operation to document the occurrence of the problem. Look for patterns, categories, frequency, and consistent differences between good and bad performance.
3. Prioritize the causes by importance, not by Pareto. In the previous chapters, Pareto's Law determined importance – the cause that was responsible for the greatest number of defects was the most important cause. In organizational problems, the guideline is different. Causes are of primary,

secondary, or tertiary importance. Primary causes are most important, like the base of a 3-level pyramid, and must be addressed first. Secondary causes are the middle layer of the pyramid, and receive attention after the primary causes have been resolved. Tertiary causes are the cap of the pyramid. Address them only after the primary and secondary causes are resolved. A variation of Failure Modes and Effects Analysis (FMEA) can be a useful tool for this assessment, especially with Multi-Vari.
4. Develop systemic solutions for the causes, beginning with the primary level causes. Fixing tertiary problems first is like rearranging the deck chairs on the Titanic. The overall impact will be minimal at best. Fix Fundamentals First.

This chapter includes two case study examples taken from the automotive industry that demonstrate the power of this approach.

The first example uses Multi-Vari to determine categories of failure in a shipping problem involving many different parts from many different suppliers to many different plants. The team identified one primary cause and two secondary causes. When they resolved the causes in order of importance, the problem disappeared. Then, they repeated the process on other problems in the system.

The second case study uses Paired Comparisons on a metal stamping operation to identify consistent differences between a company's non-competitive stamping operations and the world's most cost effective operation. The study found four systemic causes – two primary and two secondary – that limited the company's performance. The study also provided a plan for becoming globally competitive. It showed how small improvements were possible by making small changes, but that fundamental paradigms had to change before the company could compete with the best.

Solving Organizational Problems

Manage the White Space

The first step is to understand all the functions, departments, and companies involved in the operation and their roles. Create a graphic that shows them as separate entities. This is analogous to the view you would have if you flew over a farm with many silos. Managing the white spaces means understand the flow and relationships between the silos and optimizing the flow of the entire operation. This assessment reveals where work occurs, where there are redundancies and gaps, and where conflicting perceptions are contributing to the problem.

Next, understand each function's perception of the problem. Different perceptions are common in most organizational problems, especially when organizations optimize each part of the operation independently. The first step to solving complex organizational problems is for everyone to agree on a common definition of the problem.

Document the Problem

Once everyone agrees on the problem, it is time to observe its occurrence using one of two tools.

Use Multi-Vari to understand what happens when an operation works well, and when it fails. Count the number of failures for some time. Observe patterns and establish categories that describe "Like Events" and the Critical Functions that failed in each case. The largest categories are clues, but remember that Pareto is not the determinant as in the previous examples. Use the largest categories to determine the primary, secondary and tertiary causes, covered in the next section.

Use Paired Comparisons if you can compare your non-competitive operation to a best-in-class operation. Look for consistent differences between your operation and best in class. The consistent differences will guide you to the systemic changes necessary to close the gap, starting with the primary causes.

Rank the Categories and Consistent Differences by Importance

Variations of two traditional tools are useful for moving from the failure data to causes and determining the importance of each cause. The two traditional tools are Failure Mode and Effect Analysis (FMEA) and 5 Whys. The modified version of FMEA may be most useful with the Multi-Vari data, while a variation of 5 Whys may work better with the Paired Comparison data. The two case studies demonstrate both methods. When looking at your own data, consider both tools and choose the one that fits your situation best.

Assume you have a complex, multi-function operation or a supply chain problem that sometimes performs as planned, and sometimes fails to meet expectations. First, identify all the functions involved in the operation and come to agreement on the definition of the problem. Then, observe the operation and track all failures for some time. Next, apply Multi-Vari to the failure data to create categories of "like failures". At this point, either modified FMEA or 5 Whys might work.

Traditional FMEA first estimates the Severity of a failure, the likelihood of its Occurrence, and how easy it is to Detect. It creates a number scale for each with high severity, high likelihood of occurrence, and hard to detect all having the highest number value. The product of multiplying these values together gives estimated relative importance.

Traditional FMEA is a useful planning tool that forces people to think through different scenarios so they develop better plans. However, it has two significant weaknesses, the second being a result of the first. First, it uses people's perceptions and estimates, rather than hard data. Second, no one can ever think of everything, and if they did, it could take years to complete the exercise. FMEA is a good thinking exercise, but it is rarely exhaustive.

Both these weaknesses go away when you can use hard data on failures. First, the likelihood of Occurrence factor goes away because the failures have all occurred. The Detection scale shifts to measure where and when in the operation the failure was detected. If detection is immediate, the score is low. When the customer finds it, the score is high. Severity addresses impact, ease to correct, and ease to prevent.

The advantage of this modified version of FMEA is its use of hard data, not hypothetical scenarios. FMEA using real data is a powerful decision making tool. It provides accurate insight into which causes are most important and must be addressed first.

Now, consider a different situation. Assume you have a process that is non-competitive in the marketplace. It is the best you know how to do, but your competitors have a large cost advantage. The critical comparison is not your best vs. your worst, but your best vs. the best in the world. Paired Comparisons reveals the consistent differences between your process and the best process. Now, a series of "Why does this difference exist?" questions reveals the systemic issues that must be resolved to become competitive. It may take more or less than five whys to find the fundamental issue. Finally, determine the relative importance of each issue, so you resolve the primary issues first.

Fixing the Problem

The last step is acting to eliminate the fundamental issues. Sometimes this is an easy correction, as in the first case study. Some issues are rooted in management and labor paradigms that are much harder to change, as in the second example. In these situations, this approach to the complex problem provides a compelling argument for what changes are necessary, and why. The second case study provides examples of both easy and very difficult changes.

Reasoning Backward

Introduction to the Case Studies

The first example is a shipping problem among parts and component suppliers and an automotive OEM. It involved many external suppliers and several different functions with overlapping responsibilities within the OEM organization. Planning called for full truckload shipments, but quite often not everything would fit on the truck. Small, expensive, expedited shipments were necessary to achieve on-time delivery. The extra cost was over $1 million per year.

This project used Multi-Vari with the modified FMEA approach because the company was only interested in the cases where the process had failed. They first agreed on the definition of the problem and then tracked shipments for four months. They observed 652 failures and used these data to identify "like events". Then, they used the modified FMEA approach to identify the fundamental issues. Finally, they identified and addressed one easy primary issue and two secondary issues that solved the problem completely.

The second example is the metal stamping process for auto body panels. It is common to all automotive OEMs, but the Japanese producers at the time had a dramatic cost advantage over the American producers. The challenge was to learn what caused the gap, and more importantly, how to close it.

This project used the Paired Comparisons with the 5 Whys tool. The issue was not "How do we work within our paradigm to optimize our performance?" The critical question was, "What is different about our paradigm and the Japanese paradigm that gives them such an advantage?" This process identified the consistent differences between the two operations, and then asked why each difference existed. The series of whys led back to the policies and procedures that were limiting performance. It identified two primary causes and two secondary causes that were preventing the American OEMs from being competitive. This gave management a clear plan for making improvement, including a quantitative understanding of the impact of each action.

Solving Organizational Problems

Example 1 – The Shipping Problem

An American automotive OEM receives shipments of hundreds of parts and components from dozens of suppliers everyday. All its planning and scheduling efforts aim for full truckload deliveries to minimize shipping costs. However, many times trucks arrive with incomplete amounts, so suppliers have to expedite some parts to meet the on-time delivery requirements, which adds over $1 million per year of extra costs.

In addition to dozens of suppliers, five different functions within the OEM organization are involved as well. These include Material Handling Engineering, Scheduling, Logistics, Material Control Operations, and Production Material Control. Furthermore, suppliers sometimes ship to a Consolidation Center, and sometimes they ship directly to an assembly plant. A final level of complexity arises because some shipments are direct from just one supplier, while others are "milk runs", when one truck stops at several suppliers and picks up partial loads until the truck is full. Milk run trucks can go either to the Consolidation Center or to one of the assembly plants directly.

The first step was to identify all the functions involved in the operation, and then to create a graphic picture of this network, as shown on the next page.

Next, everyone agreed on the problem being solved. It was the situations where an expedited partial shipment was necessary to complete delivery of parts that had been scheduled for delivery in full truckloads. They knew from experience that this was a problem with all suppliers, with both milk runs and direct shipments, with shipments to the Consolidation Center, and with direct shipments to the assembly plants. Therefore, they designed a Multi-Vari experiment that would track all shipments for four months and record all occurrences of the problem.

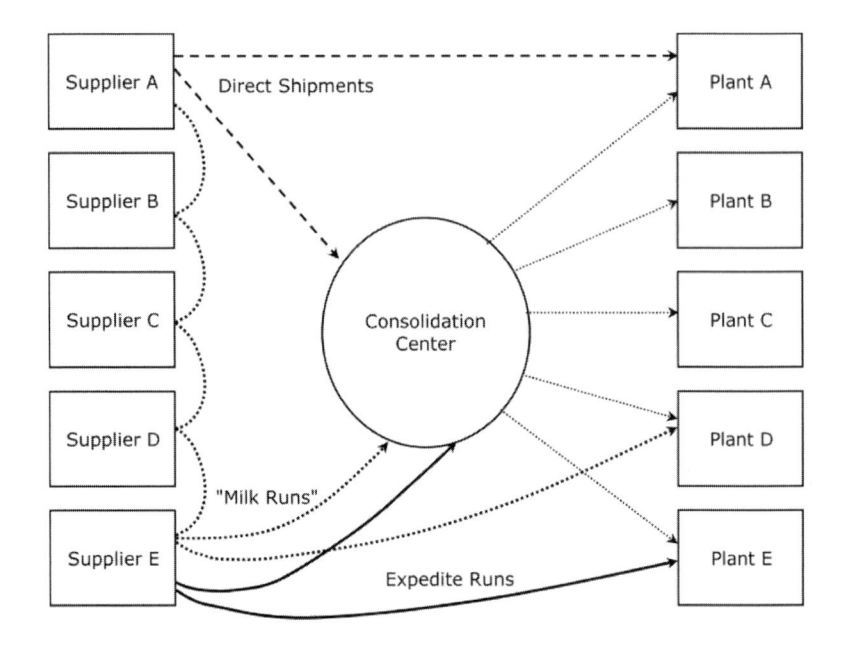

```
┌──────────┐
│Supplier A│╲  Direct Shipments                    ┌───────┐
└──────────┘ ╲──────────────────────────────────►  │Plant A│
             ╲                                     └───────┘
┌──────────┐  ╲
│Supplier B│   ╲                                   ┌───────┐
└──────────┘    ╲                              ──► │Plant B│
                 ╲                                 └───────┘
                  ▼
┌──────────┐       ⎛Consolidation⎞                 ┌───────┐
│Supplier C│  ···► ⎝   Center    ⎠ ···············►│Plant C│
└──────────┘                                       └───────┘

┌──────────┐                                       ┌───────┐
│Supplier D│                                   ──► │Plant D│
└──────────┘   "Milk Runs"                         └───────┘

┌──────────┐                                       ┌───────┐
│Supplier E│          Expedite Runs            ──► │Plant E│
└──────────┘                                       └───────┘
```

They observed 652 occurrences over the next four months. They analyzed these data to identify categories of like events and discovered three significant categories along with three minor ones. The three significant like event categories included:

- Pyramid stacking of material and pack density or container discrepancies, with 96 occurrences, 15% of the total. The critical functions that failed included conflicts in "pack size" definitions, conflicts in pack density between systems, and types of containers.
- Route design or route management problems, 151 occurrences, 23% of the total. The critical failures included designs being calculated every six months based on release forecasts, direct shipments being regularly expedited to the assembly plants, and trailer space being allocated as partial containers.
- Inaccurate daily production requirements, 232 occurrences, 36% of the total. Critical function failures included

Solving Organizational Problems

updates and fluctuations not automatically driving route recalculations and routes being modified only when reacting to differences in the predicted vs. actual trailers.

These three factors account for nearly 75% of the failures and all require attention. However, Importance, not Pareto, determines the order of attack. They realized that the container discrepancy was the primary issue because it contributed not just to pack density, but it also led directly to most of the other failures – partial loads, route mistakes, and missed predictions. While container issues were the failure mode in just 15% of the shipping problems, they were the ultimate root cause of a majority of the failures.

Closer examination revealed that entire operation included seven independent systems for pack sizes. This disparity made effective planning impossible. The primary issue that had to be resolved first was to standardize the entire operation around one container. Then, full truckloads could become the norm.

The other two "like event" categories became secondary causes. Once the container issue was under control, all the route design and management issues, whether based on semi-annual release forecasts or daily production requirements, could be resolved. Any attention to these issues before the container had been standardized would have been wasted effort. After the one standard container was in place, all the planning and management functions could begin to optimize their activities and achieve the expected results.

They used a modified version of FMEA to help assess importance. It only used the Severity and Detection criteria, and it used a 1-6 scale rather than the more common 1-10 scale of traditional FMEA.

The Severity scale reflects the impact on the end user or the next activity if the failure occurs.

> 6 = no awareness of an error. In this case, that meant people not knowing or understanding that having to expedite small loads is a failure.

Reasoning Backward

5 = no awareness of the impact of the failure on the system. Here, that meant having no reaction to the failure because the reason, cause or responsibility was ambiguous.
4 = being aware of the impact of the failure on the system, but taking no corrective action. In this case, that meant a delayed reaction but with no permanent corrective actions.
3 = being aware of the impact of the failure on the system, but with limited permanent corrective action. Here, this meant a delayed reaction with some permanent corrective action.
2 = being aware of the impact of the failure on the system and always taking corrective action. Here, that meant a proactive 24 hour notice of an expedite situation.
1 = being consistently correct. In this case, that meant consistently hitting the predicted full truckload quantities.

The Detection scale assesses the ability to detect that a failure has occurred or will occur. Any problem detected by a customer scores 6. The scale they used for this problem appears below.

6 = Reactive, using manual analysis to reconstruct the failure from historic data.
5 = Reactive, using system analysis of current data to define the root cause of the failure that has occurred.
4 = Proactive manual alert to a major exception.
3 = Proactive system alert to a major exception.
2 = Pre-load calculations within 24 hours are linked and matched to all the involved functions.
1 = Designed route always assures space on the truck.

One final note is interesting. Even though this example uses Importance rather than Pareto to address the occurrences, the results reinforce the truth of Pareto's Law. Although the pack size issue was only #3 in number of occurrences at 15%, it was the most important root cause because it contributed to well over 90% of all the failures.

Solving Organizational Problems

Standardizing pack size enabled their subsequent improvements on the secondary issues to be effective. When they tackled the issues in order of importance, they were able to make steady progress on all the issues, and eliminate the problem.

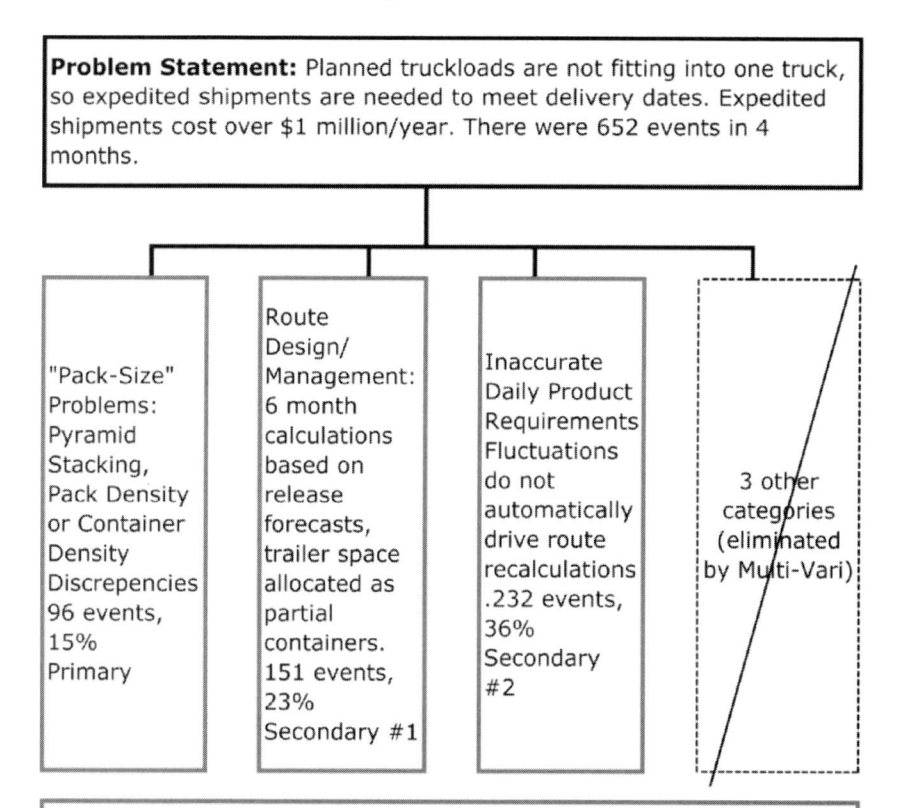

Problem Statement: Planned truckloads are not fitting into one truck, so expedited shipments are needed to meet delivery dates. Expedited shipments cost over $1 million/year. There were 652 events in 4 months.

- "Pack-Size" Problems: Pyramid Stacking, Pack Density or Container Density Discrepencies 96 events, 15% Primary
- Route Design/Management: 6 month calculations based on release forecasts, trailer space allocated as partial containers. 151 events, 23% Secondary #1
- Inaccurate Daily Product Requirements Fluctuations do not automatically drive route recalculations .232 events, 36% Secondary #2
- 3 other categories (eliminated by Multi-Vari)

Action Taken: First, reconciled pack size discrepancies between multiple systems, going from 7 to 1. Then, updated route design more frequently. Finally, made fluctuations drive daily route recalculations.

Result: Actions eliminated nearly all the expedited shipments, saving over $1 million/ year. Then, continued to upgrade primary and secondary systems and functions to achieve vision of "Integrate route and schedule to achieve maximum trailer utilization and lean material handling" to save over $15 million/year.

Reasoning Backward

Example 2 – The Auto Body Panel Stamping Operation

This project started as an effort by U.S. OEMs to reduce the cost of auto body panels. Many plastics suppliers and the OEMs considered using different types of plastic instead of steel. One company also compared the steel stamping process used by the American OEMs, the most expensive in the world, to the Japanese process, the world's lowest cost stamping operation. The company had to understand all the processing costs of each system in order to make an accurate comparison. This required the company to compare each process directly, including materials and processing costs, as well as the organizational and technical differences that affected those costs. The study used Paired Comparisons and 5 Whys as the key tools to understand the differences between five different processes. This chapter summarizes the comparison of the two different steel stamping operations, and the organizational and technical issues that made them so different.

The first step was to observe each stamping process and create a cost model for both. The second step compared the two cost models to see where they were consistently different. The third step asked, "Why do these differences exist?" The answers revealed the organizational and technical differences between the two processes, and the cost model showed the quantitative impact of each difference. The result was a clear picture of all the changes needed for the U.S. OEMs to become competitive with the best in the world.

	U.S. Process	Japanese Process	Difference $	% of Difference
Raw Material	$3.90	$3.77	$0.13	3%
Labor	$0.24	$0.06	$0.18	4%
Press Capital	$1.47	$0.56	$0.91	22%
Energy	$0.05	$0.01	$0.04	1%
Tooling Capital	$4.20	$1.37	$2.83	69%
TOTAL	$9.86	$5.77	$4.09	

Solving Organizational Problems

The cost model evaluated a generic 1000 square inch body panel and examined five factors. These included material, labor, the cost of stamping presses (including a return on investment factor), the cost of stamping dies / tooling (also including the ROI factor), and energy consumption. It first considered a run length of 200,000 units per year, and later looked at the effect of shorter and longer production runs. The initial result showed a U.S. panel cost $9.86 to make, while the Japanese could make the same panel for 41% less, at a cost of just $5.77, as shown in the table and graph.

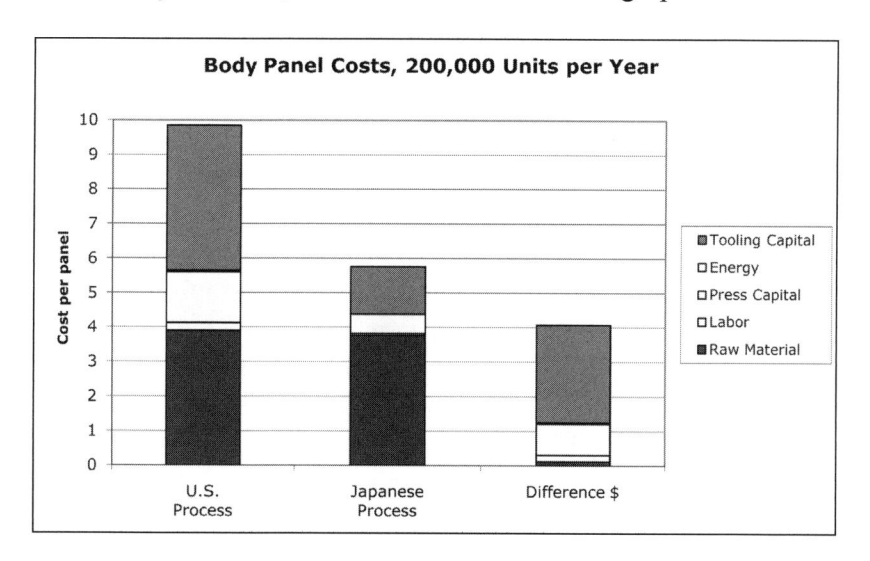

Body Panel Costs, 200,000 Units per Year

Legend: Tooling Capital, Energy, Press Capital, Labor, Raw Material

When they examined each of the cost factors separately, they discovered the two capital items, presses and tooling, accounted for 92% of the cost penalty. Raw material, labor, and energy consumption combined made up just 8% of the difference. Corporate policies and procedures that controlled capital spending limited performance. Then, they compared their procedures to Japanese procedures and discovered two primary and two secondary differences. The U.S. OEMs would have to change all four to become globally competitive.

The most important factor is the number of stamping steps needed to form the part. Steel sheet will not stretch to final shape in just one stamping step. Highly curved or complex panels require more stamping steps than shallower, simpler ones.

In the U.S., the new car designers are in charge. They create complicated panel designs that typically require 5-7 stamping steps. They work completely independent of manufacturing. They complete a design, and then hand it off to manufacturing, which must create a process to make it. Manufacturing gets no voice in the design process.

Contrast this with the Japanese design process. Corporate policy states that no panel will be stamped more than four times. Designers and manufacturing leaders work together to achieve this goal. When they begin to design a new vehicle, the designer shows the sketches to the manufacturing representative on the design team, who identifies which ones are unacceptable because they will require more than four stamping operations. Together they develop a design that achieves the style objectives and will fit into the four-stamp operation.

91% of a U.S. OEM's cost penalty ($3.74 out of $4.09) comes from the tooling and the presses required to manufacture a 7-stamp design. Introducing collaboration between marketing, design, and manufacturing during the design cycle and establishing a "No more than 4" policy saves $2.43, eliminating 59% of the total penalty.

The second most important factor is the presence or absence of a "No More Changes" date in the design process. U.S. OEMs do not use one, and Japanese OEMs do.

In the U.S., top management has always made changes very late in the design cycle. Everyone knows that something will change at the last minute, but no one knows what or when. The only way to deal with it and not lose 6-9 months building completely new tools is to make oversized tools that can be modified when someone dictates a change. This creates both short and long-term penalties. Short-term, it adds 18 months and extra expense to the design process. Long-term, the heavier tooling costs nearly twice as much to build as precision tooling. Furthermore, the large, heavy, oversized tools take longer to change than precision tooling, which creates labor and cycle time cost penalties every day for the life of the vehicle when workers changeover tooling.

Solving Organizational Problems

In Japan, company management establishes a "No More Changes" date in every design process. Everyone, including top management makes input until that date, but then the final design is set. Manufacturing then builds exactly the right tooling, knowing that there will be no last minute adjustments. One result is the Japanese design cycle takes just 18 months, half the time of U.S. OEMs. Their tools are lighter, and they use quick-change fittings to reduce changeover time in production.

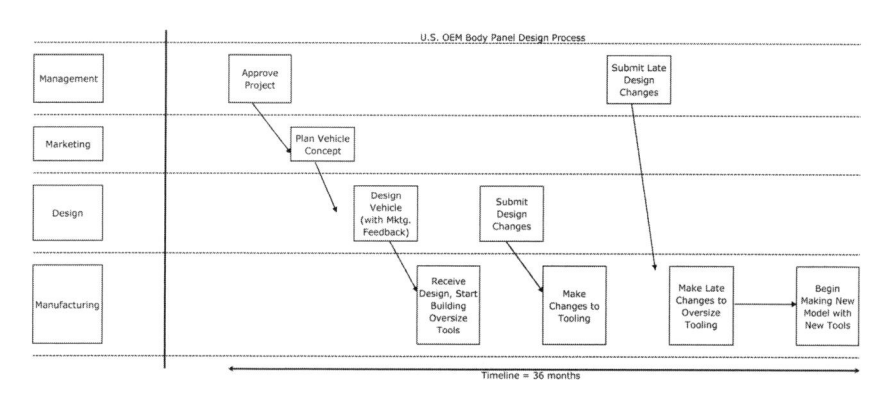

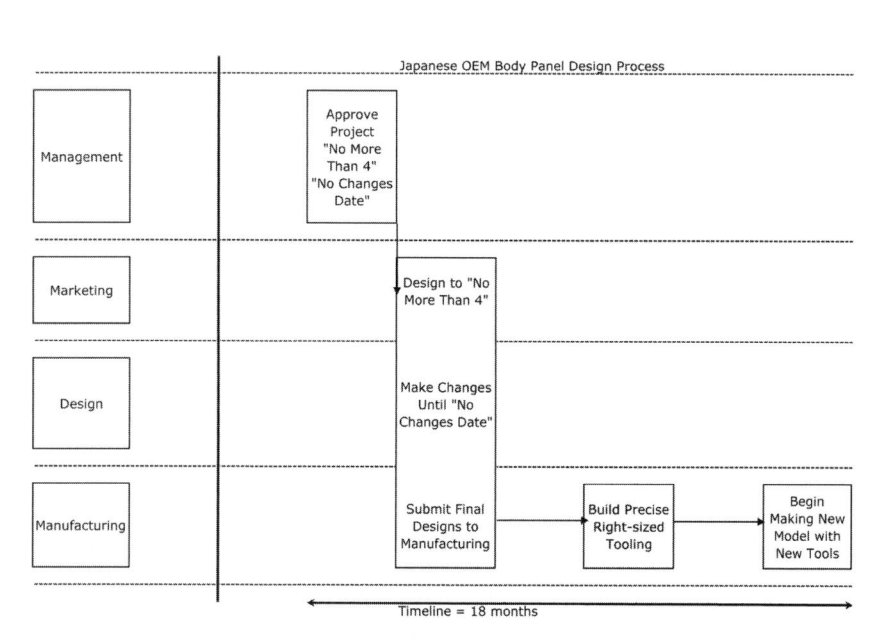

U.S. OEM Body Panel Design Process

Management	Marketing	Design	Manufacturing
Approve Project	Plan Vehicle Concept	Design Vehicle (with Mktg. Feedback)	Receive Design, Start Building Oversize Tools
Submit Late Design Changes		Submit Design Changes	Make Changes to Tooling
			Make Late Changes to Oversize Tooling
			Begin Making New Model with New Tools

Timeline = 36 months

Japanese OEM Body Panel Design Process

Management	Marketing	Design	Manufacturing
Approve Project "No More Than 4" "No Changes Date"	Design to "No More Than 4"	Make Changes Until "No Changes Date"	Submit Final Designs to Manufacturing
			Build Precise Right-sized Tooling
			Begin Making New Model with New Tools

Timeline = 18 months

The lack of a "No More Changes" date in the U.S. design process contributes multiple cost penalties. Adopting a "No More Changes" policy saves another $1.03, 25% of the total penalty.

These first two factors are the two primary issues. Together they create $3.46 of the $4.09 cost penalty, 84%. In addition, these two unresolved issues double the cost and duration of the design cycle. Eliminating each issue requires nothing more than a simple decision by top management to implement these two new policies.

The other $0.63 of cost penalty (16%) comes from two secondary causes that each contribute nearly equally. **The third most important factor is the presence or absence of a "First Part Good" policy.** This involves the relationships between the OEMs and the autoworkers unions. In the U.S., the relationship is adversarial, with no accountability or responsibility. In Japan, the opposite is true. The unions are allies of the OEMs. They work together to improve productivity. Line workers are accountable for the quality of their work. The company has a "First Part Good" policy that states the press operator is responsible for the first stamped part after a tool change being right, or it is his responsibility to make it right.

The adversarial arrangement in the U.S. has created an attitude problem. After a tooling change, the operator starts stamping parts. Sometimes the first stamped part is good, but not always. If the parts are bad, the operator stops the process, adjusts the tooling, and starts again. This trial and error continues until the parts are acceptable. This problem is even worse because the operator does not cull the bad parts. They move to the next operation along with the good parts, to be culled somewhere down the line. Even worse, some may never be culled and end up being used. Stamping operations at the U.S. OEMs typically generate 3% scrap parts for any given stamping run, and it can run as high as 5%. The combination of high scrap and 3-4 hours for tool changeover combine to make the U.S. stamping operations run at about 90% efficiency.

In Japan, the press operator is responsible for making the first part good. If there is a problem, it is his responsibility to make the part good. His job is made easier because the use lightweight precision tooling and quick-change, mistake-proof fittings, so the tooling goes in right every time. The scrap rate is <<1%. Changeover time is less than 30 minutes. As a result, Japanese stamping operations typically operate at 98% efficiency.

This change is much more complicated than the first two that simply required management to adopt a "No More Than 4" design policy and establish a "No More Changes" date. While these are both very new paradigms for the U.S. OEMs, they are unilateral actions they can make at any time. Introducing a "First Part Good" policy requires a completely different relationship with the UAW. Line workers must become accountable for quality. Line workers and the union must actively work jointly with management to improve productivity, while maintaining the legally required adversarial collective bargaining relationship. Even though this change is not readily achievable, it is necessary to becoming globally competitive. This use of Paired Comparisons gives company and union management a quantitative understanding of the impact of this issue.

The last important factor is the use of single station presses vs. four station transfer presses in the stamping operation. U.S. operations have historically used separate presses for each stamping operation. A 7-stamp design uses seven presses, which adds capital costs to the operation and increases the amount of labor required. The Japanese use one 4-station transfer press to make body panels. One 4-station press costs less than four 1-station presses and uses less labor and energy, which all contribute to reduced costs.

As long as U.S. OEMs insist on using designs that require 5-7 stamping operations, transfer presses will not help reduce costs. They would actually increase costs in the short-term because the company would have to spend new capital for the presses instead of continuing to use the single station presses it already owns. If the companies make the move to 4-stamp designs, they will achieve the immediate tooling and press savings. They should continue to use the existing presses until they wear out. Then, when they must buy new presses, they make the switch to a 4-station transfer press.

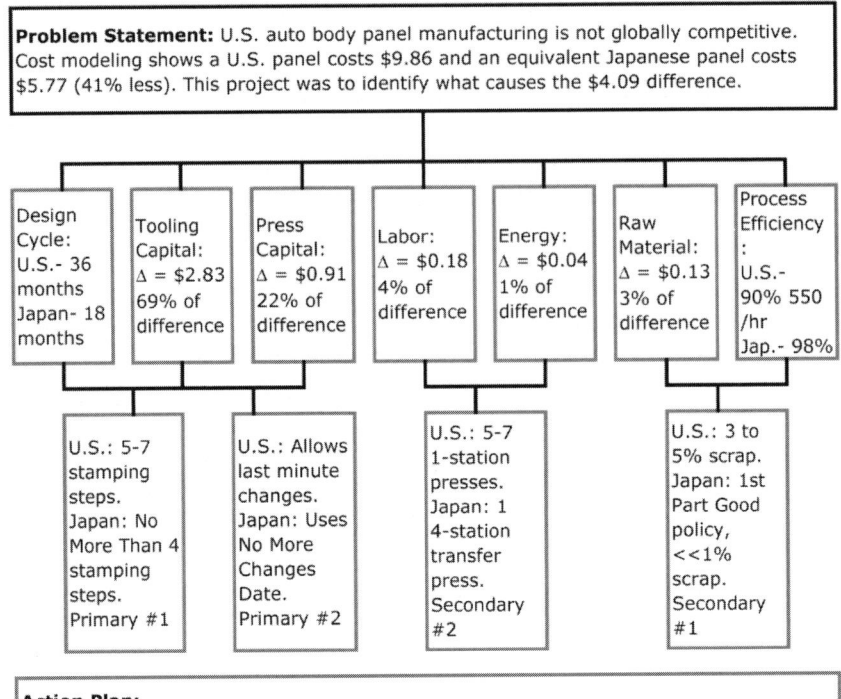

Problem Statement: U.S. auto body panel manufacturing is not globally competitive. Cost modeling shows a U.S. panel costs $9.86 and an equivalent Japanese panel costs $5.77 (41% less). This project was to identify what causes the $4.09 difference.

Design Cycle: U.S.- 36 months Japan- 18 months	Tooling Capital: Δ = $2.83 69% of difference	Press Capital: Δ = $0.91 22% of difference	Labor: Δ = $0.18 4% of difference	Energy: Δ = $0.04 1% of difference	Raw Material: Δ = $0.13 3% of difference	Process Efficiency: U.S.- 90% 550/hr Jap.- 98%
	U.S.: 5-7 stamping steps. Japan: No More Than 4 stamping steps. Primary #1	U.S.: Allows last minute changes. Japan: Uses No More Changes Date. Primary #2	U.S.: 5-7 1-station presses. Japan: 1 4-station transfer press. Secondary #2		U.S.: 3 to 5% scrap. Japan: 1st Part Good policy, <<1% scrap. Secondary #1	

Action Plan:
Primary Cause #1: Go from 7 stamps to 4. Save $2.43/panel, 59% of penalty.
Primary #2: Use No More Changes date. Save $1.03/panel, 25% of penalty.
Secondary #1: Implement 1st Part Good policy. Save ~$0.30, 8% of penalty.
Secondary #2: Replace 1-station presses with 4-station Transfer Press. Save ~$0.30, 8%

Summary:

Organizational issues were the root causes in both these examples. The first step in both examples was to understand the organization and its white spaces and to develop a common definition of the problem. In the first case, Multi-Vari then identified patterns and categories that led the team to the organizational causes. In the second case, a comparison of the company's process to the best in the world uncovered consistent differences. The differences led to the corporate policy issues that limited performance, and this led to a roadmap for improvement.

Solving Organizational Problems

These techniques have saved tens of millions of dollars in a variety of other areas, including business processes, IT systems, areas where traditional methods have failed, or where too many resources have been applied for too long and not delivered the desired results. Applications include finance, HR, purchasing, administration, asset tracking, quality systems, engineering systems, and prototyping among others, in addition to the two case study examples.

By introducing White Space Management, Holmes' "Observation, Deduction, Knowledge" process will work for any complex business problem.

Section 6
Open-ended Problem Solving

Open-ended Problem Solving Tools
- *Opportunity Analysis*
- *TRIZ*
- *Poka-Yoke*

Chapter 17

Open-ended Problem Solving

Opportunity Analysis – Developing New Products with a 95% Rate of Success

Open-ended problems that lead to innovation are how civilization moves ahead. Innovation occurs when someone identifies an unmet need and develops a solution that creates a new level of performance never achieved before. Some examples include vaccines for disease, the electric light bulb, the airplane, and the assembly line.

The historic challenge for innovation has been that most new ideas fail. The Conference Board has reported that only 11% of all commercially launched new products are successful, and the main reason for failure is poor understanding of the market need. A company invents a solution for a problem it mistakenly thinks exists, and then discovers its error when the new offering does not sell.

One approach to innovation, Opportunity Analysis, has changed the success rate dramatically. This approach tests the initial product concept in the marketplace first to validate its accuracy before developing the new offering. The historic 11% success rate is proof that the initial concept is rarely accurate. However, when a company starts with an initial idea (however flawed), tests it in the marketplace first, and adjusts its development according to what it learns, the success rate of new offerings jumps to 95%. ("3000 New Ideas = 1 Commercial Success!", *Research•Technology Management,* 40(3):16-27, May-June, 1997.)

This chapter introduces the 95% successful approach to innovation. Everyone can benefit from understanding its non-traditional methodology. It introduces a higher level of thinking so anyone can assess any situation more effectively, ask better questions, and generate better solutions.

Chapters 18 and 19 introduce two additional methodologies used in the new product development process after the real unmet need has been identified. These are TRIZ (the Theory of Inventive Problem Solving) and Poka-Yoke (Mistake Proofing). Together these three non-traditional techniques provide a roadmap for successful new product development. Not surprisingly, these techniques also depend heavily on the 10 problem solving strategies introduced in Chapter 2. The following table shows this dependence.

	Opportunity Analysis	TRIZ	Poka-Yoke
Work Backwards	***	***	***
Find a Pattern	***	***	***
Adopt a Different Point of View Act it out/Use Objects	***	***	***
Solve a Simpler Problem	***	***	***
Consider Extreme Cases	***	***	***
Make Drawing	***	***	***
Intelligent Guess & Test	***	***	***
Make an Organized List / Account for all possibilities	***	***	
Organize Data / Use a Table or Graph	***	***	
Logical Reasoning	***	***	***
Effective Strategies Used (out of 10)	10	10	8

Opportunity Analysis

The lessons of Sherlock Holmes and Sir Francis Bacon are equally relevant to open-ended problem solving as they are to closed-end problems. The fundamental principle is to examine the situation in detail, to develop in-depth understanding of the needs of the marketplace first, and then to reason backward to the winning solution before any misdirected development work occurs. Opportunity Analysis uses all of Holmes' 10 tips

"In solving a problem of this sort, the grand thing is to be able to reason backward. That is a very useful accomplishment, and a very easy one, but people do not practice it much. In the everyday affairs

of life, it is more useful to reason forward, and so the other comes to be neglected. There are fifty who can reason synthetically for one who can reason analytically."

"Once you eliminate the impossible, whatever remains, no matter how improbable, must be the truth."

"Always approach a case with an absolutely blank mind. Form no theories, just simply observe and draw inferences from your observations." "It is a capital mistake to theorize before one has data. Insensibly one begins to twist facts to suit theories, instead of theories to suit facts."

"How dangerous it is to reason from insufficient data." "Data, Data, Data! I can't make bricks without clay."

"Detection is, or ought to be, an exact science, and should be treated in the same cold unemotional manner. When you attempt to tinge it with romanticism, you produce the same effect as if you worked a love story into the fifth proposition of Euclid."

"It is of the highest importance in the art of detection to be able to recognize out of a number of facts which are incidental and which are vital."

"I can see nothing," said Watson, handing it back to Holmes. "On the contrary, Watson, you can see everything. You fail, however, to reason from what you see. You are too timid in drawing your inferences."

"I never guess. It is a shocking habit -- destructive to the logical faculty."

"Nothing clears up a case so much as stating it to another person."

"You know my methods. Apply them."

The following description includes a real business example of an exciting current opportunity, Clean the World, Inc., to demonstrate the process.

Step 1: Describe the Situation

Innovation typically begins with an idea. Someone observes some significant situation that is less than perfect and envisions a

Open-ended Problem Solving

better way. At this point, a little time spent organizing thoughts with a pen and paper can avoid hundreds or thousands of wasted hours later. Writing straightens thinking, and thinking straightens writing.

First, write a short paragraph that describes the situation, and specifically what about the situation is sub-optimal. Include any ideas about what would be improvements to the situation. Completing this paragraph will always improve your understanding of the situation and the nature of the opportunity.

Background on Clean the World

One day in late 2008, two businessmen, Shawn Seipler and Paul Till, who traveled 4-5 days every week, were leaving their hotel rooms. They saw a housekeeper changing the soap bars and shampoo bottles, and one of them asked, "What happens to the slightly used bars of soap and partial bottles of shampoo?" The housekeeper answered, "We throw them out."

This seemed wasteful, so they began to wonder if there was some way to recycle this material. A quick phone survey of several hotels revealed that everyone discarded these soap bars and shampoo bottles. No program for recycling existed.

At this point, they had a very basic idea and many questions about whether there was a real opportunity, or not. The paragraph that captures their idea and their questions at that point is as follows:

"All the slightly used bars of soap and bottles of shampoo that hotels provide to their guests end up discarded in landfills. Unanswered questions include the following.

- How much material is being discarded?

- Is there enough to be a viable resource?
- Are there processes for recycling or reprocessing soap and shampoo, and are they cost effective?
- If so, is there a viable market for recycled or reprocessed soap and shampoo?
- Are the logistics of a reprocessing operation viable – collection, reprocessing, and distribution?
- What health and safe handling issues need to be resolved?"

This paragraph with more questions than answers gave them good direction for the research they needed to complete next. They completed nearly all of it using online searches and phone calls to people who were knowledgeable about different aspects of the proposed operation.

Step 2: Formulate Hypotheses

Next, construct three hypotheses about the situation and test them to determine the accuracy of the paragraph. These are the Hypothesis of Unmet Need, the Hypothesis of the Winning Solution, and the Hypothesis of the Value of the Proposed Winning Solution. Structure these hypotheses as positively as possible to assure each is fully tested.

Note that it doesn't matter whether these hypotheses are correct in the beginning or not. The initial hypotheses may be vague and are often completely wrong. Testing these hypotheses reveals the truth, which usually forces the original idea to evolve into a revised concept. Successful opportunities generally require a series of hypotheses to fully describe the real situation, as in the Clean the World example.

Hypothesis of Unmet Need
Structure this hypothesis as follows:

"There is an unmet need for _____ because ..."

Consider an unmet need to be any shortcoming of the existing situation. Identify all the shortcomings, and the specific reasons these shortcomings exist. Be as exhaustive as possible with the reasons so the subsequent testing of this hypothesis provides a thorough understanding of the real situation.

> ### Clean the World Hypotheses of Unmet Need
>
> Their initial hypothesis focused on the Green Movement and the desirability of recycling. "There is an unmet need to remove slightly used soap bars and shampoos from landfills and recycle or repurpose them in the market place because these materials are still usable, and because it reduces the demand for landfill space." This hypothesis guided Shawn and Paul to investigate processes for recycling or re-purposing soaps, and to learn about the Green Movement and landfill utilization.
>
> Their initial research revealed both good news and bad news. A significant volume of soap bars was ending up in landfills. There was an established re-batching process for bar soap that converts soap scraps into new bars of soap. However, this process was labor intensive and not scalable to handle large volumes of soap. Furthermore, there was no driving force from the Green Movement supporting the unmet need, and there was no commercial market in the U.S. for repurposed soap. Their initial concept would not work.

This lack of a market for repurposed soap in the U.S. led them to ask, "Is there anywhere that repurposed soap would satisfy an unmet need?" They knew from the H1N1 flu situation that the best way to prevent the spread of disease is good hygiene, especially hand washing. Could repurposed soap reduce the spread of disease? They realized there was no market in the U.S., but they wondered about the third world. They looked online and discovered a large number of studies showed that simply washing hands with bar soap dramatically reduced the spread of disease, particularly acute respiratory infections such as pneumonia and diarrheal diseases, especially cholera. Hand washing with soap dramatically lowered the childhood mortality rate. For example, in one study 60% of children in one village who washed their hands with soap remained disease free, while 100% of those who did not wash were afflicted. Washing hands with soap clearly prevents disease. Studies estimate that about 3.5 million children die each year from diarrheal diseases, so the potential impact of this opportunity was huge. They had found the unmet need, but could they develop a sustainable operation that would solve the problem?

Their next unmet need hypothesis was, "There is an unmet need for a sustainable operation to make and distribute repurposed bar soap in the third world to reduce diarrheal disease and childhood mortality because:

- there is no sustainable source of repurposed bar soap today, and because
- many studies show bar soap is an effective way of reducing diarrheal disease, especially in children, which dramatically reduces childhood mortality."

Sustainability would require a reliable source of slightly used soap bars, a scalable process for converting them to new bars, a way to fund this operation, and a way to deliver the finished soap bars to the third world countries that needed them. Their next step was to investigate each of these issues to determine the hypothesis of unmet need for each issue. They discovered the following:

- Reliable source of used soap bars – hotels were a ready source and willing participants, but only if it did not cost them anything. They would not pay a processing or recycling fee to participate, even if it would generate positive public relations. It had to be net neutral, or better yet, create a positive financial impact for the hotel. There was an unmet need for a viable financial model for soap collection.

- Scalable process for converting used soap to new bars – The existing labor-intensive process was not scalable. There was an unmet need for a scalable process.

- Viable financial model for the reprocessing operation – There was an unmet need for a viable financial model that would cover the cost of collection, reprocessing, and distribution.

- Viable distribution system to reach the third world – There was an unmet need for a viable distribution mechanism. Some arrangement with another organization(s) with distribution capability was needed and did not exist then.

These unmet need hypotheses provided the basis for further investigation to clarify the situation for every phase of the process, to determine if a winning solution was possible.

Hypothesis of the Proposed Winning Solution

The first hypothesis identified the unmet need. It defined the problem, but not the solution. The second hypothesis addresses the solution.

"_____ will become the winning solution for this unmet need because ..."

This hypothesis should describe the perfect solution as completely as possible, so the subsequent testing of the hypothesis reveals the true situation and the strength of the proposed solution.

> "The winning solution must include:
>
> - A viable collection mechanism that would reward the donor for donating slightly used soap,
> - A scalable method for reprocessing soap bars,
> - A viable distribution mechanism for getting reprocessed soap into the hands of the people who need it, and
> - A viable financial model that makes the collection, reprocessing, and distribution of soap both economically feasible and sustainable.
>
> At this point in the process, they were unable to satisfy any of these four conditions.

Hypothesis of the Value of the Proposed Winning Solution

The first two hypotheses focused on the existence of an unmet need and its ideal solution. The third hypothesis focuses on how much the winning solution will be worth to the provider. Is it worth doing? Create this hypothesis as follows:

Open-ended Problem Solving

"This solution has value and is worth developing because ..."

An innovation is only successful when the solution eliminates the unmet need, and it is worthwhile for the solution provider to pursue.

Once this hypothesis is in place, the next step is testing it in the marketplace. This critical step uncovers the faulty assumptions and increases the success rate for new offerings by almost an order of magnitude.

> Because Shawn and Paul had no idea how they were going to achieve the winning solution, this hypothesis was still very general.
>
> "The winning solution creates value for everyone in the chain (the sources of the soap, the reprocessing entity, and the distribution network), so it becomes self-sustaining."

Step 3: Testing Hypotheses – the "Four Question" Framework

The exercise of formulating hypotheses is valuable because it clarifies your thoughts about what the opportunity really is, and why. However, the real power of hypotheses comes when you test them, to prove whether they are accurate, or not. Testing involves research – both online searching for information and interviews with knowledgeable people in the field. This research seeks to answer four simple questions.

- **How is this unmet need addressed now? Why?**
- **How much does it cost to address the unmet need in this way? Why?**

Reasoning Backward

- **What (if anything) is wrong with the current situation? Why?**
- **How much is the value of improving the situation? Why?**

Usually the first step is online research to learn whatever is known already, and what has been published about the situation already. Since most initial ideas are flawed in some way, online research is an easy and painless way to find that out, and then to modify the hypotheses accordingly. Quite often, that means starting over because the initial concept of the unmet need is completely wrong. When that happens, don't despair. Linus Pauling, the two-time Nobel Prize winning chemist, was once asked how he was able to have so many good ideas. He responded, "The only way to have good ideas is to have lots of ideas." Even the most brilliant among us usually starts with an imperfect concept. The key is to explore the concept in detail and allow it to evolve to a greater truth. This is the difference between the 11% and 95% success rate.

Online research usually tightens up all three hypotheses, which makes the personal interviews more effective.

Conduct interviews in person or over the telephone. Talk with people who are directly involved in the situation in some capacity. This should include people who directly experience the unmet need now, as well others who are involved indirectly, such as suppliers, equipment vendors, regulators, analysts, writers, even indirect competitors who approach the situation from a completely different perspective.

Testing hypotheses is like the parable about the blind men whose challenge was to describe an elephant. Each touched a different part of the animal and experienced something completely different. The tusk is hard and smooth like marble. The trunk is long and flexible like a hose. The ear is flexible like a piece of leather. The side is like a massive wall. The leg is like a tree trunk. The tail is like a piece of rope. Everyone was correct about his part of the answer, but no one had the complete answer. The successful analyst gathers input from a variety of sources, each with an accurate description of its specific area. The analyst pieces them all together to understand the entire situation.

Consider each of the four questions in more detail.

How is the unmet need addressed now, and why? Examine the current situation in detail. Learn exactly how the activity works, its strengths and its weaknesses. Most importantly, learn why it is done the way it is. To gather this information, interview people who are most affected by the hypothesized unmet need. This could include those who currently perform the activity, those who supply it with materials or equipment, or those who use the activity's output. The key is to develop a complete understanding of the activity, in order to understand what unmet needs truly exist. There is always at least one unmet need, to achieve the same outcome at lower cost. An innovation might be nothing more than a way to deliver the same results at reduced cost, or it could be a significant change that produces dramatically improved results.

Consider each of the four phases of the proposed winning solution for soap repurposing separately. (Collection, Reprocessing, Distribution, and Financial Model)

- Collection – They interviewed a number of hotels and received a consistent message. Hotels loved the idea but would not pay a recycling fee. For them to participate, their involvement must be cost-neutral at worst. Shawn and Paul's goal was to understand soap handling currently, and what alternatives had been considered in the past.

- Reprocessing – They discovered that no scalable process existed currently, so some process testing was required to develop a faster, less labor-intensive method.

- Distribution – They contacted several Non-Government Organizations (NGOs) to understand how materials

> are distributed now to third world countries, in order to determine if partnerships were possible.
>
> - Financial Model – They talked with the hotels and discovered that charging a recycling fee was unacceptable. Then, they explored U.S. tax code looking for tax deduction possibilities for gifts-in-kind.

How much does it cost to address the unmet need in this way, and why? Identify all the costs associated with the activity currently – raw materials, supplies, labor, equipment costs, sales and marketing, overhead, etc. The key is to understand exactly what contributes to the activity's cost in order to understand where there are opportunities to improve the situation. An innovation is only successful if it creates an improved result cost effectively, or if it creates the same result at a lower cost. Gather whatever data are necessary to quantify the current activity.

> - Collection – The cost of soap and collection was negligible.
> - Reprocessing – The cost of this process was critical. First, they had to identify a scalable process. Then, they had to determine how much it would cost.
> - Distribution – The cost of the potential partnership arrangements had to be determined.
> - Financial Model – The hotels would not accept any recycling fees. To become successful, the venture would have to discover a sustainable way of generating revenues to cover the costs of the process.

Open-ended Problem Solving

What (if anything) is wrong with the current situation, and why? In the interview process, this question can mislead the interviewer more than any other question, if they ask it in the wrong way. Always give the interviewee the opportunity to say that there is nothing wrong with the current situation. Most interviewees want to help. They understand you are looking for ways to improve their operation, so they try to be helpful. If you ask, "What is wrong with the situation?" they will try to think of something. However, if you ask, "Is there anything wrong with the way the operation is done now?" they are free to answer, "No, nothing," which gives you exactly the information you need. By letting them explain exactly what are the shortcomings of the current operation, you learn exactly how accurate the first two hypotheses are, and which opportunities do and do not exist.

- Collection – From the perspective of the hotels, there was nothing wrong with the current operation. It wasted a potential resource, but cost the hotel nothing.

- Reprocessing – This was one of two critical flaws in the current situation. The existing small scale reprocessing operation was not scalable. There was no scalable operation. To be successful, they would have to develop a viable process.

- Distribution – The existing distribution channels to the third world using non-governmental organizations operations worked well. If a viable reprocessing method could be identified, distribution would not be a problem.

- Financial Model – This was the second critical flaw. The traditional recycling fee model was not viable. A different, sustainable fee structure would be required to convert this into a viable opportunity.

Reasoning Backward

What is the value of improving the situation, and why? The answers to this question come more from follow-up analysis of the interview data than from direct questions to interviewees. People are often reluctant to discuss cost data, but they are more open with information about their operations, which allows you to reach reasonable conclusions about the value of the potential solution. In many cases, no one interviewee understands all the current costs, and why they are what they are. Gather input from multiple sources, each with their own understanding of a part of the overall operation. Combine all the data to develop a complete understanding, so you can effectively determine which situations are real opportunities worth pursuing.

- Collection – Little improvement is needed.
- Reprocessing – A scalable process of low enough cost that it creates a sustainable operation. The technology must be developed, and the financial model must be established. The two are inextricably linked.
- Distribution – Established NGO channels appear to be adequate.
- Financial Model – There must be enough value created to sustain the operation. Research and interviews must identify a viable financial model, or it will fail.

When they conducted interviews and research to test these hypotheses, they discovered that U.S. Tax Code provided the key to solving the financing/sustainability problem. When a business donates a gift-in-kind to a non-profit, 501 (c) (3) organization, it is allowed a tax deduction of double the retail value of the gift. In addition, the recycling fee the donor must pay is also deductible.

> This provision enables the hotel to accrue a net financial benefit by participating. The donated soap and fee coupled with their improved, scalable reprocessing operation enabled Clean the World to develop a sustainable non-profit operation.
>
> They also provided another community benefit by employing men from a local center for homeless men to do the reprocessing.

In this case, an interesting initial idea had to go through several iterations before it became a successful operation. Without evolving, the venture would have failed. By adapting to the situations they discovered in their research, Shawn and Paul created a viable new venture. They applied principles of the scientific method (research and observe, formulate initial hypotheses, test the hypotheses, draw conclusions, modify hypotheses as necessary, test the new hypotheses, repeat as necessary) to conduct market research, so they converted a certain failure into a viable success.

Step 4: Continue to evolve in line with changes in the marketplace

The fatal flaw in traditional new product development processes is when companies pursue their initial incorrect concepts with inadequate understanding of the market and its unmet needs. Successful new products target real unmet needs. However, needs in the marketplace change, and successful product offerings must change accordingly or become obsolete. Companies must develop strong relationships with customers and be responsive to their evolving needs to remain viable for the long term.

Clean the World's launch in 2009 with viable collection, reprocessing, distribution and financial models was successful. It started with local hotels in the Houston and Orlando areas and steadily built momentum. Its significant involvement in Haiti and Japan after the earthquakes has continued to enhance its reputation. By the end of 2010, Clean the World had nearly 700 hotel partners, and 3 months later, the number is nearly 1000. The rate of addition of new partners is accelerating, suggesting that Clean the World is reaching the tipping point. In the beginning, it had to persuade hotels to participate. Now, hotels want to participate. As it has become more widely known, more hotel guests are seeking to support the effort, so Clean the World partnerships are attracting customers.

As Clean the World has become the recycler of soaps, shampoos and lotions for hotels, additional recycling opportunities have begun to appear. Hotels are beginning to see Clean the World as their recycling partner. This momentum is causing Clean the World to evaluate other options well beyond soap recycling, such as "upcycling" some other waste streams from the hospitality industry and converting other wastes into energy and heat they can use on site to lower their utility bills while reducing the volume of material they send to landfills.

Summary

In closed-end problems, you reason backward from an existing unacceptable situation to determine its causes. In open-ended situations where no acceptable solution exists, the same Holmesian approach is equally valid. State the problem as the situation that you believe exists. Then, just as in closed-end situations, conduct research and make observations to determine if the problem exists or not. Revised hypotheses are interim conclusions, just as Sir

Francis Bacon described, and you discover the truth by gradual degrees. Development only occurs after you have identified a real unmet need.

The most important lesson is **not to fall in love with your new ideas without checking their validity. Maintain objectivity.** The biggest weakness of most new product development efforts is that they create offerings for which there is no demand in the marketplace, or not enough demand to create a sustainable business. Therefore, these new products fail. The historic success rate for new products is 11%. How can this happen? All to easily, unfortunately. Someone once said, "When Jack is in love with Jill, he is a poor judge of her beauty." When someone believes a need exists and has the creative genius to develop a solution for that need, it is only natural to become enthused about its viability. The lesson is to step back and objectively assess the situation. Are the assumptions about the unmet need accurate? 9 times out of 10, they aren't, and it's far better to discover this before committing significant resources to develop a product almost no one will buy.

Although this methodology was designed to address situations in the workplace, the principles are universal. In any endeavor, consider the ultimate goal and the specific approach. **Take a step back and go through a reality check.** As Davy Crockett reportedly said, "Make sure you're right, then go ahead." The three test hypotheses and four test questions provide a simple framework for success.

Chapter 18

TRIZ – Theory of Inventive Problem Solving
Using a System of Prior Knowledge To Develop Winning Solutions

Background and General Description:

The previous chapter addressed the identification of the right problem to solve. The outcome is a well-defined unmet need, and the initial definition of what the ideal solution would be. This chapter builds on this initial concept using TRIZ (an acronym for the Russian phrase that translates as Theory of Inventive Problem Solving), developed after World War II by Genrich Altshuller, a patent examiner in the Soviet Union.

Altshuller spent years reviewing over one million patents looking for repeating patterns. He discovered that many patents in completely different areas use the same principles to solve problems.

For example, one technique that appears in many patents uses the slow application of pressure to a system, followed by the explosive release of that pressure to cause the rupture of an object at its weak spots. One application applies pressure to rough diamonds and causes them to rupture along flaws in the stone, so they will not crush when the diamond cutters cut them. In another case, food preparers making stuffed peppers first cook whole bell peppers in a large pressure cooker, which fills the pepper with high-pressure water vapor. When they explosively reduce the pressure inside the pressure cooker, the water vapor instantly escapes through the weakest part of the pepper, the area around the stem. As it explodes, it blows all the seeds out of the pepper, leaving an empty shell, ready to receive the stuffing. Several other areas use this same technique to explosively change different materials.

Altshuller observed that patents issue when the inventor overcomes a contradiction between two features without compromising either feature – the inventive solution accomplishes both desired properties. For example, when designing many products, high strength is desirable, and so is being lightweight. Traditionally, this is a contradiction – removing weight reduces strength. One inventive solution to this contradiction is to replace steel with lighter metals and composites that are as strong as steel, or even stronger, and are much lighter in weight. Altshuller's first efforts recorded common contradictions and the inventive principles in the patent literature that have repeatedly overcome these contradictions.

The basic framework for applying these principles has four steps, as shown below.

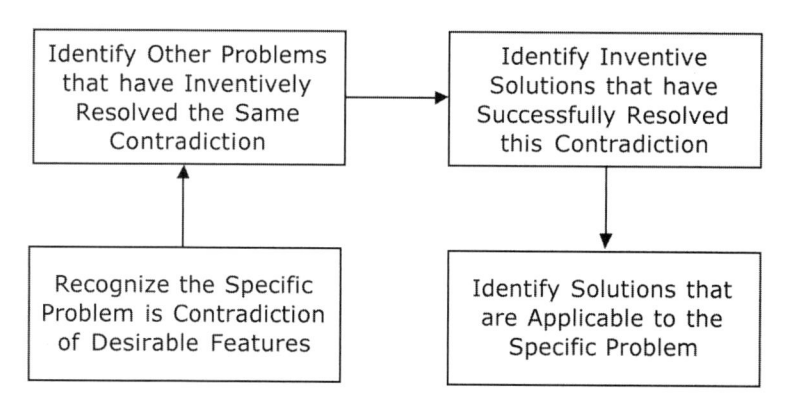

```
┌─────────────────────────┐      ┌─────────────────────────┐
│ Identify Other Problems │      │   Identify Inventive    │
│ that have Inventively   │─────▶│   Solutions that have   │
│  Resolved the Same      │      │  Successfully Resolved  │
│     Contradiction       │      │    this Contradiction   │
└─────────────────────────┘      └─────────────────────────┘
             ▲                                │
             │                                ▼
┌─────────────────────────┐      ┌─────────────────────────┐
│  Recognize the Specific │      │  Identify Solutions that│
│ Problem is Contradiction│      │   are Applicable to the │
│  of Desirable Features  │      │     Specific Problem    │
└─────────────────────────┘      └─────────────────────────┘
```

It starts by recognizing that the limits of current performance are the result of contradictions that have occurred and been eliminated in other disciplines. The specific problem is simply an example of a general problem. The general principles that resolve this contradiction elsewhere might be applicable to this specific problem.

In algebra, the technique for solving a quadratic equation follows the same methodology. The first step is recognizing that the specific equation in question is a quadratic equation. This recognition links to the general quadratic formula,

$$ax^2 + bx + c = 0$$

which has the general solution,

$$[-b \pm \sqrt{(b^2-4ac)}]/2a$$

A student simply applies the formula for the solution to his specific equation, and it provides the answer. TRIZ uses the same thinking process for other types of problems.

FEATURES

1 Weight of Moving Object
2 Weight of Stationary Object
3 Length of Moving Object
4 Length of Stationary Object
5 Area of Moving Object
6 Area of Stationary Object
7 Volume of Moving Object
8 Volume of Stationary Object
9 Speed
10 Force (Intensity)
11 Stress or Pressure
12 Shape of Object
13 Stability of Object
14 Strength
15 Durability of Moving Object
16 Durability of Stationary Object
17 Temperature
18 Illumination Intensity
19 Use of Energy by Moving Object
20 Use of Energy by Stationary Object
21 Power
22 Loss of Energy
23 Loss of Substance
24 Loss of Information
25 Loss of Time
26 Quantity of Substance
27 Reliability
28 Measurement Accuracy
29 Manufacturing Precision
30 Object Affected - Harmful
31 Object Generated - Harmful
32 Ease of Manufacturing
33 Ease of Operation
34 Ease of Repair
35 Adaptability or Versatility
36 Device Complexity
37 Difficulty of Detecting
38 Extent of Automation
39 Productivity

Altshuller observed 39 different features of an object that could be important in any given situation, and that could be in contradiction with any other of these 39 features. He further observed that inventors commonly used 40 different principles to resolve these contradictions. For a complete table of these contradictions and the principles that apply in each case, one excellent website is www.triz40.com, where you can enter the two contradicting features, and the site will present a list of the applicable principles. The two lists presented here introduce the 39 Features and the 40 Innovative Principles, with examples available from The TRIZ Journal, www.triz-journal.com. These lists are included to raise awareness of TRIZ and the types of situations where it may be applicable and to serve as a resource whenever an innovative solution would improve a situation.

40 Innovative Principles

1. **Segmentation**
   Divide an object into independent parts
   - Replace mainframe computer with personal computers
   - Replace a large truck with a semi-trailer truck
   - Break a large project into smaller pieces

   Make an object easy to disassemble
   - Modular furniture
   - Quick disconnect joints in plumbing

   Increase the degree of fragmentation or segmentation
   - Replace solid window shades with Venetian blinds
   - Use powdered welding metal instead of foil or rod to get better joint penetration.

2. **Taking out**
   Separate an interfering part or property from an object, or single out the only necessary part (or property) of an object
   - Locate a noisy air compressor outside the building where compressed air is used.
   - Use fiber optics or a light pipe to separate the hot light source from the location where light is needed
   - Use the sound of a barking dog, without the dog, as a burglar alarm

3. **Local quality**
   Change an object's structure from uniform to non-uniform, change an external environment (or external influence) from uniform to non-uniform
   - Use a temperature, density, or pressure gradient instead of constant temperature, density, or pressure

   Make each part of an object function in conditions most suitable for its operation
   - Lunch box with special compartments for hot and cold solid foods and for liquids

Make each part of an object fulfill a different and useful function
- Pencil with eraser
- Hammer with nail puller
- Multi-function tool that slices, scales fish, acts as a pliers, a wire stripper, flat and Phillips screwdrivers, manicure set, etc.

4. **Asymmetry**
Change the shape of an object from symmetrical to asymmetrical
- Asymmetrical mixing vessels or asymmetrical vanes in symmetrical vessels improve mixing (cement trucks, cake mixers, blenders)
- Put a flat spot or slot on a cylindrical shaft to attach it securely

If an object is asymmetrical, increase its degree of asymmetry
- Change from circular O-rings to oval cross-section or to specialized shapes to improve sealing
- Use astigmatic optics to merge colors

5. **Merging**
Bring closer together (or merge) identical or similar objects; assemble identical or similar parts to perform parallel operations
- Personal computers in a network
- Thousands of microprocessors in a parallel processor computer
- Vanes in a ventilation system
- Electronic chips mounted on both sides of a circuit board or sub-assembly

Make operations contiguous or parallel; bring them together in time
- Link slats together in Venetian or vertical blinds
- Medical diagnostic instruments that analyze multiple blood parameters simultaneously
- Mulching lawnmower (Also Principle 6, Universality)

6. **Universality**
Make a part or object perform multiple functions; eliminate the need for other parts
- Handle of a toothbrush contains toothpaste
- Child's car safety seat converts to a stroller

- Mulching lawnmower (Also Principle 5, Merging)
- Team leader acts as recorder and timekeeper

7. **Nested doll**
   Place one object inside another; place each object, in turn, inside the other
   - Measuring cups and spoons
   - Russian dolls
   - Portable audio system (microphone fits inside transmitter, which fits inside amplifier case)

   Make one part pass through a cavity in the other
   - Extending radio antenna or pointer
   - Zoom lens
   - Seat belt retraction mechanism
   - Retractable aircraft landing gear stow inside the fuselage (Also Principle 15, Dynamism)

8. **Anti-weight**
   To compensate for the weight of an object, merge it with other objects that provide lift
   - Inject foaming agent into a bundle of logs, to make it float better
   - Use helium balloon to support advertising signs.

   To compensate for the weight of an object, make it interact with the environment (e.g. use aerodynamic, hydrodynamic, buoyancy and other forces)
   - Aircraft wing shape reduces air density above the wing, increases density below wing, creating lift (Also Principle 4, Asymmetry)
   - Vortex strips improve lift of aircraft wings
   - Hydrofoils lift a ship out of the water to reduce drag

9. **Preliminary anti-action**
   If it will be necessary to do an action with both harmful and useful effects, this action should be replaced with anti-actions to control harmful effects
   - Buffer a solution to prevent harm from extremes in pH

   Create beforehand stresses in an object that oppose known undesirable working stresses later on.
   - Pre-stress rebar before pouring concrete

Reasoning Backward

- Masking anything before harmful exposure: Use a lead apron on parts of the body to prevent x-ray exposure. Use masking tape to protect the part of an object not being painted

10. **Preliminary action**
 Perform, before it is needed, the required change of an object (either fully or partially)
 - Pre-pasted wall paper
 - Sterilize all instruments needed for a surgical procedure on a sealed tray
 Pre-arrange objects such that they can come into action from the most convenient place and without losing time for their delivery
 - Layout tools near the location where they are used
 - Flexible manufacturing operations

11. **Beforehand cushioning**
 Prepare emergency means beforehand to compensate for relatively low reliability of an object
 - Back-up parachute
 - Manual back-up landing gear controls in aircraft

12. **Equipotentiality**
 In a potential field, limit position changes (e.g. change operating conditions to eliminate the need to raise or lower objects in a gravity field
 - Spring-loaded parts delivery system in a factory
 - Locks in a channel between 2 bodies of water (Panama Canal)
 - Skillets in a manufacturing plant that bring all tools to the right position (Also Principle 10, Preliminary Action)

13. **The other way around**
 Invert the action(s) used to solve the problem (e.g. instead of cooling an object, heat it)
 - To loosen stuck parts, cool the inner part instead of heating the outer part, or do both simultaneously
 - Bring the mountain to Mohammed, instead of bringing Mohammed to the mountain
 Make movable parts (or the external environment) fixed, and fixed parts movable
 - Rotate the part instead of the tool

- Moving sidewalk with standing people
- Treadmill (for walking or running in place)

Turn the object (or process) "upside down"
- Turn an assembly upside down to insert fasteners (especially screws)
- Empty grain from containers (ship or railroad) by inverting them

14. Spheroidality – Curvature

Instead of using rectilinear parts, surfaces, or forms, use curvilinear ones; move from flat surfaces to spherical ones; from parts shaped as a cube (parallelepiped) to ball-shaped structures
- Use arches and domes for strength in architecture

Use rollers, balls, spirals, domes
- Spiral gear (Nautilus) produces continuous resistance for weight lifting
- Compound bow instead of re-curve bow
- Ball point and roller point pens for smooth ink distribution

Go from linear to rotary motion, use centrifugal forces
- Produce linear motion of the cursor on the computer screen using a mouse or a trackball
- Replace wringing clothes to remove the water with spinning clothes in a washing machine
- Use spherical casters instead of cylindrical wheels to move furniture

15. Dynamics

Allow (or design) the characteristics of an object, external environment, or process to become optimal or to find an optimal operating condition
- Adjustable steering wheel, seat, back support, or mirror position, etc.

Divide an object into parts capable of movement relative to each other
- The "butterfly" computer keyboard (Also Principle 7, Nested Doll)

If an object (or process) is rigid or inflexible, make it movable or adaptive
- Flexible boroscope for examining engines
- Flexible sigmoidoscope and other medical "scopes" for medical examinations

16. Partial or excessive actions
If 100% of an object is hard to achieve using a given solution method, then by using "slightly less" or "slightly more" of the same method, the problem may be considerably easier to solve
- Overspray when painting, then remove the excess (Or, use a stencil, an application of Principle 3, Local Quality, and Principle 9, Preliminary Anti-action)
- Fill, then "top off" when filling the gas tank of your car

17. Another dimension
To move an object in 2 or 3 dimensional space
- Infrared computer mouse moves in space instead of on a surface, for presentations
- Five-axis cutting tool can be positioned where needed

Use a multi-storey arrangement of objects instead of a single-storey arrangement
- Cassette with 6 CDs to increase music time, variety
- Electronic chips on both sides of a printed circuit board
- Employees "disappear" from the customers in a theme park, descend into a tunnel, and walk to their next assignment, where they return to the surface and magically reappear

Tilt or re-orient the object, lay it on its side
- Dump trucks

Use "another side" of a given area
- Stack microelectronic hybrid circuits to improve density

18. Mechanical vibration
Cause an object to oscillate or vibrate
- Electric carving knife with vibrating blades

Increase its frequency (even up to ultrasonic)
- Distribute powder with vibration

Use an object's resonant frequency
- Use steel road gratings on bridges to dampen resonance and stabilize the structure
- Destroy gall stones or kidney stones using ultrasonic resonance

Use piezoelectric vibrators instead of mechanical vibrators
- Mixing alloys in an induction furnace
- Electric clock and watches instead of spring driven

19. Periodic action
Instead of continuous action, use periodic or pulsating actions
- Hitting something repeatedly with a hammer
- Use ultrasonic vibration to clean materials
- Replace a continuous siren with a pulsed sound

If an action is already periodic, change the periodic magnitude or frequency
- Use Frequency Modulation to convey information instead of Morse code
- Replace a continuous siren with sound that changes amplitude and frequency

Uses pauses between impulses to perform a different action
- In cardio-pulmonary respiration (CPR) breathe after every 5 chest compressions

20. Continuity of useful action
Carry on work continuously; make all parts of an object work at full load, all the time
- Flywheel (or hydraulic system) stores energy when a vehicle stops, so the motor can keep running at optimum power
- Run the bottleneck operation in any activity continuously, to reach the optimum pace and capability (from Theory of Constraints)

Eliminate all idle or intermittent actions or work
- Print during the return of a printer carriage on dot matrix printers, daisy wheel printers, inkjet printers

21. Skipping
Conduct a process, or certain stages (e.g. destructible, harmful or hazardous operations) at high speed
- Use a high speed dentist drill to avoid heating tissue
- Cut plastic faster than heat can propagate in the material, to avoid deforming the shape

22. "Blessing in disguise" or "Turn lemons into lemonade"
Use harmful factors (particularly, harmful effects of the environment or surroundings) to achieve a positive effect
- Use waste heat to generate electric power
- Recycle waste (scrap) material from one process as raw materials for another

Eliminate the primary harmful action by adding it to another harmful action to resolve the problem
- Add a buffering material to a corrosive solution
- Use a helium-oxygen mix for diving, to eliminate both nitrogen narcosis and oxygen poisoning from air and other nitrox mixes

Amplify a harmful factor to such a degree that it is no longer harmful
- Use a backfire to eliminate the fuel from a forest fire

23. Feedback

Introduce feedback (referring back, cross-checking) to improve a process or action
- Automatic volume control in audio circuits
- Signal from gyrocompass is used to control simple aircraft autopilots
- Statistical Process Control (SPC) – measurements are used to decide when to modify a process (not all feedback systems are automated)
- Budgets – measurements are used to decide when to modify a process

If feedback is already used, change its magnitude or influence
- Change sensitivity of an autopilot when within 5 miles of an airport
- Change sensitivity of a thermostat when cooling vs. heating, since it uses energy less efficiently when cooling
- Change a management measure from budget variance to customer satisfaction

24. Intermediary

Use and intermediary carrier article or process
- Carpenter's nail set, used between the hammer and the nail

Merge one object temporarily with another (which can be easily removed)
- Pot holder to carry hot dishes to the table

25. Self-service

Make an object serve itself by performing auxiliary helpful functions

- Soda fountain pump that runs on the pressure of the carbon dioxide used to create "fizz" the drinks, assuring that drinks will not be flat, eliminating the need for sensors
- Halogen lamps regenerate the filament during use - evaporated material is re-deposited

Use waste resources, energy, or substances
- Use heat from a process to generate electricity – co-generation
- Use animal waste as fertilizer
- Use food and lawn waste to create compost

26. **Copying**
    Instead of an unavailable, expensive, fragile object, use simpler and inexpensive copies
    - Virtual reality via computer instead of an expensive vacation
    - Webinars, Internet meetings instead of travel to meetings
    - Listen to an audio tape instead of a seminar

    Replace an object, or process with optical copies
    - Do surveying from space photographs instead of on the ground
    - Measure an object by measuring the photograph
    - Make sonograms to evaluate the health of a fetus, instead of risking damage by direct testing

    If visible optical copies are already used, move to infrared or ultraviolet copies
    - Make images in infrared to detect heat sources, such as diseases in crops or intruders in a security system

27. **Cheap short-living objects**
    Replace an expensive object with multiple inexpensive objects, comprising certain qualities, such as service life, etc.
    - Use disposable paper objects to avoid the cost of cleaning and storing durable objects. Plastic cups in motels, disposable diapers, many kinds of medical supplies

28. **Mechanics substitution**
    Replace a mechanical means with a sensory (optical, acoustic, taste or smell) means
    - Replace a physical fence to confine a dog or cat with an acoustic "fence" (signal audible to an animal)

- Use a bad smelling compound in natural gas to alert users to leakage, instead of a mechanical or electrical sensor
Use electric, magnetic and electromagnetic fields to interact with an object
- Magnetic levitation trains
Change from static to movable fields, from unstructured field to those having structure
- Early communications used omni-directional broadcasting, but new devices generate very detailed radiation patterns
Use fields in conjunction with field-activated particles (e.g. ferromagnetic)
- Heat substance containing ferromagnetic material by varying the magnetic field until temperature exceeds the Curie Point, when the material becomes paramagnetic and stops absorbing heat

29. **Pneumatics and hydraulics**
   Use gas and liquid parts of an object instead of solid parts (e.g. inflatable, filled with liquids, air cushion, hydro-reactive)
   - Comfortable shoe sole inserts filled with gel
   - Store energy from decelerating a vehicle in a hydraulic system, then use the stored energy to accelerate later

30. **Flexible shells and thin films**
   Use flexible shells and thin films instead of three dimensional structures
   - Use inflatable, thin film structures as winter covers on tennis courts
   Isolate the object from the external environment using flexible shells and thin films
   - Float a film of bipolar material (one end hydrophilic, the other hydrophobic) on a reservoir to limit evaporation

31. **Porous materials**
   Make an object porous or add porous elements (inserts, coatings, etc.)
   - Drill holes in a structure to reduce the weight
   If an object is already porous, use the pores to introduce a useful substance or function
   - Use a porous metal mesh to wick excess solder away from a joint

- Store hydrogen in the pores of a palladium sponge, the "fuel tank" for a hydrogen car, much safer than storing hydrogen gas

32. Color changes
Change the color of an object or its external environment
- Use safe lights in a photographic darkroom

Change the transparency of an object or its external environment
- Use photolithography to change transparent material to a solid mask for semiconductor processing, or change the mask material from transparent to opaque for silk screen processing

33. Homogeneity
Make objects interacting with a given object of the same material or material with identical properties
- Make a container out of the same material as the contents, to reduce chemical reactions
- Make a diamond cutting tool out of diamonds

34. Discarding and recovering
Make portions of an object that have fulfilled their functions go away (discard by dissolving, evaporating, wearing away, etc.) or modify these materials directly during operation
- Use a dissolving capsule for medicine
- Cornstarch-based packaging that reduces its volume by more than 1000x when wet
- Ice structures: use water ice or dry ice to make a template for a rammed earth structure, such as a temporary dam; then fill with earth, let the ice melt or sublime to leave the final structure

Conversely, restore consumable parts of an object directly in the operation
- Self-sharpening lawn mower blades
- Automobile engines that give themselves a tune-up while running ("100,000 miles between tune-ups")

35. Parameter changes
Change an object's physical state (e.g. to a gas, liquid, or solid)
- Freeze the liquid centers of filled candies, then dip in melted chocolate to avoid handling messy, gooey, hot liquid

- Transport oxygen, nitrogen or petroleum gas as a liquid, instead of a gas, to reduce volume
Change the concentration or consistency
- Liquid hand soap is concentrated and more viscous than bar soap at the point of use, making it easier to dispense in the correct amount and more sanitary when shared by several people
Change the degree of flexibility
- Use adjustable dampers to reduce the noise of parts falling into a container by restricting the motion of the walls of the container
- Vulcanize rubber to change its flexibility and durability
Change the temperature
- Raise the temperature above the Curie Point to change a ferromagnetic substance to a paramagnetic substance
- Raise the temperature of food to cook it – change taste, aroma, texture, chemical properties
- Lower the temperature of medical specimens to preserve them for later analysis

36. **Phase transitions**
    Use phenomena occurring during phase transitions (e.g. volume changes, loss or absorption of heat, etc.)
    - Water expands when frozen, unlike most other liquids, so when it freezes, the expansion splits rocks into smaller pieces
    - Heat pumps use the heat of vaporization and heat of condensation of a closed thermodynamic cycle to do useful work

37. **Thermal expansion**
    Use thermal expansion or contraction of materials
    - Fit a tight joint together by cooling the inner part to contract, heating the outer part to expand, putting the joint together, and returning it to equilibrium
    If using thermal expansion, use multiple materials with different coefficients of thermal expansion
    - Leaf spring thermostat: 2 metals with different coefficients of expansion linked so that it bends one direction when warmed, the opposite when cooled

38. **Strong oxidants**
    Replace common air with oxygen-enriched air
    - Scuba diving with nitrox or other non-air mixtures for extended endurance

Replace enriched air with pure oxygen
- Cut at a higher temperature using an oxy-acetylene torch
- Treat wounds in a high pressure oxygen atmosphere to kill anaerobic bacteria and aid healing

Expose air or oxygen to ionizing radiation, or use ionized oxygen
- Ionize air to trap pollutants in an air cleaner

Replace ozonized (ionized) oxygen with ozone
- Speed up chemical reactions by ionizing the gas before use

39. Inert atmosphere
Replace a normal environment with an inert one
- Prevent degradation of a hot metal filament by using an argon atmosphere

Add neutral parts, or inert additives to an object
- Increase the volume of powdered detergent by adding inert ingredients, making it easier to measure with conventional tools

40. Composite materials
Change from uniform to composite materials
- Composite epoxy resin/carbon fiber golf club shafts and airplane parts are lighter, stronger, and more flexible than metal
- Fiberglass surfboards are lighter, more controllable, easier to form into a variety of shapes than wooden ones

Summary:

The key lesson here is that **prior knowledge can be a powerful tool for successful innovation**. In situations where a breakthrough to a new level of performance is required, you do not have to wait for a flash of inspiration. By stating the problem clearly as a contradiction between two desirable features and generalizing the conditions, you can access the interactive table on the www.triz40.com website and see a large number of techniques that have successfully resolved the same contradictions in many other areas. These suggestions can lead to superior solutions. While you may not have occasion to use TRIZ frequently, it is a powerful tool to be aware of whenever the opportunity appears.

Chapter 19

Poka-Yoke: Mistake Proofing

Designs that Make Mistakes Impossible

Background and General Description:

No matter how meticulous workers are, we are all still human, and humans occasionally make mistakes. Murphy's Law (If anything can go wrong, it will) is always in play. Poka-Yoke, the creation of Shigeo Shingo, addresses this problem in repetitive manufacturing operations. Poka-Yoke operates at three levels to prevent mistakes from occurring.

At the simplest level, an alert goes off whenever a mistake occurs. The alert can be a light or audio signal that tells the worker to remove the flawed part, so no defects emerge from the end of the process.

At the second level, a warning alert sounds whenever a mistake or defect is about to occur, such as warning that a part is misaligned before it has been fastened permanently. The warning tells the worker to align the part properly before attaching it.

At the highest level, the operation prevents the worker from making a mistake. For example, a person can only insert a part in the correct way, such as the USB port or other connections to a computer. Each port has a different shape, so only the correct connector will fit, and each connection is asymmetric, so the connector only mounts in the one, correct position.

Poka-Yoke: Mistake Proofing

Poka-Yoke takes problem solving to a higher level, that of problem prevention. Manufacturing operations have traditionally used Poka-Yoke in the design of products, like the USB port, or in the control of an operation to prevent faulty product from reaching customers. However, Poka-Yoke is a way of thinking that is useful in non-manufacturing situations as well.

For example, the Spelling and Grammar checker in a word processing program is a form of Poka-Yoke. It detects a mistake, alerts the person at the keyboard, and even suggests possible corrections. The reason for including Poka-Yoke in this book is to increase awareness of this approach, so you will be better able to design mistake proof activities and products.

The easiest way to understand Poka-Yoke is to see examples of the technique.

Level 1: Alert that a defect has occurred

In this case, the operation is complete, and the defective part exists. A Level 1 Poka-Yoke sensor automatically detects the defective part and separates it from the good parts. The key benefit of Poka-Yoke is low-cost or no-cost inspection of 100% of the parts.

Consider an operation that makes a cylindrical spacer that fits around an axle. The process compresses powdered plastic into the hollow cylindrical shape. If too much or too little powder is used, then the spacer ends up too long or too short, respectively. Measuring each piece is prohibitively expensive and would be waste. The Level 1 Poka-Yoke solution is to modify the conveyer the parts go down when they leave the molding machine. First, a bar is mounted diagonally across the conveyor that exactly matches the height of the Upper Specification Limit of the part. All pieces that are too long strike the bar and slide to the side of the conveyor where they fall off into a scrap bin. Then, a second bar is mounted further down the conveyor, parallel to the first bar, at a height equal to the Lower Specification Limit of the part. This time the good pieces strike the bar and slide off the edge into the bin for good parts. Any spacer that is too thin goes under the bar and falls off the end of the conveyor into another scrap bin.

This setup assures the customer receives acceptable spacers 100% of the time. It does not prevent unacceptable parts from being made, but it can help the operator run the molding machine more effectively. For example, the two bins for defective parts can be connected to a light or buzzer. Whenever the machine makes a part that is too short and it falls into the too short bin, a warning light flashes, and the operator knows something is preventing enough powder from entering the mold. He can take action to clear the feed line, so no more short pieces occur. If a part is too long, the alarm tells the operator to find out why and eliminate the problem.

Level 2: Warning that a defect is about to occur, but can still be prevented

In this situation, something has gone wrong in the operation. In traditional operations, the process would start making defects and continue to do so until someone down the line discovers the defects, either in a subsequent process step, or during final inspection, or worst of all, a customer who discovers the problem, resulting in a product recall or a warranty claim.

In the Poka-Yoke operation, the machine automatically checks each piece after each operation, so every incorrect action is detected and corrected immediately. For example, consider a drilling operation where several drills put a pattern of holes for screws into a part. Drill bits occasionally break, which means one or more of the holes will be missing. Traditionally, defective parts would go on to the next station and the flaw would go undetected until the part reaches the station where the screws are inserted.

In the Level 2 Poka-Yoke solution, the automated drilling station includes a duplicate head right after the drilling head. This duplicate includes probes that fit into every hole that was just drilled. If a hole is missing, the probe cannot complete its stroke, which sets off a warning light or buzzer and stops the line. The operator fixes the drill, re-drills the defective part, and production begins again. Every part is 100% correct every time, with no costly human inspection.

Level 3: Defects cannot occur

Level 3 is Poka-Yoke at its best. Simple modifications to a part or a fixture make it impossible for the operation to be done incorrectly. No warning lights or flashers are necessary because the operation can only be done correctly.

Level 3 actions are obviously the most desirable because no defects ever occur. They are also the simplest because no warning sensors, lights or buzzers are necessary either. Consumer product examples include the various electrical connectors mentioned previously, as well as the door on a microwave oven that must be closed before the unit will operate. The door contains the grid that prevents leakage of high-energy microwaves into the room, which would be dangerous to living things. The consumer cannot get hurt because the unit will not operate unless the necessary safeguard is in place. Two other examples are in automatic transmissions in automobiles. One is the interlock that will not allow the driver to shift out of Park into Drive or Reverse unless the driver's foot is on the brake, preventing the car from moving unexpectedly. The second is the interlock that prevents the driver from removing the key from the ignition unless the car is in Park, thus locking the wheels against movement.

Summary:

Poka-Yoke is the design of products and processes so they become mistake proof. Simple, inexpensive modifications provide 100% inspection to completely eliminate defects, to warn a worker when a mistake is about to be made so it can be prevented, and, at its best, to absolutely prevent the mistake from ever occurring at all.

The mechanical aspects of Poka-Yoke may or may not be of immediate significance, but the way of thinking it uses is completely relevant. The key lesson is that **humans will inevitably make mistakes if the system allows them to. Building that knowledge into everything enables people to prevent problems from ever occurring, certainly the highest level of problem solving**. Always look for ways to mistake proof anything you do. This chapter simply introduces this valuable concept. Thousands of other examples exist and have been published in books on the subject by Shigeo Shingo and others, and more examples and information are available online.

Chapter 20

Summary and Epilogue

Part I – Closed-end Problems
"Fix What's Broken"

Sherlock Holmes provided the theme for all problem solving: Reasoning Backward. Think analytically, not synthetically. Begin with the end in mind. Use effect-to-cause thinking, not cause-to-effect. Observe the consistent differences and patterns when the problem exists, and when it doesn't. Use the differences and patterns as clues to discover the root causes. Never guess (hypothesize, brainstorm…) about root causes. Observe the facts, and let them lead to theories, not the other way around. Once you eliminate all the non-critical factors, whatever remains, no matter how improbable, are the critical factors, the root causes.

Closed-end problem solving is like searching for up to three M&M'S® Brand Peanut Chocolate Candies in a large pile of M&M'S® Brand Milk Chocolate Candies.

Most strategies begin with people thinking divergently, from cause-to-effect, brainstorming dozens or hundreds of possible causes to investigate. Then, they select the ones to pursue. This is like heaping more milk chocolate candies on the pile, and then sampling with a spoon. This approach may eventually find one peanut-filled candy, but it rarely finds all three. Problem solvers who use this approach usually find one root cause eventually, but rarely persevere long enough to find all three.

Reasoning Backward

Effective problem solvers think convergently, going from effect backward to cause. They observe an operation to discover the differences when it works well, and when it doesn't. In the candy example, they observe that peanut-filled candies are roughly spherical, while unfilled candies are discs. They use this difference to guide their search by pouring the entire pile of candies down a chute that passes under a bar with a 0.25" gap. All the M&M'S® Milk Chocolate Candies slide under the bar, while all three M&M'S® Peanut Chocolate Candies are captured immediately.

Three fundamental principles enable this problem solving process to be so much more effective.

- Effects have causes. Causes leave clues. Use the clues. When the operation fails to deliver acceptable results, whatever has changed will leave clues. Search for the clues. They will quickly lead to the causes.
- The Pareto Principle is universal. Whenever unacceptable results occur, no more than three critical factors are responsible for 90-100% of the problem.
- If an activity ever generates a good outcome, then it is fundamentally sound. Any time it generates the desired results, it is operating perfectly; every condition is as it should be. Whenever bad outcomes occur, something has changed.

These three principles provide three powerful strategies for identifying the critical factors in any Closed-end Problem.

- Identify categories of variation and observe which category has the widest range of variation. This category is the home of the most critical factor, the one responsible for 50-100% of the problem. Knowing where to search, and where not to search, always shortens the time needed to solve a problem.

Summary and Epilogue

- Sample the operation to discover patterns of unacceptable outcomes. Patterns provide clues about which factors are critical, and which ones are not.
- Compare performance extremes to identify consistent differences. Compare the very best outcomes to the very worst. Any consistently different factor is critical. Pursue it. Any factor that is not consistently different is non-critical. Ignore it. If no factors are consistently different, then look deeper. Something is changing. Keep looking. It may take time, but the critical factors will reveal themselves. Never resort to guesswork.

After these strategies have revealed the 1-3 critical factors, the way forward to flawless performance and zero defects is clear.

- Identify which values of the critical factors produce optimum results.
- Lock-in the proper conditions long-term to ensure the problem never returns.
- Identify dead time in the activity and eliminate it. Most activities are at least 90% dead time. Increase the overall effectiveness of the operation by reducing the dead time.

The **key lessons** from these approaches to Closed-end Problems include:

- **Never guess about root causes. Observe the activity and its outcomes. The root causes will reveal themselves.**
- **Look for non-random patterns in the activity and its outcomes to provide clues about the root causes.**
- **Compare the very best outcomes to the very worst outcomes and identify consistent differences. Any factor that differs consistently is important – pursue it. Any factor that is not consistently different is unimportant – ignore it.**

- **Verify the critical factors by intentionally varying them to turn the problem on and off.**
- **Tighten control of the critical factors to lock in flawless performance.**
- **Identify and eliminate dead time to maximize productivity.**

Part II – Open-ended Problems – Unmet Need(s) Exist – Innovation is Required

According to several Conference Board studies, only 11% of commercial new product launches are successful. The overwhelming #1 reason for failure is "Poor understanding of market need." Companies develop and introduce new products based on faulty information, only to discover too late, when their new products fail, that customers wanted something else.

The secret to effective open-ended problem solving is to understand the unmet needs of the customer before investing resources into developing the wrong offering. When companies have done this, they develop the correct offering and have a 95% rate of success.

The same critical thinking process these companies use also works whenever individuals face any situation where no acceptable solution exists, and some form of innovation is necessary. The key is to solve the right problem using the Scientific Method as the guide.

- State the initial understanding of the problem clearly. Identify the supposed unmet need or problem, the people who have this need, and why it is worth addressing.
- Test this initial concept with the people who are believed to have this need most urgently. Ask four key questions:
  1. How is the need addressed now? Why?
  2. How much does it cost to do it this way? Why?
  3. What, if anything, is wrong with this situation? Why?
  4. What is the value of improving this situation? Why?

Summary and Epilogue

- Modify the initial concept according to the results of this testing.
- If the modified problem statement indicates the problem is real and worth solving, then begin developing a solution.
- Consider using the TRIZ principles of prior knowledge to guide development, in order to develop better solutions, and to do it faster.
- Consider Poka-Yoke mistake-proofing principles when developing the solution, to create a flawless new operation where mistakes are impossible.

The **key lessons** from these approaches to Open-ended Problems include:

- Solve the right problem. Most innovations fail because they solve a problem that does not really exist. Test the initial concept with those people who supposedly have the greatest need for the innovation.
- Once a real need has been identified, make sure it is a problem worth solving. A viable solution must create value for both the user and the provider.

The most important lesson is to **Limit Brainstorming to Open-ended situations where completely new solutions are necessary. Do not Brainstorm root causes when solving Closed-end situations. The only place for Brainstorming in Closed-end situations is after the root causes have been identified, and you are considering the best possible solution to implement**.

Abraham Maslow's famous quote from *Psychology of Science*, page 15, captures the situation perfectly. "It is tempting I suppose, if the only tool you have is a hammer, to treat everything as if it were a nail."

Brainstorming is a tool. It is fun and easy. Anyone can do it. It can be helpful and appropriate in Open-ended situations, when no current alternative is adequate, when a completely new solution

Reasoning Backward

is needed. If Brainstorming were a hammer, then an Open-ended situation truly would be a nail.

However, Closed-end Problems are not nails. Closed-end Problems are the result of no more than three critical factors, out of dozens, hundreds, or even thousands of non-critical factors. Effective problem solvers refuse to guess (i.e., Brainstorm) what these critical factors might be. Instead, they use the tools from this book to **observe the problem,** to **look for patterns that provide clues,** and to **compare performance extremes**. They quickly eliminate non-critical factors, while retaining all the critical factors. After the critical factors are known, they might brainstorm possible solutions that would control the critical factors, but that is the only place that Brainstorming fits into this process. Then, they tighten control of the critical factors to lock-in flawless performance long-term. Finally, they eliminate dead time to further improve productivity.

Historically, students have left school with very few or no powerful tools for problem solving. Many only possess the hammer called Brainstorming. An examination of dozens of different approaches to critical thinking and problem solving has revealed that the slow, ineffective approaches start with Brainstorming, while the few, fast, truly effective problem solving systems use tools from this book and avoid the use of Brainstorming, just like Sherlock Holmes a century ago, and Sir Francis Bacon 300 years before that.

There was a time when we could afford to be complacent about our systems, and we were. That time is long gone. Today, we can only be competitive with the rest of the world when we are at our best. The tools covered here are the best in the world, as of this writing, proven by the results they consistently deliver. If we are going to be competitive with the rest of the world, can we afford to use anything less?

—Gregg Young
Midland, Michigan
July, 2012

Sherlock Holmes' Top 10 Tips for Effective Problem Solving

1. "What is out of the common is usually a guide rather than a hindrance. In solving a problem of this sort, the grand thing is to be able to reason backward. That is a very useful accomplishment, and a very easy one, but people do not practice it much. In the everyday affairs of life, it is more useful to reason forward, and so the other comes to be neglected. There are fifty who can reason synthetically for one who can reason analytically ... Most people, if you describe a train of events to them, will tell you what the result would be. They can put those events together in their minds, and argue from them that something will come to pass. There are few people however, who, if you told them a result, would be able to evolve from their own inner consciousness what the steps were which led up to that result. This power is what I mean when I talk of reasoning backward, or analytically." – *A Study in Scarlet*

2. "When you have eliminated the impossible, whatever remains, no matter how improbable, must be the truth." – *The Sign of Four* (and several other stories)

3. "Always approach a case with an absolutely blank mind. It is always an advantage. Form no theories, just simply observe and draw inferences from your observations." – *The Adventure of the Cardboard Box*

    "It is a capital mistake to theorize before one has data. Insensibly one begins to twist facts to suit theories, instead of theories to suit facts." – *A Scandal in Bohemia*

4. "How dangerous it always is to reason from insufficient data." "Data! Data! Data!" he cried impatiently. "I can't make bricks without clay." – *The Adventure of the Speckled Band*

5. "It is of the highest importance in the art of detection to be able to recognize, out of a number of facts, which are incidental

and which vital. Otherwise, your energy and attention must be dissipated instead of being concentrated." – *The Reigate Puzzle*

6. "I can see nothing," said Watson. "On the contrary, Watson, you can see everything. You fail, however, to reason from what you see. You are too timid in drawing your inferences." – *The Adventure of the Blue Carbuncle*

7. "Detection is, or ought to be, an exact science, and should be treated in the same cold and unemotional manner. You have attempted to tinge it with romanticism, which produces much the same effect as if you worked a love story or an elopement into the fifth proposition of Euclid." – *The Sign of Four*

8. "I never guess. It is a shocking habit – destructive to the logical faculty." – *The Sign of Four*

9. "Nothing clears up a case so much as stating it to another person." – *Silver Blaze*

10. "You know my methods. Apply them." – *The Sign of Four*

Other Sherlock Holmes Quotations on Detection and Problem Solving

From *A Study in Scarlet:*

- "It is a capital mistake to theorize before you have all the evidence. It biases the judgment."
- "Before turning to those moral and mental aspects of the matter which present the greatest difficulties, let the inquirer begin by mastering more elementary problems."
- "They say that genius is an infinite capacity for taking pains," he remarked with a smile. "It's a very bad definition, but it does apply to detective work."
- "When a fact appears to be opposed to a long train of deductions, it invariably proves to be capable of bearing some other interpretation."
- "Yes, I have a turn both for observation and for deduction. The theories which I have expressed there, and which appear to you to be so chimerical, are really extremely practical -- so practical that I depend upon them for my bread and cheese."
- "To a great mind, nothing is little."
- "Like all other arts, the Science of Deduction and Analysis is one which can only be acquired by long and patient study, nor is life long enough to allow any mortal to attain the highest possible perfection in it. Before turning to those moral and mental aspects of the matter which present the greatest difficulties, let the inquirer begin by mastering more elementary problems."

From *The Sign of Four:*

- "Eliminate all other factors, and the one which remains must be the truth."

- "It is of the first importance," he cried, "not to allow your judgment to be biased by personal qualities."
- "I never make exceptions. An exception disproves the rule."
- "How often have I said to you that when you have eliminated the impossible, whatever remains, however improbable, must be the truth?"

From *A Scandal in Bohemia*:

- "You see, but you do not observe. The distinction is clear."
- "There is nothing so unnatural as the commonplace."
- "The little things are infinitely the most important."

From *A Case of Identity*:

- "Depend upon it, there is nothing so unnatural as the commonplace."
- "It was most suggestive," said Holmes. "It has long been an axiom of mine that the little things are infinitely the most important."
- "Never trust to general impressions, my boy, but concentrate yourself upon details."

From *The Boscombe Valley Mystery*:

- "Singularity is almost invariably a clue. The more featureless and commonplace a crime is, the more difficult it is to bring it home."
- "Circumstantial evidence is a very tricky thing," answered Holmes thoughtfully. "It may seem to point very straight to one thing, but if you shift your own point of view a little, you may find it pointing in an equally uncompromising manner to something entirely different."

Other Relevant Sherlock Holmes Quotations

- "There is nothing more deceptive than an obvious fact."
- "You know my method. It is founded upon the observation of trifles."

From *The Five Orange Pips:*

- "The ideal reasoner would, when he had once been shown a single fact in all its bearings, deduce from it not only all the chain of events which led up to it but also all the results which would follow from it. As Cuvier could correctly describe a whole animal by the contemplation of a single bone, so the observer who has thoroughly understood one link in a series of incidents should be able to accurately state all the other ones, both before and after."

From *The Man with the Twisted Lip:*

- "It is, of course, a trifle, but there is nothing so important as trifles."

From *The Adventure of the Blue Carbuncle:*

- "My name is Sherlock Holmes. It is my business to know what other people don't know."

From *The Adventure of the Speckled Band:*

- "I had," he said, "come to an entirely erroneous conclusion which shows, my dear Watson, how dangerous it always is to reason from insufficient data."

From *The Adventure of the Copper Beeches:*

- "Crime is common. Logic is rare. Therefore, it is upon logic rather than upon the crime that you should dwell."

- "I am glad of all details," remarked my friend, "whether they seem to you to be relevant or not."

From *The Yellow Face*

- "Any truth is better than indefinite doubt."

From *The Musgrave Ritual:*

- "You know my methods in such cases, Watson. I put myself in the man's place, and, having first gauged his intelligence, I try to imagine how I should myself have proceeded under the same circumstances."

From *The Crooked Man:*

- "Elementary," said he. "It is one of those instances where the reasoner can produce an effect which seems remarkable to his neighbour, because the latter has missed the one little point which is the basis of the deduction."

From *The Greek Interpreter:*

- "To the logician all things should be seen exactly as they are."

From *The Hound of the Baskervilles:*

- "The world is full of obvious things which nobody by any chance ever observes."

- "We balance probabilities and choose the most likely. It is the scientific use of the imagination."

- "The more *outré* and grotesque an incident is the more carefully it deserves to be examined, and the very point which appears to complicate a case is, when duly considered and scientifically handled, the one which is most likely to elucidate it."

From *The Adventure of the Dancing Men:*

- "What one man can invent another can discover."
- "You see, my dear Watson, it is not really difficult to construct a series of inferences, each dependent upon its predecessor, and each simple in itself."

From *The Valley of Fear:*

- "There should be no combination of events for which the wit of man cannot conceive an explanation."

From *The Adventure of the Bruce-Partington Plans:*

- "We must fall back upon the old axiom that when all other contingencies fail, whatever remains, however improbable, must be the truth."

From *The Adventure of the Red Circle:*

- "Education never ends, Watson. It is a series of lessons with the greatest for the last."

From *The Adventure of the Blanched Soldier:*

- "I see no more than you, but I have trained myself to notice what I see."

From *The Adventure of the Cardboard Box:*

- "We approached the case, you remember, with an absolutely blank mind, which is always an advantage. We had formed no theories. We were simply there to observe and to draw inferences from our observations."

Reasoning Backward

From *The Disappearance of Lady Frances Carfax:*

- "When you follow two separate chains of thought, Watson, you will find some point of intersection which should approximate to the truth."

From *The Naval Treaty:*

- "The principle difficulty in your case," remarked Holmes in his didactic fashion, "lay in the fact of there being too much evidence. What was vital was overlaid and hidden by what was irrelevant. Of all the facts which were presented to us we had to pick just those which we deemed to be essential, and then piece them together in their order, so as to reconstruct this very remarkable chain of events."

From *The Adventure of the Priory School:*

- "Before we start to investigate that let us try to realize what we *do* know, so as to make the most of it, and to separate the essential from the accidental."

- "Holmes," I cried, "this is impossible." "Admirable!" he said. "A most illuminating remark. It *is* impossible as I state it, and therefore I must in some respect have stated it wrong. Yet you saw for yourself. Can you suggest any fallacy?"

From *The Adventure of Black Peter:*

- "One should always look for a possible alternative and provide against it. It is the first rule of criminal investigation."

Index

4
40 Innovative Principles 314

5
5 Whys 276, 278

A
Accounts Receivable 10, 74, 254
Active (hands-on) time 347
Adopt a different point of view 52
advertising 186, 317
Altshuller, Genrich 312, 313, 314
America 347
Another dimension 320
Anti-weight 317
Asymmetry 316, 317
Auto Body Panel Stamping 284

B
B vs. C™ 11, 58, 148, 168, 180, 181, 182, 183, 184, 186, 187, 188, 189, 191, 207, 235, 238, 347
Bacon, Sir Francis 35, 37, 46, 49, 56, 99, 117, 181, 256, 295, 311, 338
Bacterial Infection 109
Ballpark Stage 123, 135, 140, 148, 159, 165
Beforehand cushioning 318
Bhote 8
Bhote, Keki 172, 223, 230
Blessing in disguise 321
Bottleneck 263, 321
Brache, Alan 273
Brainstorming 80, 187, 337, 338

C
Capping Run 125, 132, 135, 139, 142, 148, 149, 150, 164, 168, 238
Cheap short-living objects 323
Clean the World, Inc. 296
Closed-end Closed-end Problems 23, 25, 245, 335
Closed-end Problems 338
Clue Generation 10, 42, 54, 55, 57, 58, 148, 152, 159, 162
Coefficient of Linear Expansion 202, 203
Color changes 325
Component Search™ 11, 57, 58, 69, 121, 122, 123, 125, 126, 133, 135, 136, 137, 140, 141, 148, 153, 159, 162, 163
Composite materials 327
Conan Doyle, Sir Arthur 348
Concentration Chart 10, 56, 69, 84, 87, 88, 90, 91, 92, 93, 96, 97, 233
Conference Board 294, 336
Consider extreme cases 53
constraint 262, 263, 264, 265, 266, 268, 270, 273
Continuity of useful action 321
Control 11, 12, 41, 54, 152, 153, 201, 220, 221, 222, 223, 224, 225, 226, 244, 322
Convergent thinking 9, 24, 33
Cook County Hospital 112
Copying 323
Corporate policies 285
Cost-Time.
    See Cost-Time Management
Cost-Time Management 8, 12, 61, 248, 249, 250, 256, 258, 270, 271

347

Cost-Time Profile 12, 62, 250, 253, 255, 256, 257, 259, 266, 270
Cracked Epoxy Adhesive 11, 155, 184
Curvature 319
Cycle time 12, 41, 61, 189, 216, 249, 250, 251, 252, 253, 256, 257, 266, 269, 271

D

Dairy Farms 10, 109
Decision Tree 38, 69
Deduction 37
Dictionary 42
Diode Baking Process 12, 203
Discarding and recovering 325
Divergent thinking 8, 9, 24, 39
Doyle 8
Dynamics 319

E

Edison 40
Elimination 124, 130, 135, 137, 141, 166
Emergency Room 110, 112
Employee Turnover 10, 78
End Counts 101, 102, 106, 109
Environmental Neglect 215, 349
Equipotentiality 318

F

Factorial Analysis 125, 127, 132, 135, 139, 142, 148, 149, 150, 164
Failure Modes and Effects Analysis 274
Feedback 322
Find a pattern 52
First Part Good 288, 289
First Vintage 36
Flexible shells and thin films 324
FMEA.
    See Failure Mode and Effects Analysis
Focus groups 186, 193
Fooks 8
Fooks, Jack 249
Four key questions 336
Four Question Framework 303
Fractional Factorial DOE 171
Full Factorial 11, 58, 122, 147, 148, 170, 171, 174, 177, 240, 241
Full Factorials 57, 158, 179, 224

G

Goldman, Lee 111, 112
Goldratt 8, 62
Goldratt, Eliyahu 262
Good Manufacturing Practices 215, 349
Green Y® 136
Guess intelligently 53

H

Heart Attacks 10, 110
Holmes.
    See Sherlock Holmes
Holmes' Tips 67, 80, 122, 147, 197, 249
Homogeneity 325
Hospitals 186, 193
Hotel Customer Service 10, 77
Hourmeter 11, 127
Human Shortcomings 215, 218
Hypotheses 298, 299, 303
Hypothesis of the Proposed Winning Solution 302
Hypothesis of the Value of the Proposed Winning Solution 298, 302
Hypothesis of the Winning Solution 298
Hypothesis of Unmet Need 298, 299

Index

I

Identification 11, 54, 57, 145
Ignition Amplifier 11, 199
Inert atmosphere 327
Innovation 294, 295, 305, 306, 327, 336, 337
Interacting Factors 198, 203
Intermediary 322
Invisible Inventory 251

J

Japan 24

K

Krulik, Stephen 51

L

Likert scale 85
Local quality 315
Logistics 279

M

M&M'S® Brand Chocolate Candies 46
Macro Cost-Time Management 258
Macro Cost-Time Profiles 250, 251
Make a drawing 53
Make an organized list 53
Malcolm Baldrige National Quality Award 172, 249
Management/Supervision Inadequacies 216
Market research 186, 309
Maslow, Abraham 337
Material Control 279
Mathematics problem 228
Measles Chart 97
Mechanical vibration 320

Mechanics substitution 323
Merging 316, 317
Metal stamping operation 274
Micro Cost-Time Management 172
Micro Cost-Time Profiles 251, 270
Micro-motor 102
Mistake Proofing 13, 295, 328
Most critical factor 67, 68, 70, 86, 89, 93, 97, 100, 124, 125, 130, 138, 141, 150, 162, 164, 167, 177, 179, 198, 200, 207
Motorola 8, 172, 223, 230, 242, 249, 251
Multi-Vari 10, 38, 45, 55, 66, 67, 68, 69, 70, 76, 78, 79, 80, 82, 83, 85, 100, 106, 123, 187, 273, 274, 275, 276, 278, 279, 290

N

Needles in a Haystack 45
Nested doll 317
No More Changes 286, 287, 288, 289
Non-Firing Burner 11, 125
Non-interacting factors 198
Non-random patterns 81
Novum Organum 35

O

Observation 35
Observation, Deduction, Knowledge 35, 291
Open-ended Problem Solving 12, 293, 294
Open-ended problems 24, 35, 294, 336, 337
Opportunity Analysis 12, 294, 295
Optimization 11, 59, 195, 240
Organizational Problems 12, 272
Organize data 53
Oscillator 11, 130

P

Paint Defects 10, 89
paint oven 89, 177
Paired Comparisons™ 10, 55, 69, 83, 84, 98, 99, 100, 101, 104, 105, 107, 109, 111, 113, 115, 116, 117, 118, 160, 161, 181, 183, 187, 273, 274, 275, 277, 278, 284, 289
Parameter changes 325
Pareto's Law 40, 49, 56, 97, 273, 282
Partial or excessive actions 320
Periodic action 321
Phase transitions 326
Plant/Equipment Inattention 217
Playing cards 44
Pneumatics and hydraulics 324
Poka-Yoke 13, 216, 295, 328, 329, 330, 331, 337
Population 101, 202
Porous materials 324
Posamentier, Alfred S. 51
Positrol 12, 213, 214, 216, 218, 219, 230, 243, 244
Precipitate 10, 105
Pre-Control 221, 222, 223, 224, 225, 226
Preliminary action 318
Preliminary anti-action 317
Press Brake 11, 149, 184
Princeton University 101
Process Certification 12, 60, 177, 212, 213, 214, 215, 219, 230, 243

R

Realistic Target Values 148, 198, 205, 245
Realistic Tolerances 148, 198, 205, 206, 227, 245
Reason logically 54

Reasoning Backward 4, 9, 17, 18, 20, 39, 42, 51, 333, 355
Reasoning backwards 8, 24, 39, 42
Reasoning Forwards 24
Red X® 136, 140
Rotor shaft 70
Rummler, Geary 273

S

Scatter Plot 12, 60, 197, 199, 205, 206, 209, 241
Scatter Plots 11, 59, 148, 168, 197, 198, 202, 205, 206, 207, 208, 222
Scheduling 279
Schools 51, 186, 193
Scientific Method 35, 36, 336
Segmentation 315
Self-service 322
Shainin 7, 8, 172, 249, 251
Shainin, Dorian 123, 215, 256, 258
Sherlock Holmes 1, 2, 5, 6, 8, 9, 10, 13, 17, 21, 23, 24, 25, 27, 32, 33, 37, 46, 49, 52, 99, 117, 187, 256, 295, 333, 338, 339, 355
Shingo, Shigeo 328, 332
Shipping Problem 279
Shorts in Television Sets 91
Simplex 11, 148, 197, 198, 203, 204, 205, 207
Six Sigma 1, 2, 4, 249
Skipping 321
Solve a simpler problem 52
Spheroidality 319
Strong oxidants 326
surveys 54, 77, 186

T

Taguchi 11, 171, 172, 179
Taguchi Methods 179
Taking out 315

Index

The other way around 318
Theory of Constraints 8, 12, 41, 61, 261, 262, 264, 265, 268, 270, 271, 321
Theory of Inventive Problem Solving 13, 295, 312
Thermal expansion 326
Tile Adhesion 10, 76
Time Profile 250, 266, 268
Time-to-time 68, 69, 70, 72, 82, 83, 85, 90, 93, 97, 231
Titanic 274
Total Elapsed Time 252, 259, 266, 270
Total End Count 104, 106, 109, 119, 120, 160, 183, 184, 186, 190, 191
Trends 83, 84, 186, 202
TRIZ 13, 295, 312, 314, 327, 337
Tukey 106, 183
Tukey Test 101, 103, 104, 119, 182, 190, 191
Tukey, John 101, 102
Turkeys 10, 103
Turn lemons into lemonade 321

U

Unit-to-unit 68, 69, 70, 82, 84, 85, 118, 123, 135

Universality 316
University Recruiting 10, 95
Unmet Need(s) 336

V

Validation 11, 54, 57, 145
Variable Search™ 11, 57, 58, 122, 146, 147, 148, 153, 158, 159, 161, 163, 165, 167, 171, 179, 184, 236, 238
Visible Inventory 250

W

Warped Grills 10, 11, 113, 183
Wave Solder 10, 12, 214, 224
Wave Soldering 11, 12, 93, 172, 230
Westinghouse 8, 61, 249, 250, 251, 256
White Space 273, 275, 291
Wire Bond Strength 11, 185
Within-unit 10, 68, 69, 70, 72, 82, 83, 84, 85
Work backwards 51

ABOUT THE AUTHOR

Gregg Young has helped companies solve problems, improve quality, increase profits, and develop successful new products in his capacity as President and Founder of Young Associates, Inc. (http://youngassocinc.com) Gregg spent over 30 years solving problems, leading teams, and teaching problem solving skills in both large corporations and small businesses. He experienced both successes and frustrations, so he studied dozens of processes searching for best practices he could add to his clients' processes so they would deliver bigger results faster. When he discovered that best practices do exist, it sparked his passion to share this knowledge, so that anyone can solve problems as effectively as Sherlock Holmes solved crimes. He is the author of three books. The first two focused on upgrading business processes by adding these convergent, observation-based methods to existing processes. This, his latest book, *Reasoning Backward: How Sherlock Holmes Can Make You a Better Problem Solver*, adapts these techniques for students as well as businesses, providing everyone with the skills they need to solve problems effectively and create a competitive advantage in the global marketplace. You can email him at gregg@youngassocinc.com.

CONTACT INFORMATION

- Do you want to learn more?
- Do you want to discuss your situation and explore possibilities? You can reach Gregg Young in the following ways.

Email: gregg@youngassocinc.com
Phone: 989-492-2029
Mailing Address:
Gregg Young
Young Associates, Inc.
2911 Highbrook Dr.
Midland, MI 48642 USA

Websites:
http://youngassocinc.com
http://reasoningbackward.com

TO UNDERSTAND WHY THINGS GO RIGHT, OBSERVE WHAT'S DIFFERENT WHEN THINGS GO WRONG